POISONED

POISONED

HOW A CRIME-BUSTING PROSECUTOR
TURNED HIS MEDICAL MYSTERY INTO A
CRUSADE FOR ENVIRONMENTAL VICTIMS

ALAN BELL

FOREWORD BY JAN SCHLICHTMANN

Skyhorse Publishing

Some names have been changed to protect the privacy
of those mentioned in this book.

Skyhorse Publishing books may be purchased in bulk at special discounts for
sales promotion, corporate gifts, fund-raising, or educational purposes. Special
editions can also be created to specifications. For details, contact the Special
Sales Department, Skyhorse Publishing, 307 West 36th Street, 11th Floor, New
York, NY 10018 or info@skyhorsepublishing.com.

Skyhorse® and Skyhorse Publishing® are registered trademarks of Skyhorse
Publishing, Inc.®, a Delaware corporation.

Visit our website at www.skyhorsepublishing.com.

10 9 8 7 6 5 4 3 2 1

Library of Congress Cataloging-in-Publication Data is available on file.

Cover design by Brian Peterson
Cover photo: iStockphoto

Print ISBN: 978-1-5107-0264-6
Ebook ISBN: 978-1-5107-0265-3

Printed in the United States of America

CONTENTS

Foreword

WE ALL FACE UNFORESEEN OBSTACLES in our lives. Sometimes they defeat us. Other times, with courage, we overcome insurmountable adversity.

For Alan Bell, a former organized crime prosecutor, a mysterious illness posed not just an obstacle but a near-death sentence. Forced to live in an isolated bubble in the Arizona desert for a decade, he saw his promising career evaporate and his marriage crumble. Yet, despite all odds stacked against him, Alan refused to allow his illness to define or defeat him. Instead, his ordeal transformed him, as he turned his personal misfortune into an opportunity to save others from a similar fate.

Baffled by Alan's symptoms, doctors ran test after test as they attempted to diagnose his condition, suggesting everything from chronic fatigue syndrome to a revenge poisoning by one of the criminals he'd prosecuted. Ultimately, Alan discovered a terrifying truth: his condition was caused by exposure to the same toxic chemicals we're all surrounded by on a daily basis in our homes, schools, workplaces, and neighborhoods.

Environmental toxins are devastating human health worldwide. More people become ill or die from exposure to environmental toxins than are seriously injured by AIDS, auto accidents, war, and violent crime combined. On the eve of the twenty-first Climate Change Conference in Paris, world health organizations warned of the profound impact environmental pollution has on our Earth's population. Clinicians and scientists consistently report that widespread exposure to toxic environmental chemicals is threatening healthy human reproduction and exacerbating major health disorders such as diabetes, obesity, cancer, and cardiovascular disease.

Such worldwide concern about how we are destroying our environment, and how our environment is killing us, must serve as a clarion call for our collective awakening and action on an unprecedented scale.

Alan Bell's descent into the hell of environmental poisoning puts a human face on this global issue. His journey is an alarming portrait of a tenacious and talented man's pursuit of the American dream, and how his seemingly charmed life turned into a nightmare. It is also an eternal story of how, even in our darkest hours, the healing and sustaining power of love can take root and grant us the strength to keep fighting for our lives even when all hope seems lost.

No one is immune to environmentally linked diseases. Toxicity doesn't discriminate along social, political, economic, financial, geographic, racial, or religious divides. We are all equally at risk: mothers, fathers, aunts, uncles, sons, and daughters. Like Frankenstein, mankind has created a monster. Humanity must now stop it before it's too late. *Poisoned* is an overdue call to action that we must heed.

In the words of Justice Brandeis, if there is to be *justice*, the world will need the truth. Then we must act on what we know to be true.

Jan Schlichtmann

PROLOGUE

"ALAN! ALAN!" MY MOTHER SHOUTED.

I was lying on the couch in my parents' Miami Beach condominium. My hair was soaked with sweat as I struggled to breathe.

The air around my own home was saturated with smoke from wildfires burning in the Everglades. Recently, I'd been seeking sanctuary at my parents' home as my mysterious asthma attacks became more frequent and intense. They often progressed into full-blown seizures, causing my eyes to roll back and my lungs to shut down. My arms and legs would flail, my vision would blur, my ears would ring, and stabbing pains would rocket through my body in violent waves. Any time this happened—and I could never predict when— it was like a neurological fireworks show.

"Alan!" my mother yelled again, her voice high and tight with terror.

I couldn't answer, rendered mute by lack of oxygen.

I didn't understand what was happening. Why was my body betraying me like this? I'd never been sick in my life, other than a few bouts of strange flu symptoms in recent months and now these progressively worsening attacks.

"Alan! Please, get up!" My mother, truly panicked now, was trying to help me sit up, but it felt like she was far away as I concentrated on trying to drag air into my lungs.

My father heard the commotion and hurried into the room. "What's wrong? What is it?"

"It's Alan!" she said. "We need to get him to the beach."

He quickly tried to help lift me. Despite my recent attempts to find doctors who might be able to solve the puzzle of my rapidly deteriorating health, the only tonic we'd found so far was the beach. For some unknown reason, the warm, clean air of the Atlantic Ocean always seemed to revive me.

At that moment, my younger brother, Bobby, arrived with his gym bag. "What's going on?" he asked, alarmed by the sight of my parents struggling to get me off the couch.

He didn't bother to ask twice. He knew the answer didn't matter. At this moment, all that mattered was getting me to the beach.

I was only vaguely aware of my parents and brother half-carrying me across the room to the elevator. I felt the drop of the elevator as we went down to the first floor, but it was as if I were watching the scene from outside my body.

After what seemed like years, we were finally outside the building. I could hear the noises of cars and people. More importantly, I also felt the miraculous ocean air.

I leaned heavily on my family as we crossed the street to the beach, where I collapsed on the sand with a groan and continued to concentrate on the only thing that mattered: drawing a single breath. And then one more.

I was scared. But in the weeks, months, and years to come, I was about to learn that, just when I thought things were scary, they would get a great deal scarier.

And, whenever I thought things were bad, they would always get worse.

So much worse.

1 · Trouble in the Tower

Shortly before Thanksgiving in 1988, I was sitting in the research library of my law office at 110 Tower in Fort Lauderdale, Florida, when I started perspiring and feeling oddly dizzy. It felt like I was on a ship navigating a rough sea. The room was tipping from side to side.

"What is this?" I wondered, closing my eyes.

I braced myself against the desk, waiting for the spinning to stop. After a few minutes, I felt well enough to push myself up from the chair and start gathering my files, but I still struggled to keep my balance as I staggered back to my office.

I'd been hired as an attorney by Travelers Insurance Company three years earlier. The company had moved into 110 Tower six months previously. The brand-new building had thirty floors; we were located near the top. When we moved in, many of the other suites weren't yet finished. The walls were still being painted, and new carpeting was being tacked down as I was putting my law books on the shelves.

Ours was the most impressive skyscraper to ever grace the Fort Lauderdale skyline. Located across the street from the Broward County Courthouse, 110 Tower was considered a technological marvel. These days, many of its features—like talking elevators, word processing rooms, and computerized doors that required swiping a card for entry—would go unnoticed, but back then they seemed like something out of a science fiction movie. The building had its own hotel, stores, restaurants, nightclubs, and fitness center—you literally never had to leave to do anything.

The Tower used the latest computer technology to regulate everything from the lights to the ventilation system. The windows couldn't be opened for fresh air; "sealing" the building to save energy costs prevented the influx of hot, humid outdoor air.

I didn't see that as a problem. I remember walking into my new office, with its powerful scents of fresh paint and new carpeting, and saying to my coworkers, "Breathe it in! Doesn't that smell sweet?"

I felt lucky to be there.

+ + +

At Travelers, I defended personal injury cases, typically representing Fortune 500 companies. I also had a private practice where I did criminal defense work. In conjunction with all of that, I served as general counsel for my brother, Bobby, who was growing the Banana Boat Company into one of the top sun-care companies in the world.

Juggling my professional responsibilities required me to work eighty to ninety hours a week. My schedule was brutal. Most mornings, I'd get up by five, run a few miles, shower, then jump into my silver Nissan Z and barrel down the road while listening to motivational talks from business icons like Zig Ziglar. I'd show up early at the courthouse for calendar call, then race over to my office and put in a full day's work.

At day's end, I'd hurry to the courthouse and visit my jailed criminal clients. Unlike my former work as a prosecutor with the State Attorney's Office from 1979 to 1986, where I prosecuted cases against Colombian cartels, mobsters, and other hard-core felons, my private practice allowed me to pick and choose my clients. Whenever I wasn't working, I managed political campaigns for judges who were ex-prosecutors. Inspired by my legal career, I even began making plans to run for a US Senate seat, hoping to bring about deeper, systemic change in our justice system. It was my objective to better protect crime victims whose rights were eroded in favor of safeguarding the accused.

It seemed like everything I'd been working for was coming to fruition. During one rare vacation, a long ski weekend in Colorado, I took out a pad of paper and a pen to sketch out the course of my life for my wife, Susan. I showed her how my prosecutor years provided the necessary skills to obtain this high-paying position as a defense attorney with Travelers. The job ensured that my family wanted for nothing and also left me with enough hours a day to keep my own private practice going. I really could do it all, I told her.

"One day I'll be a senator," I mused. "Then I'll be better able to make a difference for those who depend upon our government to help keep us safe."

"Florida Senate?" Susan asked.

"United States."

Susan smiled. "Senator Alan Bell."

"And his lovely wife, Susan."

The two of us looked down at our daughter, Ashlee, sleeping in her carrier. "And their darling daughter, Ashlee," we said in unison and laughed.

"Is that it?" Susan asked. "Is that where the plan ends?"

I shrugged. "Who knows?"

Who, indeed? Everything was moving so quickly that I didn't have much time for reflection. All I knew was that I was where I wanted to be: on a fast track to the future.

Back then, I had no idea that sometimes the future is much darker than you can ever imagine. To quote an old Jewish proverb, "People make plans and God laughs."

◆ ◆ ◆

Up until this point in my life, I was on a magic carpet ride to the American Dream. I had a happy childhood with loving parents who gave me every possible advantage.

South Florida seemed like paradise to me as a child. In the 1960s, downtown Miami was nothing more than a small commercial hub. We lived in the suburbs, in a new, squeaky-clean, middle-class neighborhood at the edge of the Everglades. It was a wondrous place, with alligators and armadillos roaming the streets. On weekends we sometimes drove down to the Keys, where we would swim with dolphins. We'd just jump in the ocean and they'd come right up to us.

I idolized my father, a World War II vet who had landed at Omaha Beach and fought all the way through to the Battle of the Bulge in December 1944. After being awarded a Purple Heart, he returned home to New York City and earned a law degree.

The practice of law never really appealed to him. Instead, he became a successful realtor in Miami Beach. Whenever I saw him negotiate with potential buyers, I was mesmerized by how easily my father spoke with people, taking their concerns into account, changing terms to their satisfaction, and then closing the deal. Later, when I was pursuing my own legal career, my father's persuasive salesman's strategies provided my blueprint for success whenever I spoke in courtrooms or negotiated with opposing counsel.

Our mother stayed home to raise me and my younger siblings, Bobby and Judi, while our father worked eighty-hour weeks. She was the reason why we had moved from New York to South Florida when I was six years old. She essentially put her foot down after one brutal winter, saying, "I'm sick and tired of being stuck in an apartment all winter long. We're not doing this anymore!"

For many years, our family lived modestly, while my father slowly but steadily carved out his real estate career. While many other families we knew bought their kids name-brand shirts and Weejun loafers, our mother took us to places like Zayre's, a discount department store, to buy clothes because that's all we could afford. Our only exposure to elegance occurred during occasional holidays, when my uncle—who worked as an accountant for major hotels in Miami Beach—could get us hotel rooms for next to nothing. We stayed in many posh hotels that way. Like the Beverly Hillbillies, all five of us camped out in one room and gawked at the amazing swimming pools, beautiful people, and glitzy rooms with their fine carpeting and linens.

Dad wouldn't even let us order nickel Cokes by the pool at those hotels. Our only meals out were on Sundays, when he piled us into our car, an ancient jalopy that would often break down by the side of the road, and took us to a nearby Tyler's Restaurant for the Early Bird Special. We were never allowed to order anything else off the menu because it was too expensive. I didn't mind, though, because Tyler's was in the same shopping center as the Carroll Music store, where I'd admire the drum kits.

Like millions of other kids growing up then, I was a Beatles fan. (I still am: I have a pair of Ringo Starr's drumsticks hanging on my wall and an original brick from the Cavern Club, where the band first played in Liverpool.) I dreamed about becoming a rock legend like Paul McCartney or John Lennon. My passion for the Beatles led me to take up drums, and in 1967, my tolerant parents sent me to band camp at Northwestern University. There, I was lucky enough to study with Danny Seraphine, the original drummer for Chicago, the legendary rock band.

My father tried hard to turn me into an athlete. He wanted me to play baseball so badly that he even signed up to be a Little League coach so Bobby and I couldn't escape from practice. With Bobby, the exposure to athletics stuck—he became a star at every sport he tried—but I had no interest in sports while growing up. My whole world was music.

I was lucky to have the mother I did. Her father was an opera star at Carnegie Hall, and no matter how little money we had, we always had a piano in the house. She exposed us to opera and classical music. But Mom was hip, too. Like me, she loved the Beach Boys and the Beatles, and she dressed the part of a cool, fashionable mom, in go-go boots and a beehive hairdo.

My mother was supportive of Bobby's athletics, driving him to practices and watching his games, but she and I bonded over music. I wanted to wear my hair like the Beatles wore theirs, and Mom would have let me keep it that way. Dad, however, insisted on taking Bobby and me to a local barber shop, where he'd tell the barber to give us crew cuts. I'd get upset about this, but Bobby loved having his head buzzed. His hero was Bart Starr, the quarterback for the Green Bay Packers, and Starr and all of the other athletes Bobby admired had buzz cuts.

By high school, I was old enough to run off whenever it was time to go to the barber shop. I managed to grow my hair long, and my mother talked my father into buying me a drum set just like Ringo Starr's. Music became my whole world. I played in the marching band, jazz ensemble, concert band—you name it. There wasn't much else for me to do in high school, truthfully, since I was a short, chubby nerd with acne.

Because playing the drums consumed my time and energy, I didn't have much luck with girls or pay attention to academics. I earned average grades in everything but music, where I excelled, even winning the Florida State High School Drumming Championship in 1972.

The real world knocked on my door senior year, however, when my guidance counselor took one look at my grades and informed me that I should consider trade school. "You're just not college material," she pronounced.

I was dumbfounded. All around me, my classmates were getting into prestigious colleges. Plus, my mother always said—only half joking—that I could be anything I wanted to be, "as long as it's a doctor or a lawyer."

My stubborn streak kicked in, and I applied to nearly every college and university in Florida. Every one of them rejected me except the University of Miami, where I earned a scholarship to attend their school of music. Once again, my life consisted of doing what I loved—playing drums for various bands and ensembles. Our university band traveled around the world, even winning a jazz competition in Sweden.

Yet as much as I was enjoying myself, I felt like a duck out of water the minute the music stopped. My personality was far too intense to fit in with laid-back musicians. I had changed a great deal since high school, both physically and emotionally. My acne was gone and I had shot up to six feet three inches. I became a distance runner, started playing racquetball, and had my first serious girlfriend.

Suddenly, I experienced an epiphany: I didn't need a degree to play music. I could continue to play drums in a rock band, while earning a more versatile and practical degree. After exploring several different majors, my friendships with fellow students led me to eventually transfer into the University of Miami School of Business Administration.

Finally, I began growing intellectually and socially. In business classes, I encountered classmates who were the children of bankers, Fortune 500 executives, and even senators. They were ambitious and driven to succeed despite the University of Miami being known back then as "Suntan U."

Being among these movers and shakers motivated me to up my game. I joined a professional business fraternity and became active in student life, serving as student body treasurer, president of the Omicron Delta Kappa fraternity, and Chief Justice of the Student Supreme Court. In 1976, I graduated magna cum laude, in the top 2 percent of my class.

Now I faced another fork in the road as the real world beckoned. I decided to study for the CPA exam, figuring that was the next logical professional step. I quickly discovered accounting wasn't for me. The profession seemed to be filled with Poindexters who navigated their world with numbers. In contrast, I was a "people" person who loved to socialize and debate about topics ranging from music to politics. What else could I do?

And then it came to me: law school. I'd grown up watching the *Perry Mason* television show—one of my mother's favorite dramas—on a small, oval-shaped television with rabbit ears. Because Perry Mason was one of my mother's heroes, he became one of mine. Perry Mason was a smart, articulate, and quick-thinking trial lawyer. I wanted to be just like him, only instead of being a defense lawyer, I wanted to argue cases in front of juries and put bad guys behind bars.

Why not? My other dreams had come true.

2 ◆ Lessons in the Courtroom

In law school, they don't warn you that the legal profession isn't all that glamorous. Most lawyers never see the inside of a courtroom. Instead, they spend their lives drafting contracts, making deals, and pushing papers. Trial lawyers like Perry Mason—known as "litigators"—are an elite breed: the courageous, risk-taking fighter pilots of the legal profession. I was determined to become one.

At the University of Miami Law School, an exciting opportunity arose. Students in their final year of law school had the option of signing up for an internship program instead of taking classes. Eager to test-drive my skills, I jumped at the opportunity to work at the State Attorney's office under Janet Reno, who would later serve as Attorney General of the United States for President Bill Clinton.

I took every case that came along and got my clock handed to me over and over again. It was humiliating at times. However, my early days as a prosecutor taught me essential lessons about justice and power that would prove to be not only key to my success in the courtroom, but also vital to my survival when I later became a victim imprisoned in my own body.

I learned my initial lesson when I prosecuted my first case in a courtroom as an intern. I was only twenty-three years old and still very wet behind the ears. I took comfort in the fact that I was being closely supervised by an experienced attorney who tutored me every step of the way.

The defendant, a large black man, was accused of hitting a police officer. Officially, this was "battery on a law enforcement officer," a third-degree felony in Florida punishable by up to five years in the state prison. Since he was a first-time offender, if the man had agreed to a plea bargain, he would have been placed on probation. However, because he maintained his innocence and refused to take the plea, his fate would be decided by the judge.

I walked into the courtroom and stood before the judge. Although I was nervous, my supervisor was by my side, monitoring and correcting every move I made. My case was simple: the defendant hit a police officer. No injury, no weapon, and two witnesses. In my mind, this was the kind of case where the judge would be lenient and give this man another chance. I figured the State had given a green intern like me an opportunity to prosecute it because there wasn't much to lose if I screwed things up and the guy walked out of the courtroom a free man.

I was confident that I had done my homework. I was fully prepared to question the police officer and two witnesses on the stand. However, the judge was so authoritative and had such a loud, intimidating voice that I was suddenly gripped by stomach-churning fear. I felt like the scarecrow quaking in front of the all-powerful Wizard of Oz as she bellowed, "Call your first witness."

The minute I began direct examination of the cop, everything changed. Immediately after he identified the defendant as the man who'd hit him, the judge interrupted and said, "Mr. Bell, you're done with the direct testimony of this witness, correct?"

"No, I'm not," I said. We were only halfway through the cop's testimony, and I was stunned that she didn't want to hear any more.

I turned to look for guidance from my supervisor, who was seated at the table next to me, and was shocked to see that he'd covered his eyes with his hands. What had I done wrong? Had I messed up so badly that the judge was going to throw the case out of court?

"Mr. Bell, we're finished with this witness, are we not?" the judge asked sternly.

Now I received an even bigger shock: my supervisor looked up at me and made a slashing motion across his own throat, an obvious signal urging me to comply with the judge's wishes and terminate my direct examination of the police officer.

"Yes, Your Honor," I muttered reluctantly. "I guess we're done."

Once the judge dismissed the cop from the stand, I said, "Your Honor, I have two eyewitnesses who saw the incident take place."

The judge snapped back, "The State rests, correct, Mr. Bell?"

"No, Your Honor," I replied in confusion. "We have two eyewitnesses." Hadn't I just told her that?

She raised her voice even more. "The State rests. Correct, Mr. Bell?"

I looked over at my supervisor for guidance, wondering what I was supposed to do. Had I really lost my first case as easily as that? I'd never been so embarrassed.

My supervisor hissed, "Say 'yes,' Alan. You're done, kid."

Sadly, I complied. "Okay. I mean, yes, Your Honor. The State rests."

My supervisor tugged on my jacket, and I finally sat down next to him, feeling completely defeated.

Then the biggest shock of all came: the judge hit her gavel and said, "I find the defendant guilty, and sentence him to five years in Florida State Prison." She then ordered the bailiff to remove the defendant and called, "Next case."

I walked out of the courtroom feeling a turmoil of emotions: happy that I had somehow "won" my first case, but stunned and heartsick because that man didn't deserve to be put away for five years. The judgment, I now saw, had been predetermined, and the facts of the case weren't all that important.

It was then that my supervisor explained that the judge was widely known as "the hanging judge" because she prided herself on being "America's toughest judge." She had formerly been Florida's first female felony prosecutor. Now that she was a judge, she nearly always handed out the maximum sentences possible—no matter what the crime or circumstances.

For me, this was a sobering moment. It was my first real encounter with the criminal justice system, and I had witnessed firsthand just how flawed it could be. My life lesson: people in positions of power are not always motivated to do the right thing.

◆ ◆ ◆

While I was earning my legal chops, crime in South Florida was heating up. The best and most expensive lawyers followed the money to Miami to represent celebrities, mobsters, and Colombian cartel kingpins. They were a virtual legal who's who, national headline makers like F. Lee Bailey; Roy Black, who represented William Kennedy Smith; Albert Krieger, who represented John Gotti; Frank Rubino, who represented Panama's ex-dictator, Manuel Noriega; and Gerry Spence. Despite my heavy caseload, I was determined to learn how to win, and I earned an amazing education by watching these masters at work.

I devoted every spare moment to sitting in different courtrooms, studying these esteemed legal experts while taking notes. I analyzed their actions and questioned them about their tactics. Gradually, I figured out how the game was played and started winning, too.

In one of those courtrooms, I observed the accused rapist and serial killer Ted Bundy—a third-year law student just like me—representing himself in front of a jury. Bundy was arrested in 1978 and was charged with assaulting and murdering numerous young women and girls. To this day, his victim count remains unknown, but before his execution in 1989, Bundy confessed to thirty homicides committed in seven states between 1974 and 1978.

To put it mildly, Bundy was the very face of evil. Yet, as I watched him represent himself in the courtroom, it was easy to see why he had so readily earned the trust of his young female victims. He was handsome, personable, poised, and articulate.

Years later, as an organized crime prosecutor, I decided to visit the state prison where many of the most hardened criminals I put away were housed. I wanted to see firsthand where I was sending our convicted criminals. To my surprise, while I was touring the facility, the warden asked if I'd like to meet Ted Bundy. By then, he was their most infamous prisoner.

When I agreed, the warden woke Bundy in his cell on death row. Bundy was sleeping on his cot beneath a thin blanket; he stirred, rubbed his eyes, and climbed out of bed to greet me. He was wearing a nightshirt and a pair of boxers. His skin was pale, almost milky white, and his eyes were a piercing bright blue. He looked like an anchorman on the evening news.

This infamous serial killer was articulate, friendly, disarming, and engaging. We could have been in a barbershop or at a backyard picnic talking about local sports teams and politics. I left Bundy's cell feeling chilled to the bone, wondering how this blandly "normal" man could possibly have committed such horrendous, heartless acts. He was an infamous murderer awaiting execution, yet even face-to-face with him, I could perceive no evil residing in Ted Bundy.

I'd learned another valuable life lesson: evil can be found anywhere, even in our everyday environments and in seemingly "good" people— including, I would later find out, those in government organizations and Fortune 500 corporations. I vowed to keep my antenna up for evil I might encounter in my future work as an attorney.

◆ ◆ ◆

As I grew and changed, so did South Florida. These were the Reagan years, a time when business bustled and new buildings were springing up like mushrooms. In 1979, the year I graduated from law school, a deadly shoot-out in broad daylight at the Dadeland Mall between Colombian drug traffickers highlighted the fact that Miami had become the locus of mob violence and turf wars over illegal narcotics.

I was living just two blocks away from where the shooting occurred, but I wasn't shocked by it. This kind of violence had become the new normal: every day, bodies turned up on beaches, in the streets, in the Miami River, and in the Everglades as the homicide count skyrocketed.

Most of the cocaine and marijuana entering the country at that time was trafficked through South Florida, drawing ruthless drug cartels as well as exiled dictators, con men, international weapons traffickers, and the idle rich. Miami also served as the Mafia's winter home. Mobsters came south every winter for extended vacations, financing and running businesses, many of them illicit. They invested in strip joints, bars, drugs, and prostitution.

This booming trade brought millions of dollars into the region, and nobody was shy about spending it on fast boats and even faster cars. South Florida rapidly became a glamorous destination for the rich, famous, and beautiful. There were three women for every guy in the nightclubs. The disco scene was heating up and the partying never stopped. Nothing was too excessive or outlandish. South Florida sizzled, pulsed with bright colors, and danced to a sexy Latin beat as everyone basked in the sunshine by day and partied all night.

Because I was from South Florida, I assumed the whole country was like this. When the TV show *Miami Vice* aired in 1984, everyone thought it was an exaggerated view of what was going on in the city. It wasn't. In fact, the show minimized our extreme reality.

I was the youngest prosecutor in the State of Florida when I joined the Dade County Prosecutor's Office in 1979. As I worked my way up through the legal ranks in the State Attorney's office, I advanced from prosecuting traffic tickets and misdemeanors to serious felonies, until eventually I was trusted to handle cases involving homicides and organized crime.

In 1982, I prosecuted my first felony trial. This case was a slam dunk—or so I thought. The defendant had committed aggravated assault with a firearm, an offense punishable by five years in prison, with a mandatory minimum of three years because a firearm was used.

The defendant was a young white guy who worked with the Mafia. He was represented by the godfather of all criminal defense attorneys, John Baron, who was in his mid-seventies by then. Baron commonly bragged that while not all of his notorious mobster clients "got off," not one was ever executed.

I didn't see how I could lose this case. The defendant had pointed a gun at the victim, cocked it, and threatened to shoot him in front of two eyewitnesses during a dispute. The victim had called 911 after the defendant left, and had given an accurate description of the vehicle. The police had found the car. The gun was still in it, and the defendant had confessed to the crime.

Judge Joe Mosey sat on the bench for that trial. I called the victim and two eyewitnesses to the stand, as well as the police officer who testified that the defendant had confessed the crime to him. I then introduced the gun into evidence. By contrast, the defense attorney had no evidence or testimony to contradict my case.

And yet, as I sat there waiting to taste sweet victory after proving my case, Judge Mosey instantly made his decision after everyone had testified: "Not guilty!"

I was flabbergasted, then infuriated. Afterward, I learned that Judge Mosey had previously worked as an attorney for Baron. When Mosey ran for judge, Baron had supported his candidacy and helped get him elected. As a representative of the people of the State of Florida, I had been set up to lose the case: they had cleverly plotted to waive a jury trial so Mosey could take care of his buddy. Years later, I learned that Judge Mosey's nickname was "Let 'em go, Joe."

After that case, I vowed to become a skilled enough attorney to outwit even those who abused power, in the courtroom and beyond. I was going to do whatever it took not to lose another case.

+ + +

The more I practiced law, the more I loved the excitement of the job, especially as I began specializing in organized crime cases. My job was to convict and put away murderers, mobsters, drug dealers, and other lowlifes.

One of my most entertaining cases involved international drug smuggling by the Colombian cartel. In this case, the cops had brought drug-sniffing dogs into the Fort Lauderdale airport and discovered several kilos of cocaine inside a suitcase on the conveyor belt. The two men who had checked in the luggage were arrested. Even half a kilo in those days warranted a mandatory fifteen-year sentence, and these men were smuggling five kilos. Things didn't look good for them.

My intelligence source informed me that one of these guys was a kingpin in the cartel. The other one was a lower-level guy, or what we called a "mule." Naturally, we wanted to nail the kingpin, so I made a deal with the mule, offering him only five years in state prison if he'd flip on his boss. He took the deal. The kingpin went to trial; he got on the stand and claimed the suitcase wasn't his and that the cocaine belonged to the mule.

Before the trial, I had meticulously examined the contents of the suitcase and found clothing as well as cocaine. I noticed that the shirt inside the suitcase was monogrammed with the initials "JAR." The defense had no idea that his shirt was inside the suitcase; they had never even bothered to look inside it to catalog the contents. As I cross-examined the kingpin on the stand, I seemingly went easy on him, but asked him write his name on an easel in front of the jury before he stepped down from the witness stand. He did so.

Then I asked, "So that's your name? Juan Alfonso Rodriguez? Your full name? The name you've written on that easel?"

"Yes," he said.

"And you're telling the jury that's not your suitcase?" I asked. "That you never even looked inside it?"

"Yes, that's what I say."

"So it's absolutely impossible that any personal items of yours are in this suitcase?"

"Yes, that's what I say," the defendant repeated.

"You're sure of that? As sure as you are that this cocaine is not yours?" I demanded.

"Yes," he said.

I dismissed him from the stand, saying I had no further questions for the witness. This left the defense attorney gloating, thinking I'd gotten nowhere. Even the judge—a close friend of mine—said, "You're in trouble, Alan," when we happened to meet during a recess. "You're not going to win this case."

I laughed. "Just relax, buddy. You'll see."

During closing arguments, I had a field day. I went easy during the first part, but after the defense attorney finished his closing argument, I took the suitcase and easel and put them right in front of the jury. Then I removed a pair of shoes from the suitcase and asked the defendant to try them on. "Your Honor, can you please order this defendant to try on these shoes?"

They fit. The defense attorney was still gloating; I knew he'd argue that the shoes were a common size.

But then I pulled a shirt out of the suitcase, too, saying, "Well, let's see what else is in here. Wow, what do you know. A shirt! And look at these initials on it right here!"

I went over to the easel and circled the three initials of the defendant's name—written in his own handwriting—showed the jury that the initials on the shirt matched, then said, "Your Honor, please order the defendant to try on the shirt."

Of course, the shirt fit. I smiled at the jury and said, "The State has nothing further. Thank you."

The jury was out all of five minutes before they returned to the courtroom and convicted him. I was getting better, making good on my resolutions.

◆ ◆ ◆

During my time with the State Attorney's office, I prosecuted tens of thousands of cases. Hundreds of these involved the Mafia or drug cartel criminals. People often asked if I was scared for my own life, but I wasn't. I figured that prosecutors were a dime a dozen. If they murdered me, the State could always find another prosecutor to try the case.

My career was exhilarating, but it was also exhausting, demanding twelve-hour days and involving frequent adrenaline rushes while working closely with local police departments. The cops often put me on the front lines as they made their busts. They didn't want the criminals getting off because of procedural or technical errors, so I accompanied them as an on-site legal advisor to make sure everything stuck in court.

Working with the police was like being thrown into a real-life *Miami Vice*. I sped around in cop cars with sirens screaming and joined SWAT teams on drug busts and raids. I flew to crime scenes in helicopters and landed on remote airstrips in the Everglades. I even rode in police speedboats, giving chase to smugglers. On these raids, I typically wore a badge and bulletproof vest. I also carried a .357 Magnum four-inch-barrel pistol in a shoulder holster in case things turned really ugly.

Although at times South Florida felt like the Wild West, it was gratifying work. I felt like I was making a difference.

I had no idea how abruptly my exciting career was about to end, or how important these early courtroom lessons would be to me later in life.

3 · FAMILY LIFE

IN 1982, I ATTENDED MY ten-year Coral Park High School reunion at the Fontainebleau Hotel in Miami Beach. I'd dressed up for the occasion in one of my favorite charcoal-gray gray three-piece suits and spent the first part of the evening catching up with classmates I hadn't seen in years.

Suddenly, a waiter brought me a drink on the house. Then one more, and another.

The drinks kept coming, but whenever I asked the waiter who was sending them, all he'd say was, "You have a secret admirer." I looked around the room, yet I had no idea who it might be.

Eventually, an attractive woman walked up to me and said, "I'm Susan. Did you like the drinks?"

Although Susan had been in my high school class, she might as well have gone to school on another planet. Our social circles never intersected. I was an overweight, pimply percussionist who had actually been to band camp and enjoyed it. She was runner-up to the Homecoming Queen with a star quarterback for a boyfriend. Need I say more?

Yet, by some stroke of luck, this attractive, friendly, auburn-haired woman made it abundantly clear that she was interested in me. Susan was divorced from her first husband and had moved back in with her mother. She worked full-time as the manager of a medical practice, but seemed eager to fit into my busy world. We began dating seriously, and she made a point of getting close to my mother. We moved in together two years later; when I proposed marriage, she offered to convert to Judaism without me asking.

Susan and I were married in 1986 and built a brand-new house in the upscale neighborhood of Coral Springs outside of Fort Lauderdale. She was sweet and attentive, got along well with my family, and didn't seem to mind that our social life consisted of my family, friends, and work colleagues.

Looking back on things now, I realize how immature I was when we got married. I didn't know what depths of communication every good marriage requires. I hadn't had many long-term relationships with women because I started dating later in life. I simply accepted Susan as she was and felt grateful that she didn't mind my busy schedule. She seemed happy to quit her job, and we had a maid who took most of the housework off Susan's shoulders, leaving her free to socialize with her own friends during the day, shop, or go to the gym.

When we were together, Susan was enthusiastic and athletic enough to keep up with any adventure I suggested. We traveled a great deal whenever I could get time off from work. We took trips through Europe and went skiing in Colorado. We played racquetball on weekends and took scuba diving lessons together before embarking on a fabulous diving trip to the Cayman Islands. In the evenings, we ate out whenever I got home early enough, and we went to the movies a lot. Weekends were spent socializing with my law practice colleagues.

Susan got along well with my sister, Judi, too. I really appreciated this because Judi and I had always been close. During our adolescent years, Bobby was the athlete in the family and I was the musician; he and I often got into scrapes and egged each other on during our various adventures, like wrapping houses with toilet paper. Many times, we drove our poor mother to say, "You boys just wait until your father gets home. He's going to hear about this!"

Judi, on the other hand, was a quiet, intellectual kid who always had her nose in a book. Because my father frequently worked long hours and I was six years older than Judi, my little sister looked up to me as a surrogate father in his absence. If she ran into any kind of trouble, she could always count on me for protection. When it was time for her to go to college, I was the one who drove her to Gainesville and helped her move into her dormitory. I visited Judi about once a week during the time she lived in Gainesville, and later I helped her find her first job.

When Judi earned her chiropractic license and opened an office in Deerfield Beach, Susan worked right alongside my family as we helped Judi launch her career and make a success of her fledgling practice. Susan helped select the location—she was the only one of us who was experienced in managing a medical practice—and chose the teal carpeting and the linen-white walls for Judi's office décor. Bobby provided the seed money to get things up and running, and my father handed out fliers advertising free initial visits to get patients into her office. I loved it that Susan was so willing to pitch in whenever it came to family activities.

It didn't take long before I realized that balancing a family with my work at the State Attorney's Office would be much more difficult now that I had a wife to consider. Even when I was out all night investigating crime scenes, my schedule demanded that I still return to the office the morning after, often preparing for back-to-back trials. Sometimes I'd have to face up to ten new cases a day.

I was extremely earnest and idealistic about practicing law. However, since I'd been raised in a traditional household, where my father was the one who worked long hours so my mother could be at home with the children, I decided it was time to take another professional leap. I wanted to provide better financial support for Susan and, hopefully, for our children one day. I had grown up with the benefits of a happy, secure family life, and now I longed to recreate that scenario for my own kids.

It felt like the right time to look for an opportunity in private practice, learn about civil litigation, and do defense work. I accepted a position with an insurance defense firm representing Travelers Insurance Company and Fortune 500 companies. This career move not only provided a significant pay raise, but also afforded me opportunities to keep learning as a litigator. I didn't stop there, though: I also represented private practice plaintiffs during my off hours.

I took criminal cases that interested me—usually for teenagers or the elderly—that I often defended pro bono. I was focused on reaching out to the underdog partly because I always carried that chubby band geek inside, the one who was counseled in high school to apply to trade schools because he wasn't "college material." I knew what it felt like to be kicked around.

Fulfilled by my marriage and my career, I was riding high, making my parents proud and embracing every challenge that came my way.

My life was transformed once again in 1988, when Susan gave birth to our daughter, Ashlee. She went into labor on Super Bowl Sunday while we were having breakfast with friends. I took Susan to the hospital and stayed by her side through the birth of our blessedly healthy daughter. Of course, I thought Ashlee was the most beautiful baby I'd ever seen.

I left the hospital at 5 o'clock in the morning after kissing my wife and child. Despite having been up all night, I felt energized and drove straight to work. As the sun rose over I-95, the inky black sky faded and then brightened to pink while I experienced the most incredible feeling of joy. This was a new dawn in my life. I vowed to be as loving a parent to Ashlee as my own parents had been to me. The word *dawn* meant so much to me that we gave it to Ashlee as her middle name.

In the months to come, I worked harder than ever while Susan stayed home with Ashlee. She had become president of a local Jewish group in Fort Lauderdale and socialized with the women she met there. She also took Ashlee to Mommy & Me classes and worked out at the gym. On evenings and weekends, she and I reveled in parenthood together. We took Ashlee everywhere: to the beaches and parks, to restaurants, and to visit family and friends.

I embraced my blessed life with no foreshadowing of what was to come. Maybe that was a good thing, given what I would soon have to endure.

◆ ◆ ◆

Shortly after I began working at my new law firm at 110 Tower, I began experiencing odd symptoms. I'd wake up in the morning and feel fine until I reached the office. After an hour or so there, my sinuses would clog up. My eyes burned and my nose seemed to run constantly. I couldn't swim in the usual community pool without my eyes and skin stinging from the chlorine, and I felt increasingly short of breath any time I exerted myself swimming. I tried pool after pool with the same results. Yet I felt fine whenever I swam in the ocean, and at home on weekends I was usually well enough to take a walk with Susan and Ashlee.

One day in 1989, I suffered an intense episode of vertigo. Even worse, this time the dizziness was accompanied by a high fever, sore throat, and aching joints.

I was thirty-five years old, healthy and fit, still running and working out in the gym every day. It must be the flu, I told Susan. What else could it be?

"Hey, buddy, do you know a good doctor?" I asked a friend. "I don't have my own physician. I think I'm coming down with something."

My friend sent me to his internal medicine practitioner, who thought I probably had a virus. The doctor prescribed antibiotics "just in case."

In time, my symptoms improved, though they didn't go away completely. I still felt like I was fighting off a low-grade cold.

About three months later, I experienced a relapse. This time I suffered from an even higher fever. Incredible hot flashes swept through my body like flash fires, causing me to feel so nauseated that I would vomit. It felt like an elephant was sitting on my chest. Even climbing stairs was a challenge, despite the fact that I'd been running over three miles every morning since college.

I returned to the doctor and told him about the relapse.

"We'll put you on a different antibiotic, something stronger," he said confidently and sent me away again.

He was the guy wearing the white coat, so I followed his instructions to the letter. I carried Ashlee in my arms into the pharmacy to pick up my new prescription, wearing a surgical mask to prevent her from catching whatever strange virus I had.

The antibiotics helped, but I still wasn't myself. Whenever I tried running, my knee joints felt like they were on fire, so I stopped. Even working out on the machines in the gym was too much for me. I constantly felt like I had the flu: exhausted, wrung out, occasionally feverish, and wheezing for breath.

"What do you think it is, Alan?" Susan kept asking. "I'm worried about you. Maybe you ought to get another antibiotic or something. It seems like this thing is still hanging on."

"I probably just need more time," I reassured her. "I think I'm just burning myself out by working too many hours."

I tried slowing down my pace at work, taking on fewer cases and sometimes handing things off to my coworkers. Occasionally, I even worked from home if I felt really terrible; still, after a few hours, I had trouble concentrating. I'd sit up in bed to work on a case, and the minute I opened up my legal books, my eyes would start burning. I couldn't understand it.

Our social life slowly began drying up. I started declining invitations to dinner or the movies, avoiding social situations the same way someone who's coming down with the flu might. I just wanted to lie on the sofa in front of the TV and go to bed early. Susan tried hard not to complain, but every now and then she'd turn to me with a beseeching look and say, "Really? You want to stay home again? But it's Saturday night, Alan! Can't we at least go out for a little while?"

"I just can't do it," I'd tell her. "I'm too exhausted and sick. You go."

To her credit, Susan stayed home with me most evenings despite her obvious restlessness. And, no matter how lousy I felt, I continued doing my best to be a good father. I spent time with Ashlee on weekends any way my limited health would allow. Sometimes, if my energy level was particularly low, all I could do was take her for a spin in my car. That was fine with Ashlee: my daredevil daughter loved racing around corners in our neighborhood with the top down and feeling the wind blowing through her fiery red hair.

Whenever I felt well enough, I took Ashlee to the playground so she could toddle around with other kids. Ashlee was over a year old by then; it was agony to watch her master crawling and then walking without feeling well enough to play with her. All I could do was watch her and marvel at all the new things my little girl was learning and doing.

The third time I relapsed, I ran a high fever and felt so weak and dizzy that I could hardly stand up. I felt not only frustrated, but angry, too. Being sick was never part of my life's plan. Not one of my inspirational Zig Ziglar tapes had ever covered illness. There was no such thing as a problem without a solution! Not unless you were a total loser!

I still believed that if you worked hard enough, you could achieve any goal. Obviously, I wasn't working hard enough to kick this illness. I would look for a different doctor, I decided, because the one I'd seen so far must be incompetent.

By the time I found a new physician—recommended by another colleague—my fever had soared to 104 degrees. My ears were ringing, my vision was blurred, everything hurt, and I was wheezing and spitting up green sputum. This doctor put me on a course of even stronger antibiotics. He also prescribed an additional medication.

"Here," he said. "I want you to take these steroids, too. That should help with your breathing."

I took the antibiotics and religiously sprayed the steroid into my nose as directed. In my view, these doctors were professionals, the next step down from God when it came to health. I never thought to question anything they prescribed.

The next morning, I felt slightly better. I knew that Susan was at the end of her rope with my health complaints, so I suggested that we put Ashlee into her stroller and go out with another couple, my former prosecuting partner, Andy, and his wife. We went to the local Coral Springs carnival, where I was determined to enjoy the day.

It was a beautiful day, the sort of sunny afternoon in early spring that draws people trapped in snow-burdened states to Florida. A salty breeze blew in from the Atlantic as I pushed Ashlee in her stroller past craft vendors selling brightly colored goods. The air was redolent with delicious smells from the Cuban and Latin American food stalls all around us.

Suddenly, I started sweating profusely; waves of nausea swept over me. "Not again," I thought, as I gripped the handles of the stroller and struggled to stay upright.

It was as if all of the blood were being drained out of my body. My brain was like a loose light bulb, slowly blinking on and off: one second I was there, the next second I was gone. My legs gave out from under me. I would have hit the ground if Andy hadn't grabbed me around the waist and helped me to a park bench.

My head was spinning, and it seemed like everything was coming toward me at top speed. At the same time, everything was bizarrely happening in slow motion. I wondered if this was what it felt like to die.

"What's wrong, Alan?" Andy asked.

"I don't know," I managed to wheeze.

"We're having the devil of a time figuring out what's going on with him," Susan said.

I closed my eyes, worrying that my wife's patience with my ongoing problems might start wearing thin. What if she lost her patience altogether? She'd married a dynamic, athletic prosecutor. Now I could barely push our daughter's stroller.

◆ ◆ ◆

I checked myself into our local hospital after collapsing at the fair. The doctor on call diagnosed atypical pneumonia when I listed my symptoms. "I'll put you on an IV with antibiotics and steroids," he said.

I nodded weakly in agreement. Who was I to question him?

Within a few hours of being put on the IV, I had this incredible burning inside my chest, as if someone had lit a fire inside my rib cage. The flames burned up to my throat, searing the inside of my esophagus.

I screamed and writhed in pain. The hospital staff hurriedly wheeled me into an operating room, where they sedated me and performed an emergency endoscopy. When I came to, the surgeon visited my room to report the results.

"Your esophagus is covered with candida fungus," he said. "That's why it feels like you're burning up inside."

"Why would that be?" I asked, still half out of it from the procedure.

"It's usually the result of a weakened immune system," he explained. "Small amounts of candida are always present in our mouths and digestive tracts, and in other parts of the body, too. Normally they're kept in check by bacteria and other microorganisms. You were probably on antibiotics for so long that the 'good' bacteria in your body was wiped out. That left you totally susceptible to the fungus, which is eating away at your esophageal tissues."

"I don't understand," I said. "I took the antibiotics just as prescribed. Is there anything else that could be causing my immune system to break down?"

"It could be a virus," he said. "We'll run some tests. Have you ever been tested for AIDS?"

I shook my head. I'd never even heard of AIDS at that point in my life.

My AIDS test was negative, and other diagnostics were inconclusive. Nevertheless, the doctor prescribed antifungal drugs, without any positive test result supporting this aggressive "shotgun" method of treatment. "We'll start you on a new IV," he said.

"No," I answered. I couldn't handle the thought of taking one more medication that might cause me even more pain. It sounded to me like this doctor was only guessing. For the first time, I questioned the competency of the "almighty" medical profession, and I wanted to do my own research and find a specialist before I agreed to any other treatments. My very life was at stake.

I removed the IV line from my arm, staggered to my feet, and somehow pulled on my clothes. I managed to get myself out of the hospital and into my car, but I couldn't make it very far. I pulled over and called Susan to come meet me in a park because I was too weak to drive all the way home.

Susan spread a blanket out on the ground when she arrived. I stretched out on it and closed my eyes, trying to gather enough strength to move again. Something was totally broken in my body.

There was a deep-seated feeling of darkness inside me now. For the first time, I felt like I had come face-to-face with my own mortality.

I wasn't afraid to die. But I was beginning to feel scared my little girl would grow up without her daddy.

◆ ◆ ◆

The day after Susan picked me up from the hospital, I called the University of Miami Medical School. I was still putting my faith in the medical establishment; I was convinced that my getting well was just a matter of finding the right professional, someone with the expertise to diagnose and cure me.

At the University of Miami, I saw a hematologist, who ordered blood tests and offered a new diagnosis: Epstein-Barr virus, the virus that causes mononucleosis.

"Your antibodies are through the roof," he said. "All you need to do is rest, and it will go away. Give it time."

I took him at his word because he had offered me solid, scientific, irrefutable proof: antibodies to the Epstein-Barr virus were in my blood. We finally had an answer!

Relieved, I continued working, putting one foot in front of the other. Every day, I'd reduce my high fever by loading up on aspirin and go sit at my desk in the 110 Tower. I tried hard to work, but often did little more than stare out at the ocean, feeling like I was in a boat on a pitching sea. My joints were on fire; my whole body ached. I worked at home on my worst days and asked for help on my cases whenever I could, telling myself, over and over, that it was just a matter of time before I beat this thing.

Meanwhile, more odd symptoms appeared. It seemed like I was making my way through a maze of new obstacles every week. I'd always loved the smell of certain women's perfumes, but now, within moments of becoming aware of someone wearing perfume

31

and thinking it smelled good, I'd double over in pain. If I was driving in traffic with the windows down, the car exhaust would make my lungs seize up.

Back then, cigarette smoking was still allowed in the courthouse. I'd never minded this before. But on the increasingly rare occasions I went to the courthouse, I'd walk through billowing clouds of smoke in the hallways and feel like I was being poisoned. My eyes teared up, and I could hardly breathe. On the even rarer occasions when Susan and I ate out, if someone lit a cigarette at the next table, I'd have to leave the restaurant with my food still untouched.

"Come on, Alan, this is silly," Susan said after one such incident. "What are you doing? You can't possibly be this sensitive. You didn't even eat your dinner, and we still had to pay for it."

"I'm sorry," I said. "I can't tolerate cigarette smoke anymore. Maybe I'm allergic to it or something. I don't know."

Driving in my new car was starting to make me feel nauseated, and I could no longer tolerate air-conditioning. Anyone who has ever lived in South Florida knows that air-conditioning isn't a luxury—it's an absolute necessity for survival in this region's hot, humid climate. But I simply couldn't handle it. One night, my shivering and wheezing got so bad, I had to retreat to the patio and sleep outside. Susan found me there one morning.

"What are you doing out here?" she asked, obviously bewildered. "How can you sleep on that lounge chair?"

"It's better than the air-conditioning," I replied. "I don't know if it's the quality of the air or the temperature, but I can't stand it anymore."

"What do you mean? That's crazy! You can't sleep out on the patio every night!" She shook her head and left me there.

Another day, while I was walking on my treadmill at home in a desperate attempt to keep up my muscle tone, an exterminator came to spray for pests. In South Florida, it's common to have your house sprayed regularly for bugs; I'd grown up being around these pesticides. But this time, when the guy started spraying around me, I passed out on the floor.

I didn't understand why all of this was happening to me. I'd never been allergic or even sensitive to anything the way I seemed to be now.

As a college athlete, I had learned how to train through pain. I opted for the same stoic approach now, refusing to cave in to my symptoms completely. I did whatever I could to live a normal life. I had a family to provide for and clients who depended on me. I continued spending time with Ashlee whenever I wasn't working.

Being at the beach always seemed to make me feel better—although I had no idea why—so we started spending more time there. Once, I felt well enough to dive into the ocean and retrieve a starfish that Ashlee carried in her hand everywhere she went. We named him Billy.

When feeling too sick to move, I'd lie on the floor and let Ashlee use me as a human jungle gym. The sight of her grinning always lifted my spirits.

Eventually, I began having real trouble breathing. I literally couldn't draw a full breath of air into my lungs and started wheezing constantly. My colleagues at Travelers continued trying to cover for me, but my work was definitely suffering. I wasn't getting enough oxygen to think straight. Sometimes I felt so ill that I'd have to postpone my private cases, too, because dragging myself across the street to the courthouse became practically impossible.

On the rare days I managed to get myself to the office, I was so exhausted by the end of the day that I struggled against dozing off at the wheel as I drove home. When I arrived, I'd hug Ashlee and play with her a little if she was still awake, then crash into bed. The next morning, I'd wake up and do it all again. I was hardly eating and started losing weight.

Susan had to gradually take over more and more household responsibilities. By now she was doing most of the child care, even at night, plus all of the grocery shopping and meal preparations. We were forced to eat at home nearly every night since I usually didn't feel well enough to go out. As a precaution, I avoided all artificial or processed foods, which added to Susan's burden in the kitchen. I tried ordering takeout food from the Chinese and Italian restaurants I'd always loved, but I couldn't hold down the food. Even pizza no longer agreed with me.

If we had to deal with anyone outside the house—our car mechanic, the yard crew, delivery people—Susan had to be the one to do it. She also took over managing our finances. That proved to be a disaster. Within a year, she managed to bounce fifty-two checks. I happened to stumble upon this fact by accident one day when I pulled open a desk drawer and realized it was full of overdue notices.

"What's all this?" I asked, staring helplessly at the jumbled piles of bills and notices. "Why are all of these papers stuffed in the drawer?"

"It's nothing, Alan," she said. "Come on. Lie down. I'll take care of it."

"What do you mean, it's *nothing?* Susan, you can't just toss bills in a drawer. And how did these checks bounce? We have plenty of money."

She looked down at her feet and mumbled something about forgetting to transfer money from one account to the other. I was angry, but I felt bad about losing my temper with her, too. Susan hadn't signed on to be my accountant any more than she'd signed up to be my nursemaid. I felt sorry that I was putting her in this position, but I didn't have the energy or cognitive ability to do more than survive one day at a time. I pushed the envelopes back into the drawer and left them.

4 ⋅ The Doctor Shuffle

As I stared at the ocean outside my window in 110 Tower, my body was bathed in sweat as I struggled not to vomit. I tried my best to stay still, hoping the nausea would dissipate before my court hearing scheduled for later that afternoon. Otherwise, I'd never make it through.

My phone rang as I was mopping my forehead for what felt like the thousandth time. It was the judge's assistant calling to reschedule the hearing. *Thank God*, I thought. Now I wouldn't have to be the one to cancel—again.

As we spoke, the assistant could hear me sniffling and wheezing. "Are you sick, too?" she asked.

"Yeah. I've been fighting allergies or some sort of flu," I said.

"It's the building, you know."

"I'm sorry?" I thought I must have misheard her.

The assistant explained that the judge she worked for had fallen ill and blamed it on mold in the courthouse. She went on to say that she'd heard of other people who worked in the courthouse falling ill, as well as in new buildings like 110 Tower.

"It's because there's no fresh airflow in these buildings," she said. "The closed ventilation system is a serious problem. There's mold and all kinds of bad stuff in the carpet and paint."

"Huh," I said, already turning my attention to the next item on my "to do" list. "That's all very interesting."

I must have sounded dismissive, because the assistant became agitated and adamant. "Let me tell you something right now, son," she said. "You've got to get out of that building immediately. Run, don't walk! The judge can hardly work or function. You need to get out while there's still time!"

I hung up the phone while staring out the window, shaking my head. That woman sounded like a lunatic.

◆ ◆ ◆

No matter what the outcome, I was determined to get to the root cause of my illness. Although I finally had to admit that I was no longer a bulletproof athlete and attorney, I remained convinced that there had to be a physician somewhere out there with the expertise to "fix" me.

During the next year or so, I left no stone unturned, doing what I dubbed the "doctor shuffle." I saw physician after physician, eventually losing count. *It only takes one good doctor*, I kept reminding myself. *Then my life can return to normal.*

The doctor shuffle usually began with me in an exam room as a physician breezed in with an air of confidence, asking how he could help me today. I would list all of my symptoms as the doctor flipped through my ever-growing medical file and nodded.

By now, I'd accumulated a host of symptoms and hundreds of test results. I'd earned diagnoses of fatigue, fibromyalgia, cognitive dysfunction, short-term memory loss, disorientation, blurry vision, impaired coordination, inflamed joints, gastrointestinal dysfunction, respiratory distress, asthma, and seizures.

Each time I saw a new physician, more tests would be ordered and I'd be sent away until the results arrived. Every time the results arrived, the doctor ordering them seemed slightly less cheerful and confident, or maybe even angry, as if I were part of a conspiracy to confuse him. It was as if eventually I'd hit a weak point in every physician's psyche, that secret fear that they didn't know as much as they thought they did.

This doctor shuffle would typically end in an awkward silence or something vague and noncommittal when they realized I had exhausted the limits of their knowledge. "It's a virus. I don't know what else to tell you," some said.

"Maybe it's an infection we can't detect," others suggested.

As I left one exam room after another, I could almost hear the physicians muttering, "Got to be a psych case" under their breaths.

I faced disappointment after disappointment, but every time I looked at my beautiful little girl, I became more determined than ever to keep going. I longed to watch my daughter grow up and to celebrate a golden wedding anniversary with Susan. The idea that I might have an untreatable illness never once crossed my mind. Up until that point in my life, I had never experienced pain, failure, or deep unhappiness. I was still an innocent.

The other person who kept me going was my brother, Bobby. Unlike Judi and me, Bobby hadn't pursued a four-year degree. He had chosen to attend a junior college and then transferred to the University of South Dakota, where he was the star quarterback on their football team until he decided cold weather wasn't for him. He returned to Florida and became a delivery truck driver for the Banana Boat company, a mom-and-pop operation that sold suntan lotion.

The owners were basically running the company out of a garage. They sold it to my brother for a small amount of money. I helped Bobby incorporate the company, served as his legal counsel, and helped him connect with an accountant, my good college friend and former fraternity brother, Barry.

When we were in high school, our father made a small fortune in real estate by selling property to tourists in a central Florida community known as Lehigh Acres. Dad's job often involved meeting and greeting potential customers in the lobbies of Miami Beach hotels; because of his various hotel contacts, Dad knew many of the hotel owners and was able to get Bobby and me jobs as lifeguards during the summers when we were in our teens. Bobby often heard people complaining about greasy suntan lotion while lifeguarding, so he started mixing different ingredients—everything from coconut and fruit to baby oil and iodine—to see if he could create a more effective tanning formula. Although he had no formal education in chemistry, Bobby was creative and risk tolerant, and he possessed the instinctive gift to sell. Imagine this young, eccentric guy experimenting with all kinds of ingredients like a mad scientist: that was my brother.

Up until the mid-1980s, sun-care products were developed to help people tan, but by the time Bobby bought Banana Boat, there was evidence linking sun exposure to skin cancer. This prompted him to research and develop high-SPF sunblocks. Bobby remembered the western TV shows we'd both loved as kids, and how gunshot wounds were often treated with aloe plants. He decided to research skin-care products using aloe to help heal sun-damaged skin.

When Banana Boat brought Aloe After Sun Gel to the market, Bobby saw his company boom as the gel became its bestselling skin-care product. With him as CEO, Banana Boat grew to become the second-largest sun-care brand in the world.

Ironically, during the years my brother was building his business, my health and career were declining rapidly. My work at Travelers Insurance began to unravel as I kept getting sicker. It killed me to ask others to cover for me and do my work—I had always prided myself on performing my responsibilities at the highest possible level—but I had to accept the help. My private practice trickled down to nothing. Eventually, I had to face the reality of my plight and step away from my professional responsibilities.

I'd always been the big brother, the one my younger siblings looked up to whenever they had problems that needed solving. Now the tables were turned. Bobby stepped up to the plate.

"Don't worry, Alan," Bobby said. "I've got your back. Whatever happens, I'll be there for you."

He was, too. Bobby kept me on as general counsel for Banana Boat, a job that was flexible enough for me to do during times I felt well enough to work. Later, he'd save my life again and again with his brotherly support.

◆ ◆ ◆

Thanks to the support of Susan, Bobby, and the rest of my family, I had the resources to begin searching for the best allergy and immunology specialists across the country. My first stop was National Jewish Health in Denver, Colorado, an academic medical research facility dedicated exclusively to the research and treatment of respiratory, allergy, and immune disorders. I saw Dr. Charles Kirkpatrick, a physician and professor in the division of allergy and clinical immunology at the University of Colorado.

Dr. Kirkpatrick was tall and silver-haired, with a commanding air of authority; he was clearly well respected. Because National Jewish Health is a teaching hospital, he entered the exam room accompanied by a flurry of assistants and associates who seemed to hang on his every word, as Dr. Kirkpatrick flipped through my blood work and frowned.

"This red blood cell count looks really low for a young guy like you," he announced and sent me off for an endoscopy at the University of Colorado right away, along with a battery of other tests.

The next time I saw him, Dr. Kirkpatrick had the test results in hand. "I thought you might have internal bleeding, maybe bleeding of the esophagus, because your red and white blood cell counts are so low," he explained. "Now these tests show that your liver enzymes are off, too."

I remained quiet, recognizing that Dr. Kirkpatrick was acting like a medical detective. He was intrigued by my case and tried to puzzle out the clues. "This is so odd," he said. "None of this adds up, unless—" he began, then stopped.

"Unless what?" I asked.

He looked at me. "Unless you were poisoned. That's how it appears to me. What do you think?"

"Poisoned? Like food poisoning, you mean? I don't think so. I haven't eaten any bad fish or anything."

"No, that's not what I'm talking about," Dr. Kirkpatrick said. "Listen, I know you're a lawyer, but where do you work?"

"I'm a litigator for Fortune 500 companies."

"And how long have you been doing that?"

I told him, then added, "Before that, I was a prosecutor for the State Attorney's Office."

"What kinds of people were you prosecuting?"

"I was in the organized crime unit."

His eyebrows shot up. "Any chance one of those guys might have poisoned you for revenge?" Dr. Kirkpatrick said.

"I don't know," I said. "I don't think so." This whole idea seemed pretty far-fetched to me.

"Look, how many people did you put away?" Dr. Kirkpatrick asked.

"I can't count how many," I said. "Lots."

"And did any of them get out recently and maybe come see you?"

Dr. Kirkpatrick was clearly serious about this possibility, so I thought hard. "You know, something did happen recently," I admitted.

I told him about pulling up to a pump at a gas station near the courthouse not too long ago. As I was filling the tank of my car, a tall, muscular guy in ragged clothing came up to me and said, "Hey, remember me?"

I looked up at him—he must have been really tall, since I'm over six feet—and I told him I didn't know who he was. The guy responded, "Yeah, well, I remember you. Is you a lawyer?"

"Yes," I said.

"Well, is you a prosecutor?" he asked.

By then, I was alarmed enough by his appearance and behavior to hide my identity. "No, I'm not a prosecutor," I said, "and I've never seen you before in my life. You must have the wrong guy."

The man would not give up. "I just got out of the jailhouse, and you put me in there," he insisted.

"I don't put people in the jailhouse," I said.

"No, I think you did. I never forget a face," the man said.

I shrugged, trying to act nonchalant, but my heart was pounding as I got back into my car and drove off, feeling the guy's eyes on me.

I described this incident to Dr. Kirkpatrick, then said, "But I don't see how that guy could have done anything to me."

"You'd be surprised," he said. "There are all kinds of chemicals people can use if they want to poison someone. These substances are easy to put in your drink or your food. If the poison doesn't kill you, it leaves you permanently impaired. I'm telling you, Alan, this really manifests like a poisoning case."

I was still skeptical. "Okay, but can you find out what it is?"

"Maybe," Dr. Kirkpatrick said. "I'll run some basic test panels to screen for the most common toxins."

More tests followed. The results suggested that my immune system had been exposed to a toxin of some kind, Dr. Kirkpatrick reported during my next appointment. "Unfortunately, we don't have the technology to identify what that poison might have been," he said. "All I can tell you is that your blood test results are abnormal in a way that suggests you were poisoned, but we have no way to diagnose the root cause of your malady. I'm sorry, Alan. There's nothing more I can tell you."

Susan had traveled with me to Denver. At night, we'd drive around the local neighborhoods looking at houses, imagining what it would be like to live here instead of in Miami. I talked with Susan about Dr. Kirkpatrick's poisoning theory. She thought it was absurd.

"Come on, Alan. That's ridiculous. How would anyone get to your food?" she demanded.

I'd asked myself the same question. On the other hand, talking with Dr. Kirkpatrick had also made me think back to the hundreds of high-level mobsters and drug dealers I'd put away during my time as a prosecutor. What if somebody like that cocaine kingpin who left his shirt in the suitcase had a long memory and a thirst for revenge? Even if he was still in prison, it would be easy enough for him to order one of his underlings to go after me. Perhaps I *should* have been concerned for my life while I was putting criminals away. Was it possible that my past had caught up with me?

But Susan wasn't buying this theory, so we didn't talk anymore about it. Instead, as we were leaving National Jewish Health for good, Susan said, "We'll get through this, Alan, and maybe when you're feeling better, we'll come back here to ski."

"That sounds great, honey," I replied as I held her hand. "I'd love that."

I was glad to hear that Susan seemed as certain as I was that I would eventually kick this thing one day.

◆ ◆ ◆

When we arrived home from Colorado, I was exhausted, but I continued to mull over Dr. Kirkpatrick's theory. I still thought it was pretty crazy that, after all this time, somebody would come after me. At the same time, Dr. Kirkpatrick was a prestigious, well-qualified physician with a workable hypothesis. What if he was right? And what if we could discover the source of the poisoning, leading us to an antidote?

My legal training prevented me from accepting anything as truth without adequate proof. On the first day of law school, the dean told us, first-year students, "When you leave here, you will never be the same again. Look at your fellow classmates sitting next to you. Some of them will fail to become lawyers because they will not have learned to change the way they think."

I walked out of that class feeling concerned, thinking, "I don't want to change how I am. I like the way I think!"

I was twenty-one years old, tall and athletic, with beach-blond hair. I was a former lifeguard and musician. On the first day of that class, I was wearing my favorite faded blue-and-white striped T-shirt. Despite all of my academic accomplishments, I was still a naive kid.

But the dean was right. In order to become a successful attorney, you must change the way you approach, analyze, and solve problems. In the courtroom, everything must be proven by solid evidence. If you can't see something, smell it, hear it, touch it, or taste it, it doesn't exist.

After spending many years gathering evidence, building legal cases, and proving them beyond a reasonable doubt, I'd learned that you can't convince juries to convict criminals and put them away unless you give them hard evidence. It was the only way I knew how to navigate my world.

My well-trained prosecutor's investigative mind kicked into gear after our return from Colorado. If this were a criminal case I needed to solve, I wondered, then how would I approach it? How could I find out if I'd really been poisoned? And, if so, by whom?

I decided to investigate my alleged poisoning the way I would any other crime. I called a buddy of mine, Ben, a former detective for the Oakland Park Police Department, and asked if he'd look into this for me.

"What do you want me to do?" he asked.

"Sniff around and see what you can dig up, maybe develop some leads on who might have wanted to poison me," I told him.

"Leave it to me, Alan," he said.

I knew what Ben would do from there: he'd reach out to our confidential informants, the petty street criminals who fed cops information about the mob in exchange for lighter sentences after they were busted for a less serious crime. These informants would know of any rumors about someone acting on a vendetta against me.

Ben wouldn't stop there, either. He was a good detective: I knew he'd also start nosing around my office building, the courthouse, the restaurants I frequented, my gym, you name it. He would casually strike up conversations to see where they'd lead. If somebody *had* poisoned me, Ben would find out who had done it and why. I felt confident of that.

Meanwhile, I continued my own parallel investigation, doggedly searching for medical answers. My next appointment took me to the Mayo Clinic in Rochester, Minnesota. Susan accompanied me, and, once again, I saw a primary physician who would serve as my guide through their ranks of specialists.

"Look, we'll get to the bottom of this," he vowed, "but you'll need to stay here a week so we can check you out. You'll have to promise that you'll see every doctor I refer you to, all right?"

"Fine," I said, scanning the list of referrals he'd given me. "I'll do whatever it takes." Just then, I noticed the first specialist on the list was a psychiatrist. "Wait a minute," I said. "What's this about?" It was the first time a doctor had ever openly suggested that my illness might be psychosomatic.

Calmly, he told me, "I want to rule out everything by making sure there's no mental component to your experience."

"Fine," I agreed. "Here's the deal. I'll see everyone you send me to, even the psychiatrist. But at the end of it, I want you to promise you'll find out what's wrong with me."

"You've got yourself a deal," he said.

I went to the psychiatrist, who sat me at a desk in a tiny room. I answered hundreds of multiple-choice questions, looked at inkblots, and told him what they looked like. I passed these psychological assessments with flying colors—no surprise to me—and made it to the next round of tests.

The Mayo doctor sent me to specialist after specialist. Susan and Ashlee shared a hotel room with me, and every day, the three of us went to laboratories and doctors' offices from morning to late afternoon.

Whenever I wasn't at a medical appointment, Susan and I toured the area with Ashlee. We were especially fascinated by the Amish communities, and loved seeing how simply they lived, whether they were baking their own bread or driving a horse and buggy down the road ahead of our car. Susan provided a comforting presence, helping me look toward the future rather than feel stuck in this bewildering present.

The lab results from Mayo Clinic confirmed much of what I'd already discovered at National Jewish Health: my red blood cell count was low, causing anemia and low oxygen levels. My low white blood cell count indicated a condition called "leucopenia," which caused me to be prone to infection.

In addition, I had high carbon dioxide levels—probably because of the low oxygen—and my liver enzymes were all abnormal. I still had high Epstein-Barr viral titers.

Translation? I wasn't getting enough oxygen to feel or think normally. My severely compromised immune system meant I was vulnerable to constant viral attacks, and my liver couldn't cleanse my body of toxins.

"Is it possible I was poisoned?" I asked the Mayo Clinic doctor.

"All I can tell from the tests is that you have chronic fatigue immune dysfunction syndrome caused by the Epstein-Barr virus," he replied.

Epstein-Barr is a virus that causes mononucleosis, and many people carry it without getting sick. However, people who do exhibit symptoms of Epstein-Barr might experience a rash, fever, drop in appetite, sore throat, fatigue, swollen glands, and sore muscles.

These symptoms typically improve after a few weeks, but the fatigue can linger much longer—even for months.

Chronic fatigue syndrome is a complicated (and still controversial, in some circles) disorder. It's also characterized by extreme fatigue, which may get worse with physical or mental activity, and doctors still haven't pinpointed an absolute causal factor for the condition. Theories range from psychological stress to viruses; most medical professionals today believe chronic fatigue syndrome is triggered in certain individuals by a combination of factors. Treatment is focused on helping reduce the symptoms. There is no medical cure.

This doctor's diagnosis was consistent with my symptoms of fatigue, muscle and joint pain, cognitive and gastrointestinal dysfunction, respiratory distress, and seizures. "Go home and rest," he said. "There's nothing more we can do for you."

"Wait a minute," I said. "Hold up. You're saying the only advice you have for me is to *rest?* There's no medicine you can give me to at least make me feel better?"

"No," he said. "I'm sorry. It's really just a matter of giving the body time to heal itself."

"I don't have that kind of time," I said. "I can't do my job, I can't go out with friends, and I can't run around with my kid. I can't even think straight most days."

"I know it's difficult, but only time will help heal you," the doctor said. "That's my diagnosis. Go home, Alan."

After we returned home, Susan said, "See, Alan? I knew there wasn't really anything wrong with you. You just need to take it easy, honey."

I didn't argue with her, but at this point, I was secretly hoping my investigator would discover that someone had tried to poison me after all. At least then I'd have an actual reason for feeling so ill. And if we could find out what poison it was, maybe there would be an antidote, too.

5 ⋅ A Diagnosis without a Cure

WEEKS AND MONTHS PASSED. I didn't feel any better physically, and I was feeling increasingly despondent and hopeless. I had consulted with any and all specialists under the sun, including immunologists, neurologists, toxicologists, gastroenterologists, hepatologists, virologists, endocrinologists, pulmonologists, hematologists, rheumatologists, cardiologists, and more. I had seen over one hundred doctors in all; I was radiated like a well-done steak and felt like a pincushion from all the needles. Not one ounce of my body was left untouched by medical tests.

Even worse, I realized that my earlier worries about Susan eventually losing patience with this whole doctor shuffle—and with me—weren't completely unfounded. My wife was withdrawing emotionally.

One evening, I collapsed on the couch with Susan, lying with my head in her lap. I felt totally messed up and disoriented, and grateful to feel her comforting hand stroking my hair.

But when I opened my eyes and looked up at her, the expression on Susan's face terrified me. She had let her mask slip for a split second, and as her eyes met mine, her stony gaze revealed the truth: she really didn't want to be with me, doing this. She simply did not want to be in this situation.

No feeling of compassion emanated from her, and there was no attempt to connect with me. She was simply staring off in the distance with a trapped look that said, "Get me out of here."

Suddenly, Susan blinked and looked down at me with her usual warm smile. The mask was fastened tightly back in place. "How are you feeling now?" she asked.

"Not great," I said.

The truth? At that moment, I felt absolutely terrified of losing her. Illness, especially chronic illness, can take a terrible toll on a marriage. Would my marriage to Susan survive if I didn't get better fast enough?

◆ ◆ ◆

In the meantime, Ashlee was developing fast, as all kids do during the toddler years. I loved seeing her toddle toward me on her chubby legs, arms outstretched for me to pick her up. She was acquiring new words and cognitive skills quickly while I was fading. Sometimes, I could actually feel the light and energy draining from my body, robbing me of precious time with Ashlee. I could no longer take her on car or bike rides, to the playground, or out to a restaurant. All I could do was sit on the floor and read her a book. Even that was exhausting.

More than anything, I longed to be the strong father that every child deserves, rather than this fragile shell of a man. I couldn't give up the fight to solve my mystery illness.

Someone suggested that I call the Cleveland Clinic, which had a local branch near Fort Lauderdale. Once again, I saw a new primary doctor who evaluated my case and referred me to various specialists for tests. But this time I heard something new.

"There's something wrong with your heart," he said, reviewing my tests. "You've got a prolapsed valve."

I was still in my thirties and thinner than I'd been in years. "How is that even possible?" I demanded to know. "I've had a million tests, and nobody has ever said there's something wrong with my heart."

"Oh, it's possible." The doctor then went on to say something even more astonishing: "You know, all of your symptoms point to something environmental."

"What are you talking about?"

"Well, when did you first get sick?" he asked.

I gave him the same date I'd given every other doctor.

"No," he said. "I mean, what were you *doing* when you started to get sick? Where were you in your life?"

I wasn't following the connections he was making. Then he asked, "What building were you in?"

"110 Tower," I said. "I was spending most of my time either in my office there or in the Broward County Courthouse."

"That might be your answer, then: one of those buildings. Probably 110 Tower, since that's where you started really feeling ill."

Even though I was capable of connecting the dots—I'd never been sick until I worked at 110 Tower—I couldn't fully grasp what this doctor was saying. How could I have been poisoned by a building? This theory was even more far-fetched than Dr. Kirkpatrick's suggestion that I'd been poisoned by a criminal.

"That's impossible," I said. "Flat out impossible."

"I know it sounds incredible," the doctor said. "But look. Do me a favor. I want to refer you to this guy who specializes in environmental illnesses. If you go see him, maybe he can help you figure this out."

◆ ◆ ◆

How ironic: after searching all over America, Dr. Albert Robbins, the man designated to solve my medical mystery, was located less than a half hour's drive from my house.

His office building resembled a miniature two-story hospital from the outside, but inside, it looked nothing like any hospital I'd ever seen. Air purifiers hummed, and there was no carpeting anywhere. I checked in at the front desk and was sent upstairs to the sparsest, whitest, most sterile office I'd ever seen in my life.

Dr. Robbins was a doctor of osteopathic medicine. He had a master's degree in public health and was also an allergy and environmental health specialist. He shook my hand in the exam room and looked me over with his piercing eyes as he asked about my medical history.

I rattled off the high and low points of my odyssey and handed him the test results I'd collected. My medical file was a giant cement block of papers, but Dr. Robbins zeroed right in on my environmental history rather than the multitude of test results in his hands.

"Tell me about when you were a little kid," he began. "Where did you grow up? Were you ever exposed to any pesticides?"

I told him how, as children, my brother, sister, and I loved riding through the sweet-smelling mist of pesticides sprayed by mosquito abatement trucks as they cruised through our family's suburban neighborhood near the Everglades.

Dr. Robbins also asked about my house and car, as well as the buildings I'd worked in through the years. He asked question after question, and I dutifully answered each one as thoroughly as I could. His mind busily processed and analyzed the data I was feeding him. He was connecting dots I couldn't even see, much the way I did as a lawyer presented with a challenging legal case.

Finally, I stopped him. "Come on, why are you asking me all this stuff? Let's get on with the testing or whatever you're going to do."

At that, Dr. Robbins leaned back in his chair and shook his head. "I'm not going to order any tests," he said. "You've had enough of them. Besides, I know exactly what's wrong with you."

I stared at him in disbelief. Nobody had ever said anything like this to me before. "Oh, yeah? What's that?"

"You have an environmental illness brought on by 'sick building syndrome.'"

"*What?* What's that?"

"In simplest terms, the building you were working in made you sick," he said. "Certain buildings are toxic environments."

Chemicals commonly found in buildings can affect individuals in a variety of ways, he explained, depending on factors relating to genetics and length of exposure. "Over time, cumulative exposures can reach a threshold that will injure the human body by weakening the immune and nervous systems."

My mind was racing to keep up, but I wanted to shut out his words because I didn't want to believe what I was hearing.

"So why did all of the other doctors I've seen tell me I have chronic fatigue syndrome, anemia, and Epstein-Barr virus?" I challenged him.

Dr. Robbins shrugged. "Your body is in overdrive because your immune and nervous systems are compromised. But those viruses aren't the things making you sick. It's the other way around: your body can no longer defend itself against viruses like Epstein-Barr because it's injured."

Most people exposed to these viruses don't become ill, "because their immune systems are strong," he continued. "Your body was injured by exposure to toxic chemicals inside your office building, and this injury weakened your immune system to the point where your body is no longer capable of defending itself against other environmental exposures. In other words, you have become hypersensitive to various things, including molds, pollen, foods, and chemicals found in everyday products and environments. Anything from chlorine to deodorant is enough to set you off."

This all sounded impossible to me. Yet a part of my brain was analyzing the evidence along with him. Before this moment, I hadn't restricted any of my activities: not my diet, not my outings to hotels, and not my brand-new car rentals. What if Dr. Robbins was right and I was reacting to the chemicals in the environment?

No. This was too crazy.

Dr. Robbins continued explaining his diagnosis to me, saying I'd been in a chronic state of illness, so my reactions to these things were masked over. But over time, I had become hypersensitive to most chemicals found in our environment. That's why I felt like a rookie soldier suddenly dropped into the middle of a jungle war zone, with hidden adversaries shooting at me from all directions. I didn't know where the bullets were coming from. I only knew I had to run for my life.

I thought of that brand-new car smell I'd loved in my Z, and the home Susan and I built in the fancy Coral Springs development. Our home was filled with the smells of new paint, new carpet, and fresh building materials. Was my car toxic to me? Was my house? It couldn't be true!

As Dr. Robbins continued to quiz me, I answered his questions with an eerie sense of dread. I told him about the various things I'd noticed, like how walking past a swimming pool caused me to start wheezing; how I'd passed out when pesticides were sprayed around my treadmill; and the many times when perfume or cologne scents were so overpowering, they caused me to double over in pain.

If Dr. Robbins was correct, then I was like one of those canaries in the coal mines. If dangerous gases like carbon monoxide accumulated in the mine, the birds would keel over and the miners would know to exit the mine before they died from exposure to the same dangerous chemicals. Was I that canary for everyone around me, everywhere I went?

As we continued talking, I recalled how, during my time as a prosecutor, I'd moved to a different part of the courthouse and started getting flu-like symptoms. When I asked to be moved back to my old office, the symptoms went away soon afterward. Had my prior exposure to pesticides, molds, and other toxic chemicals made me more susceptible to the chemicals in the sealed environment of 110 Tower?

No. That was completely and totally *insane*. Period.

"I can't believe this," I said, shaking my head as Dr. Robbins walked me out of his office. "It's impossible. The government would never approve dangerous chemicals in building materials. Besides, if what you're saying is true, other people working there would have gotten sick, right?"

"There is no government regulation of most chemicals used in building products, only in foods and drugs," he countered. "And there probably are other colleagues who got sick. They just may not be as disabled as you are. It is true. I'm sorry." Dr. Robbins offered me a little smile. "By the way, Alan, you're wearing cologne and it's making *me* sick." He pointed to the sign on the front desk saying, *Please, no perfumes or colognes.*

"What's that about?" I asked. "I wear this stuff every day."

"It isn't helping you," Dr. Robbins said. "In fact, your cologne is aggravating your condition."

"So what will help? What's the cure?"

"There isn't one, I'm afraid," Dr. Robbins said. "Your body has been permanently injured. Now you must learn to live with these injuries and do your best to keep the symptoms at bay."

"How do I do that?" I asked desperately, ready to grasp at any straw.

"I can work with you here to stabilize you, but because your case is so extreme, you should go to the Environmental Health Center in Dallas," he said. "I know of a doctor there, William Rea, who's the top guy in this field."

Dr. Robbins explained that Dr. Rea was trained as a thoracic and cardiovascular surgeon. He'd developed a strong interest in the environmental aspects of health and disease, which led him to found the Environmental Health Center. Dr. Rea, he said, would identify what specific environmental chemicals were triggering my symptoms.

"You'll have to stay away from those chemicals," he added. "All of them."

"Stay away from them?" I echoed. My mind was reeling. "How?"

"By living your life in a radically different way," Dr. Robbins said. "Basically, you have to steer clear of anything in the environment that can trigger your body's reactions. That means you must pay attention to how your body responds to different stimuli, so you're aware of the causes and effects different chemicals have on your body. For starters, get rid of your bed and buy an organic cotton mattress. Remove any furniture made out of particleboard. You can no longer live the way other people do, Alan. This is going to call for a radically different lifestyle, one where you live in an environment that's virtually chemical-free."

"I can't do that," I said, stunned. "That's too much. My wife will never tolerate it. And what would be the point, anyway, if you're saying there's no cure for this whatever-you-call-it, this environmental illness?"

"I know it won't be easy, but the point is to keep you alive," Dr. Robbins said. "We can hope your body will heal itself a little over time, but you'll always be sick. You simply must accept that you're permanently injured from toxic exposure."

◆ ◆ ◆

I went home feeling angry, disheartened, and confused. My prosecutor's skepticism kicked in again, just as it had when Dr. Kirkpatrick suggested I'd been the victim of some kind of revenge poisoning by a criminal I had prosecuted in the past. It defied logic that there were things in the environment I was reacting to that nobody else even noticed.

Plus, as I'd told Dr. Robbins, I didn't believe for one second that our government would allow people to be subjected to poisons. If these buildings were so dangerous, then surely experts would have identified the problem and people wouldn't be allowed to work or live in them.

Most of all, I refused to accept that there was no cure. According to Dr. Robbins, this thing was a death sentence unless you lived in a sterile bubble for the rest of your life. I couldn't swallow that idea. Not with my wife and Ashlee depending on me. Not with my whole life to live.

I wanted to think Dr. Robbins was a quack like that crazy judge's assistant who had claimed the courthouse and 110 Tower were making people sick. How dare he tell me I was going to be like this forever? And how could he have the audacity to take money from patients he couldn't cure, especially when he couldn't cure *himself* enough to even tolerate my cologne?

If I was skeptical of the diagnosis, Susan was downright furious. She refused to believe there was any truth in what Dr. Robbins said.

"I don't buy it," she said flatly. "There's just no way that you could be hypersensitive to so many things in the environment. What about all of those other doctors you went to? They never said anything like this. Nope, I just don't buy it. That guy's a nut."

With her blessing, I returned to the doctor I'd seen at the Mayo Clinic in Minnesota. When he called me into his office, I said, "Look, you told me that if I rested, this thing would go away, but it hasn't."

I went on to describe my visit to Dr. Robbins and his bizarre diagnosis. "You never mentioned this possibility to me," I said. "Why not?"

He sighed. "Look, this is a controversial diagnosis, Alan," he said. "There's no proof that multiple chemical sensitivity exists. There are three camps of doctors. The first group is the majority who don't believe the diagnosis is real. The second group consists of quacks who prey on unfortunate patients by putting crazy ideas in their heads about things that don't exist."

"The third camp," he explained, "is an emerging group of doctors who believe there are, indeed, cases of human environmental poisoning. This poisoning causes a breakdown of the immune and nervous systems, rendering certain people defenseless against diseases that might have otherwise been contained—even cancer."

I was so tense by now that I could hardly breathe. "So what's the Mayo Clinic's position?"

"I don't know," the doctor said. "The truth is, nobody really knows about this stuff yet. But if this Dr. Robbins is telling you that he might be able to help, what do you have to lose by following his advice? We don't know what else to do for you. Medicine is an art, not a science, and medicine is archaic. We know about 1 percent of what's really going on in the human body. In fifty years, they'll look at us as practicing medicine in the Dark Ages."

I went back home and sank into an even darker place. A big part of me still wanted to reject everything I'd heard. I had no idea where to turn next.

Then my detective buddy, Ben, called me. We hadn't spoken in months; I perked up at the sound of his voice saying, "Hey, Alan. I've got something interesting to tell you."

"Yeah, what?"

"Well, I didn't find anybody who wanted to poison you, but listen to this. There's a whole list of people who got sick while they were working in that 110 Tower building. Dozens and dozens of 'em! One judge's daughter even died." (She was a young lawyer working on the floor below me, who was suddenly stricken with a crippling respiratory ailment.) "Think maybe the building could have made you sick?"

I closed my eyes. "I don't know," I said. "Maybe. Thanks for telling me."

We hung up. I pressed a hand against my eyes, as if I could block out the truth. The last thing I wanted to sign up for was a school of thought dooming me to suffer from these crazy symptoms forever.

But, like it or not, if Ben said dozens of people in my building were sick, then what choice did I have but to accept my plight?

If I were in court prosecuting a murder, I'd call this the "smoking gun": here was solid evidence. I couldn't keep my head buried in the sand any longer. I had been injured, probably permanently, by the toxins in my fancy office at 110 Tower.

Only now did I remember another omen I'd ignored: a conversation I'd overheard soon after I started working at 110 Tower. I was in the elevator of that building with a friend of mine whose father was a judge. "Where are you off to?" I asked.

"I don't know, but I'm getting out of here," she said. "Something about this building is making me sick."

At the time, I thought she was delusional. I had smiled politely and changed the topic. Now, I began wondering if things might have been different for me if I had listened to her and that judge's assistant, and paid better attention to the signals my own body was sending every time I worked at 110 Tower.

By now, it was 1991, and my condition had deteriorated to the point where I could no longer work. I often had trouble breathing, was in almost constant pain, and had to sleep many hours each day. Other than being with my daughter, the joy in my life was slipping away. I'd been sick for two years, and was getting worse by the day. I knew the Mayo Clinic doctor was right about one thing: I didn't have much to lose by letting Dr. Robbins treat me, because I'd lost nearly everything already. I was fighting for my life.

◆ ◆ ◆

Dr. Robbins did his best to stabilize my health in the coming weeks. He gave me immunotherapy and vitamin injections, instructed me to sit in saunas to sweat out toxins, told me to eat organic foods, and made it clear that I wasn't to go near perfumes and most chemicals.

He also gave me books to read. Ever the diligent researcher, I read them all. Nothing I learned made me feel any better.

I learned, for instance, that during the energy crisis in the 1970s, many new homes, schools, and office buildings were sealed to contain energy costs. That meant toxic chemicals outgassing from building materials were sealed inside as well. As the awareness of this brand-new "sick building" syndrome grew, so did the number of people complaining of symptoms brought on by exposure to various toxins in their home and work environments.

Perhaps the most ironic of these cases involved the Environmental Protection Agency's Waterside Mall headquarters in southwest Washington. In this complex, the windows didn't open and there were signs warning of asbestos fibers in the ceiling. Many of the 5,500 employees at the EPA headquarters complained of symptoms like mine: headaches, rashes, nausea, fatigue, blurred vision, chills, sneezing, fever, irritability, forgetfulness, dizziness, and burning sensations in their throats, ears, eyes, and chest.

When surveyed, many of those affected believed their health problems were caused by the building. The EPA ended up spending hundreds of thousands of dollars in upgrading the air-handling systems and tearing out the building's new carpeting, which contained toxic adhesives.

"Sick building syndrome," though a relatively unscientific term, was becoming more commonplace when describing patterns of health symptoms associated with lousy indoor air quality in workplaces, schools, homes, and other buildings. Poor air quality is caused by inferior ventilation and many pollutants, including insulation, formaldehyde from pressed-wood products, and volatile organic compounds (VOCs) seeping out of building materials, paints, copying machines, carpets, and adhesives, among other things. Unhealthy air is also caused by mold and other biological contaminants from dirty ventilation systems or water-damaged carpets, ceilings, or walls, as well as radon, pesticides, and combustion by-products.

It's challenging for victims to prove their claims involving "sick buildings," however, because it's difficult to specifically pinpoint, link, and prove that exposure to specific toxins definitively caused their various health complaints.

If I'd been well enough, I would have put my skills as a prosecutor to work, investigating each sick individual in 110 Tower to prove the building was responsible for our plight. But I was now in survival mode and barely hanging on. All I could do was feel sorry for these other people, and somewhat grateful that maybe I wasn't completely delusional.

It would be another decade before the news would break that the Broward County Courthouse I had worked in was also a sick building, inundated with toxic black mold. Judges, police officers, clerks, administrators, and attorneys all fell ill while working there. Certain judges who spent a lot of hours in the building became disabled.

It was starting to look like everything Dr. Robbins told me was true.

◆ ◆ ◆

Despite Dr. Robbins's efforts to stabilize my health, my condition continued to deteriorate. By 1992, I could barely tolerate a trip to the playground with Ashlee. Nonetheless, sometimes I went, simply to be with her somewhere other than inside my grim, claustrophobic world, which consisted mostly of my couch and bed. Just seeing the ice-cream man show up at the playground in his truck, playing that familiar chiming music, and watching my little girl grin as a Popsicle dripped bright colors down her fingers brought a smile to my face. But these joyful moments were becoming increasingly rare. Each drained what little energy I had, taking me days to recover to my baseline: a flu-like state of aching joints, headaches, wheezing, and fatigue.

As my health and spirits sagged, Dr. Robbins referred me to the Human Ecology Action League (HEAL) based in Atlanta, Georgia. "You should join this support group," he urged. "They've got enormous contacts and research on how to cope with chemical sensitivities."

Susan, who'd driven me to his office for that visit, walked out of there shaking her head. She was worried about money and still couldn't accept the idea that I suffered from an illness caused by an invisible injury. Nor could she believe that my bizarre symptoms were triggered by exposures to environments that other people seemingly tolerated just fine.

"This guy is a quack, Alan," she insisted. "He's putting crazy ideas in your mind. You need to find a different doctor."

I stared at her. "Can't you tell I'm reacting to stuff all around us?"

"No," she said stubbornly. "I still don't buy it. And I will not let you waste our money by going to Dallas, either. Don't you dare even think about going there for treatment."

I agreed with her: I wasn't ready for something so drastic as traveling to Texas just to see a doctor there when I'd already seen so many physicians. But I did attend meetings with HEAL members at a local chapter, listening to doctors talk about how chemicals of the modern world were killing their patients. I also contacted members of HEAL by phone to hear their stories. Many were like me—too ill to meet in person—so this was our only way of communicating. These people came from all walks of life and suffered from a variety of disorders brought on by environmental poisoning of one kind or another.

Some of their stories were frankly terrifying, especially the ones from people who had been suffering for decades. If they couldn't find a cure, what hope did I have? On the other hand, what could I do but hope?

Finally, I had to admit that living in humid, hot South Florida in a house that was emitting toxic chemicals was killing me. Dr.

Robbins advised me to find a place far away and hope my body could heal itself. This meant finding a place with clean, dry air and a chemical-free dwelling.

"The environment is a huge factor in how you feel," one guy from HEAL reminded me. "You've got to get out of South Florida."

I began forming a plan of action. I wondered if I should try a place I'd heard about, Seagoville, a community of people suffering from chemical sensitivities located near Dr. Rea's practice in Dallas. I phoned other patients I'd met through HEAL to ask their advice. They told me that some Seagoville residents had gotten better, but out of the thousands of people Dr. Rea had treated, few, if any, had been cured. Those were dismal odds to face.

I decided I'd be better off just trying out a new climate and a "safe" house. After doing some research through the HEAL network, I finally found what seemed like the ideal spot: Elgin, a small town about a hundred miles from Tucson, Arizona. I'd never been there, but it was cooler and drier than Florida; in addition, there were few cars, no industry, and no smog to pollute the air.

There wasn't much to Elgin. The town consisted of a gas station, post office, and a 7-11. But it had an environmentally safe place I could buy: an 800-square-foot adobe brick house specially constructed by a woman who'd suffered from multiple chemical sensitivity before she passed away.

I'd found the house through an ad in one of the HEAL magazines. It had tile floors and everything inside it was metal or glass, including the table and chairs. There were no drapes, just metal slats on the windows. When anyone went inside or out, air locks on the roof would kick in and prevent irritating chemicals from entering this environmentally controlled bubble. The kitchen was built fifty feet away from the house to avoid cooking fumes, in a detached building barely big enough for a stove, refrigerator, sink, and table.

It sounded sterile and therefore perfect.

I signed my house in Florida and my beloved car over to Bobby. "Here," I said. "Take care of these things for me." I was heartsick at the loss of both, but especially my Z—this car had been a symbol of my dedication to my profession and my vehicle for wild rides in our neighborhood with Ashlee. But it was the only choice I could make, given that I really didn't know if moving to Arizona would kill or cure me.

Susan flew out to Elgin first to scout out the house and pronounced it environmentally safe. My parents put me on the plane alone in West Palm Beach. The only way I could travel was with an oxygen tank; it was the first time I'd ever used oxygen on a plane, and I was embarrassed. All my life, I'd been strong and fit, but now I looked like an invalid. No, I didn't *look* like an invalid. I had *become* one.

I sat in a special seat with the tank on the floor. As I breathed in life-sustaining oxygen and watched the ground fall away beneath me, I felt anxious and deeply sad. I was leaving the only home I'd ever known, my family and friends, and the career I loved. I didn't know if I'd see any of these places or people ever again.

Despite this sobering thought, I had little energy to spare for reminiscing or contemplating the past or future. I had never felt more alone. I was trapped in this present moment, assaulted from all sides by the world around me, imprisoned in a body that had betrayed me.

6 ◆ Life on Mars

When I arrived in Tucson, Susan was waiting at the airport with Ashlee. I was too exhausted to make much conversation as she drove us to Elgin. I was engaged in the fight of my life—or, rather, in a fight *for* my life.

Everything had been stripped from me: my health, my profession, my friends, and the only place I'd ever called home. I felt exposed and vulnerable. *Raw:* that's probably the best word to describe my state of being at that time. The only way I could keep myself from sinking into despair was to tell myself that this move to Arizona was only a temporary stepping-stone before I could escape this nightmare and return to my "real" life. I would breathe clean air and heal myself in Arizona. Then I'd go back to Florida and resume my normal life.

Meanwhile, staring out at the Arizona landscape surrounding us only amplified the shock I was experiencing after landing. My surroundings were so vastly different from Florida's that I might as well have landed on Mars. Instead of the fast-paced city life, we were surrounded by expansive desert vistas. The foliage was made up of cacti and tumbleweeds instead of palm trees and jewel-colored flowers. Snow-covered mountains rose where I expected to see ocean, and the air was cold and dry instead of hot and humid. As far as our eyes could see—fifty miles in every direction—there were no cars, roads, buildings, or people.

Total isolation was just what I needed to get better, I reminded myself.

I'd seen pictures of the house, but I still wasn't prepared for this reality. To reach it, we navigated a dirt road about a mile long. It had so many ruts and potholes that, under different circumstances, it could have been an exciting amusement park ride.

At the end of the road, in the middle of three barren acres surrounded by desolate high desert studded with saguaro cacti, the house rose like a tiny bump on the landscape against a backdrop of jagged mountains. Its brick color matched the desert terrain.

We quickly named our new residence "the bubble" because it was so sterile looking: no art on the walls, no carpets to muffle sound, no fabricated furniture, and no drapes. I was entombed in a tiny fortress of glass, metal, untreated wood, and brick. Everything inside the bubble was composed of inert substances to prevent the outgassing of volatile organic compounds, which triggered my symptoms.

Susan and Ashlee lived in the house with me, but Susan had to prepare meals in a small outbuilding fifty feet away from the house, because cooking fumes sent me into seizures. We called it the "cookhouse." Susan set up a home office in it, as well as a play space for Ashlee.

I drank water only from glass bottles because plastics had an adverse effect on my body. I limited my diet to organic foods, though haphazardly, since I still wasn't sure what might set me off. Back then, I had no idea that gluten was one of my triggers.

When Susan returned with residual scents on her body from her excursions to the outside world, it triggered my symptoms when we shared a bed. If that occurred, I had to sleep in a customized trailer parked on the property. This was an environmentally sealed unit made of steel and glass on wheels that protected me from outside chemicals.

I couldn't travel long distances in conventional vehicles because of their unsafe plastic and vinyl materials, so we used my customized trailer to transport me to doctors for experimental treatments or emergencies, calling it my "hospital on wheels."

Fortunately, because I was bombarded with fewer chemicals in the desert, my physical symptoms improved during those first few months in Elgin. I began feeling hopeful that my health was stabilizing. I could even go entire days without oxygen, except when something unusual happened.

For instance, shortly after moving into the bubble, a babysitter wearing perfume came over to pick up Ashlee for an outing. Seconds after her arrival, my fingers, toes, arms, and legs began twitching violently. Soon, my joints were cramped. I became dizzy and struggled to swallow. My vision blurred, and the room began spinning around me. I couldn't speak. Suddenly, my legs gave out and I crashed to the floor.

When I awoke, Susan was frantic, hovering over me to wipe the sweat off my forehead and clean drool from my mouth. She was ghostly pale.

I blinked at her, still disoriented. The right side of my body ached, bruised from the fall. The muscles on the left side of my face didn't seem to work right, and when I saw myself in the mirror, I looked like a stroke victim.

But I hadn't had a stroke. I'd had a grand mal seizure.

This experience taught me something new: any time someone entered the bubble, he or she had to shower outside with special soap and change into freshly washed, unscented clothing, which we kept in an outdoor closet. Most people who visited were neighbors, friends, or babysitters. Sometimes they declined the outdoor shower and change of clothes, communicating with me through the door instead. For someone like me, who had always reveled in conversations with people, this isolation was torture.

Susan spent a lot of time in Tucson, shopping or eating out. She often took Ashlee with her. Other times, she went alone, taking breaks from her role as caretaker. She decided to return to school because she'd never earned a college degree. My family agreed to pay for her tuition, so she took courses in Tucson a few nights per week.

Although Susan hung out with Ashlee and me sometimes, I could feel that she was still extremely withdrawn emotionally. This made me feel uneasy and insecure, but I lacked the energy and skills to draw her out.

Besides, I sympathized with her plight. Susan hadn't signed up for this situation any more than I had. She was stuck in the middle of nowhere, separated from her friends and missing out on any sort of normal life, trapped with an invalid and a small child in an alien landscape. She couldn't go on dates with me, wear nail polish, or even get her hair done at a salon, because these simple things caused me to experience adverse reactions.

Ashlee was three years old by then, and I did my best to be an involved parent for her despite my physical limitations. We didn't receive broadcast television stations, because there wasn't any cable or satellite reception then in Elgin, so we had to resort to watching the same VHS tapes over and over. We must have seen *The Wizard of Oz* twenty times in the first few weeks there. Later, I would be deprived even of this small pleasure.

I also tried to read to my daughter. I'd discovered that even the ink letters on the pages of a book would set off an allergic reaction. Fortunately, I quickly hit upon a solution: I bought a reading box made of glass on three sides. I put the books inside it when we read; it had two holes underneath the top glass with built-in gloves. When I slipped my hands into the gloves, I could turn the pages. It was as if I were dealing with nuclear waste instead of my daughter's beloved picture books.

One day, I saw Ashlee standing by herself in the yard. I felt terrible because she had so little to entertain her. There was nothing but nothingness all around us. There certainly weren't any other children.

I decided that, no matter what toll it might take on my body, I would build her a swing set. I'm not handy by any stretch of the imagination, but I had a kit delivered and put the swing set together myself. It was probably a small miracle the thing didn't fall down.

Between our December arrival in Elgin and April, my condition remained stable, or even improved in small increments. Suddenly, that spell of relatively good health came to a crashing halt.

When the spring wildflowers and desert grasses started blooming, the landscape was magically transformed into a thing of beauty. Unfortunately, it also became another hellish version of my kryptonite. The spring pollen caused my entire body to shut down with a vengeance. I couldn't breathe, my throat burned, I had intense headaches, and my eyes were swollen shut. I began experiencing seizures on a regular basis. My respiratory system shut down, making it nearly impossible for me to breathe. We used my "hospital on wheels" to transport me to doctors who brought me back to life with cortisone shots, inhaled bronchodilators, or adrenaline.

Before my arrival, I believed that escaping chemicals would solve my health problems. I was mistaken and still understood very little about my own body and what could trigger these extreme and potentially lethal allergic reactions. Here I learned—quickly—that pollen could be as toxic to me as any chemical.

The glass bubble I'd created for myself started shrinking. When we first arrived in Elgin, I was well enough to eat at a natural foods restaurant that Susan and I both liked if I used my oxygen tank. However, by spring I could no longer enter the place without something setting my body off, so I had to wait in the car while Susan and Ashlee ate in the restaurant. After a while, I couldn't do even that much. I stopped leaving the bubble because I was too ill to do more than lie in my bed or sit hunched over in my wheelchair, sucking on a tube connected to my oxygen tank.

I lost track of time and often didn't know what day, week, or month it was. At times I didn't even know where I was. I suffered constant physical pain with little relief, imagining it was like enduring Chinese water torture. Isolated from most of society, and with little hope of recovery from my illness and almost no belief in the medical profession, I descended into severe depression.

Probably one of my lowest points was a day that Susan told me she was going to Tucson. She'd hired a young woman to care for Ashlee; this babysitter, a lovely girl in her twenties, often came to stay with Ashlee whenever Susan went to a night class, worked out at the gym, saw friends, or ran errands. On that particular day, the babysitter arrived as I was lying on the cookhouse floor because I was too ill to stand. As Susan was leaving, she looked down at me for a moment, then put a bowl of food on the floor next to my head before stepping over my body and leaving for the day, as if I were her ailing pet rather than her husband.

Maybe, like an ailing pet, it would be better for everyone if I were put out of my misery, I thought, as I closed my eyes and lay there, scared and helpless.

✦ ✦ ✦

When you become seriously ill, you learn who your true friends are. Many of my colleagues and friends from Miami and Fort Lauderdale were busy; when I stopped communicating with them, they went on with their lives and disappeared. I couldn't really blame them; I was so ill by the time I was living in Elgin that I often couldn't speak or function. It was hard for me to even comprehend words people were saying at times.

Fortunately, I did have a few good friends who stayed loyal and continued calling and writing me. Some even visited. They came from every phase of my former life: my friends Jeff and Tiny, who played in the marching band with me during high school; my college fraternity brother, Barry, who became my brother Bobby's accountant; my friend Steve from law school; and my prosecutor colleagues Paul and Mark. By the looks on their faces, I could tell it was daunting for my friends to see me in this condition. I was a pale shadow of the man they remembered.

It was embarrassing for me to feel so vulnerable and exposed to my fellow adventurers, risk takers, and colleagues. But it was heartwarming to feel their love and loyalty. I could not have made it through this bleak time without them.

Another good friend who unexpectedly offered his support was Alex, who had been my hairstylist since 1978, when I was still in law school. Despite the fact that Alex had become one of Miami's premier stylists, sought out by celebrities like Gloria Estefan and Julio Iglesias in his Fort Lauderdale salon, he and I had remained close through the years. Alex was a broad-shouldered, six-foot-five-inch Aussie. With his long, wavy blond hair and piercing blue eyes, he looked like an oversized Roger Daltrey from The Who.

In one of the most generous gestures extended to me during that time, Alex flew out to Arizona to cut my hair. When he saw what I looked like—I was down to a scrawny 145 pounds by then—this tall, burly man broke down and cried. But Alex quickly pulled himself together and went to work, creating a makeshift salon in the bubble. It was the first time my hair had been professionally styled since I'd been in Arizona, and it gave me some semblance of normalcy. You don't realize what a privilege it is to have someone care for you until you can't take care for yourself anymore.

◆ ◆ ◆

In the early 1990s, very little was known about the links between toxic chemical exposure and human disease. I was blindsided by invisible chemical exposure leaving no evidence behind, like a stealth bomber that inflicts its damage in the dead of night without a trace. But I was lucky in one way: many people are struck down by environmentally induced illnesses before they launch professional careers and develop a skill set. In contrast, I was fortunate enough to have made it through law school and forged a successful career as an attorney. This made it possible for me to tap into my legal training to research every possible cure.

I still couldn't bring myself to see Dr. Rea at his Environmental Health Center in Dallas. This was largely because I knew I'd have to live in Seagoville, a community that seemed like the place of last resort. Everyone I talked to in my network said it was crowded with people suffering from chemical sensitivities who had run out of options, and I couldn't imagine anything more depressing than that.

Now that my belief in the medical establishment had been shaken to the core, I began exploring innumerable alternative "cures." An entire circus parade of healers came through my bubble in Elgin.

One notable participant in my curative attempts was a doctor from Seattle with stellar credentials: he held both an MD and a PhD, and headed up a brain injury clinic affiliated with a university hospital. This doctor was researching a drug he claimed could reverse brain injury.

I paid for him to travel to Elgin. In the bubble, the doctor examined me, then proceeded to dose me with his specially formulated medication. The guy gave me two pills, looked at his stopwatch after a few minutes, then gave me two more. He looked at his watch again, and when an hour had passed, he told me to take two more tablets.

Suddenly, I felt a seizure coming on. I was light-headed, weak, and dizzy. My hands and feet began twitching as I was abruptly thrust into what felt like an alternate dimension. I was experiencing a grand mal seizure. Although I wasn't in pain, I was aware of my head smashing to the ground. A whirlwind of colors blended and swirled around me. It felt like I was in a wind tunnel.

I didn't black out, exactly, but I woke up not knowing exactly what I'd missed. The look of fear in the doctor's eyes and the rage on Susan's face told me that whatever had happened was pretty bad.

The doctor called a cab and disappeared down our dirt road in a cloud of dust. Meanwhile, Susan helped me into the sauna, where I sat and sweated out the potent drug he'd given me. Afterward, I called the medical board in Washington and discovered this quack had numerous complaints pending against him. I lodged one more.

Still, I was desperate enough to try anything. One Chinese healer traveled to Elgin from Los Angeles. He mixed up herbal potions for me to drink. These did nothing, but at least they didn't send me into a seizure.

Another woman, who claimed to heal with energy, asked me to lie face down on a massage table. She proceeded to lay her hands on my body, "harnessing energy from the universe," and explained that she was infusing energy into my body to make me healthier. That had no effect, either, but it was nice to be touched.

Of the dozens of healers who arrived on the doorstep of my bubble in Elgin, the strangest was probably the "psychic surgeon" from the Philippines. This practitioner told me to lie down on a table with my eyes closed while he lit candles around me, explaining that he would be inserting his hands through my skin—literally, he would make an incision using his bare fingers, no knives involved—to remove pathological matter from inside my body. Afterward, he added, "your incision will spontaneously heal."

Naturally, I was skeptical of that guy, but I let him proceed. I had little left to lose.

+ + +

One of my most bizarre and disheartening experiences during this time took place in a famous hospital in Tijuana, Mexico. Tijuana had become a busy center for alternative health-care treatments, particularly for cancer and AIDS patients who had run out of options on our side of the border.

This hospital advertised "metabolic" therapies that included detoxification through enemas, fasting, injecting vitamin and glandular supplements to boost the immune system, and treatments using Laetrile—an extract from peach pits that supposedly cured cancer.

"At least going to Tijuana will get me out of this pollen," I told Susan.

She wasn't convinced that the trip was a good idea. This act of desperation would most likely prove to be a big waste of energy and resources, she said.

"You go if you want, but I'm not coming with you," she announced. "Anyway, somebody has to take care of Ashlee."

"You know I can't fly alone," I protested.

Susan's solution was pragmatic, though it left me feeling more emotionally cut off from her than ever: she sent me to San Diego with Ashlee's babysitter as a companion. This feeling of being an outcast from my own country—and even from my own family—was amplified when I boarded the plane with only this young woman and my oxygen tank for support. Other passengers seemed to visibly shrink away from me, afraid of catching whatever disease I had.

I couldn't blame them. I didn't want what I had, either.

My father met us at the San Diego airport, put me in his rental car with my oxygen tank, and drove us across the Mexican border to Tijuana. We were stunned to discover that the Mexican hospital was an absolute dump, filthy and rundown.

I couldn't be an inpatient at the hospital because of the abundant chemical smells of the disinfectants, nor could I stay in my father's hotel room with the curtains and bedspreads infused with fire retardants. So, each day, I'd meet my dad at the hospital, have treatments, then drive to a cliff on the seashore while on oxygen. I'd sleep fitfully in the car for a few hours, then reverse direction in the morning and return to the hospital for more treatments.

I still have no idea what potions they gave me. A German doctor injected fetal cells from sheep using a giant needle—supposedly to help my body regenerate white blood cells—and I was on IV drips of medication they promised would clear up my candida. I was surrounded by American patients paying large amounts of cash for questionable treatments. It was a real mill, and the worst part about it was that, after four days, I was even worse off than when I'd arrived—something I didn't think was possible. I returned to my Arizona bubble in defeat.

Other than spending time with my father and feeling his love and support, the only good thing that came from the trip was the reminder that the ocean proved to be the best thing for my breathing. So I decided to try living in a California beach town. I was hopeful that I could somehow cure myself by breathing the pure air blowing off the Pacific Ocean—despite the fact that, by now, my belief in miracles was shaky at best.

+ + +

I had traveled to California years earlier as a prosecutor and recalled Santa Barbara as laid-back and clean. I chose this small city as my next destination. At least there would be no pollen like what I'd encountered in Elgin.

Susan and Ashlee flew with me to Los Angeles. By now, I knew that new-car smells set off a reaction, so we called Rent-a-Wreck and secured an older car to drive to Santa Barbara from the airport. Through my growing network, I found a nice guy with a house to rent in Montecito, a suburb of Santa Barbara. This was a beautiful, comfortable neighborhood close to amenities like restaurants and shops. I hoped Susan would be happier there than in the isolation of the Arizona desert.

Unfortunately, the minute we arrived at the house, I realized I couldn't even enter it without having seizures. Because we had already signed the lease, and Susan and Ashlee needed a place to stay, my only choice was to leave them there, go back on oxygen, and drive to a cliff overlooking the ocean, where I slept in our Rent-a-Wreck.

It was torture, not being with my family and having to live in a car like a vagrant. But given how weak I was physically, emotionally, and mentally by then, I couldn't find my way out of that situation for months. It seemed like I'd lost the ability to tolerate any indoor spaces at all. During daylight hours, I'd return to the house and spend time outside with Ashlee, who, despite only being three years old, had long surpassed me in her physical abilities. Whereas I could only hobble or shuffle, she was leaping, jumping, running, and growing taller and heavier by the day.

Meanwhile, I desperately continued trying various "cures." Since Santa Barbara is a part of the world that attracts people interested in exploring alternative lifestyles, there was no shortage of things for me to try. I paid handsomely for all sorts of useless treatments, including colonics, herbal remedies, and even spiritual cleansings.

I had come from a world of skeptical lawyers who don't believe anything exists unless you can see it, smell it, touch it, hear it, or taste it—or, preferably, all of the above. I had spent decades proving truths in court beyond a reasonable doubt by harnessing these five senses.

Now, however, I could "feel" chemicals harming me, even though nobody else could sense these same chemicals in the environment. Knowing that "invisible" things caused my body to react, I started opening myself up to other intangible possibilities: what else might exist that even I couldn't sense? I kept making new leaps of faith, convinced something would heal me eventually.

As the days passed, I spent whatever daylight hours I could with my family, and nights in a broken-down jalopy on the cliff. Susan brought me food when I was too weak to leave the ocean shore. At night, I'd lie down on the back seat and try to sleep—a nearly impossible feat, since I was too tall for the seat and in constant pain.

Then, one night, I'd dozed off in the car when there was a tap on the window. A pair of police officers were peering inside; one of them was using a flashlight to knock on the glass.

"Open the door and step out of the car," one of them ordered.

I had worked long enough with cops to know that I'd better do as I was told. I also knew how I probably looked to them: like a homeless, emaciated drug addict.

"Put your hands on the hood and spread your legs," they said once I was standing outside.

"You don't understand." I tried to explain my situation.

"Be quiet and listen to us," the other cop barked as he handcuffed me and prepared to take me away, presumably to a jail, a psychiatric ward, or a homeless shelter.

"Wait a minute," I protested. "You can't do this."

"You're a bum and a trespasser," they insisted. "We're removing you and your car from the property."

I continued talking fast. I'm sure I sounded desperate or insane—or maybe both—as I explained that I was actually a prosecutor from Florida who'd become too ill to stay in my own house.

"Look, there's my oxygen tank," I said, "and you can check my wallet. I have a prosecutor's ID card. I know this probably sounds nuts to you, but I live in Montecito with my wife and daughter. I understand what you're thinking, but believe me, this is true. I can't sleep in my own house because it makes me sick."

At long last, they took the cuffs off me and said, "Get out of here. And don't come back."

I drove away slowly, thinking how ironic it was that I'd once been a prosecutor accustomed to having police officers take my orders.

I had experienced very few failures in my life. Now I felt like I was failing every minute, just in the business of ordinary living.

After that night, I became even more itinerant. California has a long coastline, and over the next few months, I must have slept in dozens of different places, always in the car, waiting for the next cop to find me.

Finally, one night I woke up shivering and realized I couldn't keep doing this. It was late fall in California, and the nights were getting colder. We returned to Elgin, defeated once more.

The only option left for me to try was Dr. Rea and his Environmental Health Center in Dallas.

7 · The Leper Colony

SUSAN PUT ME ON THE plane with oxygen in Tucson, and my father met me at the Dallas airport. He wasn't about to let me go through this alone. Susan promised that she and Ashlee would join me in Dallas in a few weeks.

As Dad and I drove thirty miles down Highway 175 from Dallas to the Seagoville Ecology Housing area, he said, "Don't worry, Alan. You're going to get through this. I'll be with you every step of the way. You're going to beat this thing. I know you can do it."

Hearing my father say these words reminded me of the time he taught me to ride a bike when I was in elementary school. He had jogged alongside my two-wheeler, holding the bike upright as I pedaled, constantly murmuring encouragement despite having to huff along.

Finally, when my bike went fast enough for me to balance on it, he let go. I didn't realize this at first; I was too focused on cycling as hard as I could. Then I turned around and looked at him as I pedaled away.

"I knew you could do it!" Dad shouted.

The joy and love in his eyes made me realize I could do it, too. Having him believe in me made me believe in myself.

I didn't feel nearly that confident now, even with my father beside me, but I was comforted by his presence. He continued talking on the drive to Seagoville, probably knowing how nervous I was, repeating, "I know you can beat this, Alan. We're going to do it."

But when we reached Seagoville, both of us fell silent. All we could do was stare at this new version of hell in disbelief.

Seagoville Ecology Housing was an independently managed, special environmental housing village billed as a place where the air was clean and the well water on the property was filtered and free of chlorine. Residents had to be under a doctor's care, and most were Dr. Rea's patients at the Environmental Health Center.

Susan had called this place "the leper colony" when I described it to her, and I had to agree that the name fit. My first thought upon seeing it was, "This is the last stop. I'll never make it out of here alive."

The housing units were customized mobile homes constructed of porcelain, steel, and glass. Instead of typical paint, wood, fabric, and carpeting, the interiors were built with these inert materials that didn't emit fumes and sicken the community's inhabitants. The units were raised off the ground on cement blocks; this allowed air to circulate underneath them, preventing the growth of mold. Each trailer had its own air filter and organic cotton bedding, but not much else inside.

Thirty-gallon metal trash containers were scattered around the village; these served as storage lockers for personal articles that might otherwise convey toxins into our living spaces. There was one large community kitchen with refrigerators to store our food; we could also get organic food delivered there.

Despite the obvious lack of curb appeal, this all might have been tolerable for me, since I was accustomed to living in a car. However, this place was inhabited by people who looked like victims of war, plague, or some horrible natural disaster. The residents wore white uniforms and gloves as they shuffled from one trailer to the next. Most of them were attached to IV poles. The housing units had metal roofs, many of them rusted blood red.

I couldn't bear the thought that these sick people had been dumped out here in the middle of nowhere, in this awful place. Most were literally dying in isolation because their families and spouses had left them, unable to cope with having such fragile, chronically ill people in their lives.

"Jesus," my father muttered under his breath. "I was in the Battle of the Bulge, son, and this place looks worse than the foxholes I hid in during the war. Are you sure about this? Because we can turn around right now."

I shook my head. What choice did I have? "I don't think there's any turning back for me, Dad," I said.

He helped me to the small trailer that would be my home for the next five months. Suddenly the heavens opened up and a heavy downpour began. As my father left the trailer to retrieve our luggage, someone began screaming. I looked out the window and saw him trying to help lift an older woman who had fallen and was now sitting in mud as a hard rain fell.

"Leave me alone!" the woman yelled. "Don't touch me. I don't want help! I just want to die! Put me out of my misery!"

I could only watch helplessly as my father stood there dumbfounded. Finally, the woman crawled to her feet and staggered in the direction of the infirmary.

The next morning, I watched as an ambulance pulled up with no lights or flashing sirens. The attendants took out their gurney, then wheeled out the woman's lifeless body. The woman was finally free of Seagoville and all the troubles of our toxic world.

◆ ◆ ◆

My father stayed at a local hotel. There was a shuttle service for Dr. Rea's patients between Seagoville's Ecological Housing and the Environmental Health Center. My father met me at the Center each morning and stayed until I went home in the afternoon.

To our immense relief, the health center looked like a well-run hospital and was very modern and high-tech. Patients came here from around the world and from all walks of life. It was a humbling experience for me to be one of them.

Epiphanies come in all shapes and sizes. For me, this was the first time I could see for myself that there were many, many people who had, like me, been injured by exposure to chemicals in their environments. Whereas before I had felt alone and ostracized, now I was one of many people who would suddenly start wheezing or experience a seizure if we breathed in or touched the wrong thing.

Seagoville residents rarely left the property, except to get treatments at Dr. Rea's clinic in Dallas. They had to travel in retrofitted cars and vans, older models stripped of all carpeting and plastic and equipped with air filtration systems. Even then, the patients needed oxygen tanks or cotton face masks while in transit.

One of these outings nearly ended in tragedy when two of my fellow residents ventured out to a Whole Foods store as a nearby bank was being robbed. The criminals were driving an older car described as being similar to the one used by the Seagoville residents. The cops descended on Whole Foods and, when the two residents exited with their bags of groceries, wearing their cotton face masks, the police leveled shotguns and pistols at them. It took a lot of explaining to convince the officers that, despite all appearances, these people were probably the least likely bank robbers in Texas.

◆ ◆ ◆

During my first visit with him, Dr. Rea—who served as the Environmental Health Center's medical director—explained that he viewed his work as "pioneering." I remained skeptical, but felt slightly comforted by the fact that he was a reputable physician. In 1963, Dr. Rea was on duty as a thoracic surgeon on the day President Kennedy was shot, alongside John Connolly, who was then governor of Texas.

Dr. Rea is credited with performing the surgery that saved Governor Connolly's life.

In the intervening years, Dr. Rea continued his work as a surgeon until becoming ill from chemical sensitivity, a condition he associated with breathing in too much anesthesia in operating rooms. This spurred his interest in environmental illnesses and led to the founding of the Dallas Environmental Health Center in 1974, which, by the time I was a patient there, employed dozens of clinicians.

Dr. Rea's associate, Dr. Alfred Johnson, was my primary physician in Dallas. He explained that everyone has a different biochemical fingerprint and a unique capacity to detoxify chemicals. One person might be able to detoxify a chemical exposure thousands of times greater than another.

Dr. Johnson's goal was simply to stabilize my health enough so that I could live independently, albeit in environmentally controlled circumstances. Or as he put it, "Our aim is to teach you how to prevent yourself from dying."

An amiable Texan who served on the State Medical Board, Dr. Johnson explained that my diagnosis of "multiple chemical sensitivity"—also known as MCS—was a term that had only recently been coined for people who react to many different types of chemicals. According to him, the onset of this syndrome is triggered by a significant toxic exposure, such as a dangerous chemical or a pathogenic mold that injures the immune and nervous systems. When this happens, cascading hypersensitivities develop to most chemicals, pollens, and molds found in everyday environments.

"Toxic chemical exposure damages the nervous system," he explained, "and the symptoms resulting from such exposure are dependent upon which nerves have been damaged. If damage occurs to the brain, the onset of MCS occurs, resulting in a myriad of symptoms, including numbness, headaches, extreme fatigue, disorientation, and impaired thinking. In the worst cases, people become disabled or die."

Toxic exposures also lead to cancers, autoimmune diseases, and Parkinson's, he added. The ultimate result of toxic exposure depends on each victim's biochemical predisposition as well as the types and concentrations of each exposure.

"In general, people in your situation often become outcasts," he said. "Many of you have already been through numerous physicians and have taken all kinds of medications that didn't work, or exacerbated your conditions and made you sicker."

That was certainly true in my case, I had to admit.

"Patients isolate themselves to avoid exposure to toxins," Dr. Johnson went on, "or because they're embarrassed and fearful of their own unpredictable reactions to the environment. They are often misdiagnosed as having a mental illness, because they've stopped functioning in any 'normal' way."

When I first saw Dr. Johnson in 1991, physicians didn't have advanced diagnostic tools—or even correct theories—to confirm exposure to environmental toxins. All they could do were skin tests to determine what an individual was sensitive to, from an allergy standpoint. Initially, Dr. Johnson ordered a series of tests that mostly involved taking fat samples from my buttocks to determine what chemicals my body was storing so that he could pinpoint my initial toxic exposure.

Besides being a human pincushion, my regime at the Environmental Health Center involved a variety of diets, colonics, and other detoxification therapies. I spent a lot of time hooked up to an IV in a room with up to twenty people also being infused with various nutrients, antioxidants, and medications. Dr. Johnson put me on a rotation diet, so my immune system wouldn't become overexposed to the limited foods my digestive system could tolerate. He also believed in daily saunas as a means of sweating toxins out of my body and making my symptoms more tolerable.

Being treated at the clinic felt like a full-time job. Daily, I'd board the shuttle to go there, spend the day being poked and treated, then stagger back to the shuttle and return to the leper colony. Most of the other patients were staying in the same Seagoville housing community. Those who could tolerate it stayed in a nearby motel instead of the dismal leper colony.

Sadly, despite the doctors' efforts and mine, my condition didn't improve.

◆ ◆ ◆

In talking with other patients, it became clear that my condition was as bad as any they'd ever seen. A few even brazenly told me I might as well make sure my legal and financial affairs were in order, because they didn't expect me to make it out alive.

It didn't help my state of mind that Susan, who had promised time and again that she would be joining me, now sent word that she wasn't coming. There was no fight, no argument, nothing like that. She simply said she wasn't coming, despite Dr. Johnson's treatment plan including a "transfer factor" from Susan's blood to mine.

The procedure was a simple one: Dr. Rea would take some of Susan's white blood cells—the "transfer factor"—and inject them into me to boost my immunity to whatever chemicals we were both exposed to in our home environment. Susan's immune system clearly tolerated these chemicals, but mine didn't. Transfer factor was supposed to convey Susan's immunity into my body. It was an experimental procedure but a safe and simple one.

Susan wanted no part of it. During the time I was trapped in the leper colony, she had moved out of the bubble in Elgin into an environmentally controlled home on the outskirts of Tucson. This was a home I had found before leaving Arizona. It was located on three acres of land and, because it had been retrofitted by another patient of Dr. Rea's with air filtration locks, among other things, it was the perfect place for me to come home to once I finished my treatments in Seagoville.

"What do you mean, you're not coming to Dallas?" I asked Susan. "I need you here."

"I'm sorry, Alan, but I can't do it," she said. "I have to stay home and work on personal issues."

It was such a vague and awkward excuse that, even now, years later, I can't forget her "explanation" for why she couldn't join me in Dallas. I realize now that Susan was struggling with the idea of having to live her life with an invalid, and she felt guilty about that struggle. That's why she couldn't bear to face me in person. But even though I understood her complicated emotional state and sympathized with it to some degree, I felt abandoned by my wife. There's no other way to put it. I tried not to judge her actions—I knew that family breakups were common for people suffering from chronic illnesses—but I was devastated.

Even worse, I missed our daughter. Ashlee obviously didn't comprehend much of what was going on; our phone conversations were all too brief and infrequent, since I could only call in the evenings and Susan usually claimed Ashlee was either unwilling to come to the phone or already asleep. I missed my little girl desperately and had horrible nightmares of dying without ever being able to see her again.

I didn't make many friends in Seagoville. During conversations with residents of this environmental illness community, I discovered they had unique rules. We didn't talk about our former occupations, our backgrounds, or our families. We'd left all of that behind. Instead, we typically started our conversations with, "What got you sick?" It felt like I was an inmate talking to my fellow prisoners about their crimes.

One of my favorite people in Seagoville was Tom, a big-bellied tugboat captain who started suffering from MCS after helping clean up the *Exxon Valdez* oil spill in Alaska. He began suffering flu-like symptoms after a cleanup helicopter flew over the site and sprayed chemicals on the spill, dousing him as well.

Tom made a big impact on everyone he met because he was such a fun-loving, lighthearted, bigger-than-life personality who added levity to almost any situation—including our dire predicament. He had no problem coming right out and admitting to Dr. Rea that he practiced his four-day rotation diet by eating fast food from McDonald's one day, Burger King the next, then Taco Bell, and so on. Boy, did that guy like food, and it showed. But he wasn't the least bit self-conscious about his appearance or his lifestyle choices. His attitude seemed to be "Hey, here I am. What you see is what you get."

Tom gave us all a good example of how necessary laughter is in the face of adversity. There's probably no better weapon against your darkest hours.

I also formed a close bond with Anthony, a former medical student who fell ill after developing a hypersensitivity to formaldehyde and other laboratory chemicals. He wasn't as sick as I was, but he struggled, and he didn't have financial resources or family.

"You know, Alan," he said one day as we were sitting together, "our situation reminds me of moths that land in a swimming pool. Most just flap and flap their wings until they wear themselves out and drown. But a few get to the edge, gain a foothold, dry their wings off, and fly away. You're going to be one of those moths that fly away."

I could only hope he was right.

After five months of barely surviving in that horrible Seagoville trailer, I told Dr. Rea I'd had enough. It was time for me to leave. In addition to feeling frustrated by my failure to get better, I was feeling angry over the financial cost of my treatments. On the other hand, I couldn't direct those feelings toward Dr. Rea and Dr. Johnson. They, at least, were among the few who believed my illness was "real," and they were trying their best to humanely treat a desperate patient population.

Susan finally visited Seagoville to try the transfer factor injections before I left. The treatment didn't take, but at least I knew my wife still cared about me.

When I announced I was finished with Seagoville and my treatments at his center, Dr. Rea suggested one more option: a patient of his, Carla Tyson, the daughter of former Tyson Foods executive Don Tyson, had successfully recuperated from her chemical sensitivities in a three-story, 10,000-square-foot stone castle carved out of a cliff on the Gulf of Cortez in Cabo San Lucas, Mexico.

"Do you want to try and recover there?" Dr. Rea asked.

"Let's see," I said. "You're asking if I'd rather stay in a crappy little mobile home on a dry and dusty Texas prairie, or in a beautiful castle above a sandy beach bathed in fresh ocean breezes? What do you think?"

Still, I decided to check the place out myself before moving there—a move that would be complicated by my special needs. I asked Dr. Rea for Carla's phone number and called her. I explained that I was a patient of Dr. Rea's, then asked her about the castle and whether staying there had really improved her health. (By this time, I'd been burned enough to view everyone and everything that promised to make me healthy again with a certain degree of cynicism.)

"I just want to know one thing, Carla," I said after we'd chatted for a few minutes. "Did you actually get well staying at the castle?"

"I sure did, honey," Carla answered in her Southern drawl. "The ocean air is so clean and so pure there, it's like you're on *Gilligan's Island*. You've got to try it! The castle is amazing. When you get down there, you call me and let me know how you're doing, okay? I go down to Cabo San Lucas every now and then just to get recharged for a weekend. Will you do that? Will you call me?"

I promised that I would and made the necessary arrangements with the castle's owner to rent the place. When I excitedly told my friend Anthony about my plan to leave Seagoville, he asked if he could join me and volunteered to split the costs. I immediately agreed. I felt better going off to Mexico with someone else. In addition, since Anthony was healthier than I and a far better cook, I volunteered to pay him to make our meals.

Escaping the leper colony and persuading Susan to join me in Mexico with Ashlee provided me with a small but bright glimmer of hope. I offered to fly them to Cabo, excited about a possible reconciliation, but Susan declined to move there with me. She would stay in Arizona, Susan said, "but I promise that Ashlee and I will visit you every weekend."

Just before I left Seagoville, Susan sent me a birthday card. In it, she promised to stand by me, writing, "No matter how bad it gets or what happens to you, look to the past and I was there, look to the present, I'm here, and look to the future; I'll be waiting for you."

I kept the card close to my heart, longing to believe her.

8 · A Castle by the Sea

Once Anthony and I arrived in Cabo San Lucas, I discovered that the "castle" was aptly named: it had a forbidding medieval décor, with stone walls and floors. It was perched on a high cliff overlooking the Pacific Ocean and blessedly clean of chemical compounds, as Dr. Rea had promised. We gleefully moved in, feeling like prisoners who had somehow managed to break free of Seagoville.

"It's our *Papillon!*" I exclaimed, referring to a conversation we'd once had about that movie, which features an amazing prison break.

"The moths will not die in the pool," Anthony agreed, making us both laugh as we placed our five-gallon bottles of drinking water and oxygen tanks against the wall.

In reality, though, the castle felt as much like a prison as Seagoville, despite the welcome sound of crashing surf. On the first floor, the only furniture was a glass kitchen table and a few chairs. My bedroom, located in a second-story room with a balcony overlooking the ocean, had nothing more than a cotton mattress on the floor surrounded by mosquito netting draped from wooden beams. To me, it looked like a casket.

I had arranged for Susan to buy organic food and ship it from Tucson to the Cabo San Lucas airport, a tiny airstrip in the middle of nowhere. Anthony and I hired an ex-con who was living down in Cabo to pick up the food for us and drive it to the castle. We had also bought bottles of filtered water in Texas, which Dr. Rea's son loaded onto his truck, along with our organic bedding and six months' worth of other supplies that we considered essential to our daily lives. Dr. Rea's son drove the truck from Texas to Mexico.

If we hadn't had those minimal supplies, I don't know how I would have survived that place. It was just as bad as Seagoville. There was no air-conditioning, and the windows had no screens. During summer months, the humid heat was unbearable, and the place was infested with mosquitoes. Despite the bare floors and walls, I had trouble tolerating whatever chemicals they'd painted on the floors. At night, I slept on a hammock outside the second floor balcony after Anthony had encased me in mosquito netting so that I wouldn't get eaten alive.

As in Seagoville, I gave my best effort to remain in contact with Ashlee, mailing her messages and songs I'd record on cassettes every week using a small tape recorder. Often, these were sweet children's songs, like "House at Pooh Corner" by Kenny Loggins, which I'd sing and record while playing my portable keyboard synthesizer.

I worried that my health would continue to deteriorate to a point where I might not be able to travel and see my daughter again, or—God forbid—that I might not even live long enough to see Ashlee finish school, grow up, get married, and have children of her own. These fears seemed well-founded, especially when, out of the blue, Susan mailed me a "Dear John" letter. The letter was long and convoluted, but basically said she couldn't do this anymore and needed to "move on with my life." Her words sent me spiraling deeper into despair.

Apparently, Susan had moved out of the house we'd rented in Tucson and was now living in an apartment closer to the city. She'd gotten a job, too—all without telling me. I was heartbroken almost as much by her deception as I was by her decision to leave. But I knew there was nothing I could do to force her to stay. I had to accept her decision.

Meanwhile, with no phone, television, radio, or newspapers, Anthony and I were effectively cut off from the world. I felt isolated and alone as I hit a new low.

I had always prided myself on being resourceful, but I couldn't see how I was going to survive. Part of me didn't even want to, now that Susan had left. Besides the debilitating heat and humidity of Cabo, there was mold in the castle, and the air was thick with smoke from burning garbage and pesticides being sprayed.

Fortunately, the minute they heard the news about Susan, my parents, brother, and sister flew out to Cabo San Lucas to spend Thanksgiving with me. Over dinner, we had a family powwow about where I should try living next, since Mexico clearly wasn't the solution. Although we didn't come to any conclusion, before my family flew back to Florida, we all agreed that I needed to be near Ashlee in Arizona.

To my surprise, soon thereafter, I received another letter from Susan, admitting she'd made a mistake in asking for a divorce. "I'm sorry," she said. "I want to get back together with you."

Of course, I had no idea that she'd been fired from her job. All I knew was that I was glad my wife hadn't left me.

My health continued spiraling downward. I couldn't cook or walk without crutches. The castle was three stories high and my bedroom was on the second floor. I didn't have the strength to navigate stairs. Even if I *could* have gone down the stairs, I didn't have the strength or cognitive ability to drive my car. I was a prisoner.

One day, I asked Anthony to call Carla Tyson the next time he drove into town to get our mail from our PO Box. We didn't have our own phone line at the castle and we were half an hour's drive from any sort of civilization.

"Just tell her how we're doing," I said. "She asked me to call."

To my surprise, one day Carla showed up unexpectedly, walking right into my bedroom like she owned the place. I was lying in the hammock, too weak to move. She stayed the whole day. The only other person I had face-to-face contact with was Anthony, whose health actually did seem to be improving with the sea air. He was still doing all of the cooking, and whenever I needed something, he'd go into town and get it.

Finally, though, Anthony became so concerned about my health that he called my family and told them they had to come get me. "You have to do something, or Alan's not going to make it," he said.

Susan flew to Cabo San Lucas at that point. "Alan, you can't live like this anymore," she declared. I could hear the fear in her voice; I'm sure she was shocked by my appearance. "I'm taking you back to Arizona with me."

I returned to Tucson in an air ambulance, tethered to my oxygen tank, clinging to my one comfort: I was going to be reunited with my wife and daughter at last.

◆ ◆ ◆

Despite everything she and I had been through, it was clear that Susan still harbored some illusion that I could live a semi-normal life. Our ranch house outside of Tucson, like the smaller place in Elgin, was built to accommodate patients with chemical sensitivities. It had air locks and a special air-filtering system. There was an outdoor shower for anyone who had been outside the house to rinse off outdoor pollutants before entering. In other words, it was bigger and more comfortable, but still as much of a bubble as the Elgin house. It was exactly the sort of chemical-free environment I needed to survive.

However, when we arrived in Tucson, I discovered that Susan had furnished the place with a brand-new couch, chairs, drapes, rugs, and television. I'm sure she had fun decorating, but I couldn't tolerate any of it and told her we had to get rid of everything immediately.

"The house is safe for me, but these furnishings aren't," I explained.

"You can't possibly be hypersensitive to the TV," she argued.

"Yes, I am," I insisted. It was true: through speaking with other patients at Seagoville, I now understood that televisions emitted electromagnetic frequencies that triggered adverse bodily reactions.

If I came near a TV when it was turned on, I'd feel the muscles in my chest contract and experience uncontrollable twitching in my arms and hands. My heart would start beating erratically and I might even suffer a seizure. I didn't understand why this was true, but it definitely was: I could tell if a nearby TV was turned on, even if the sound was off and my eyes were closed.

Once we removed the television, most of the furniture, drapes, and carpets, the only items left in the house were an old leather couch, a glass table and chairs, and organic cotton beds. There was no furniture in the living room, and we kept the television outside. Ashlee had toys in her bedroom; that was fine, as long as I never entered her room.

When the summer temperatures soared to 120 degrees, it became clear that Susan and Ashlee needed air-conditioning, which I couldn't tolerate. We rented an apartment five minutes away for them to live in, except for the few hours they spent with me during the cooler hours of the day. Susan also continued taking classes at a school in Tucson, and ventured out to the mall, movies, and restaurants. Occasionally, she'd take Ashlee with her to visit her grandmother, who lived in Las Vegas.

Even as bare as the house was, one of the rooms still smelled like perfume. The smell was infused into the walls, so I lined them with sheets of tinfoil to encapsulate the smell. From then on, we referred to this as my "war room," the place from which I waged a war against my illness, making phone calls and writing letters as I doggedly pursued a cure.

My best bet was pursuing alternative medical treatments, because orthodox medicine had nothing to offer me. I read any book I could, still using my reading box, and relied on the telephone as my lifeline to the outside world. I networked with other patients, read medical articles, and called doctors who had helped other patients. When speaking with these doctors, I painstakingly quizzed them about their treatments, costs, and history of results.

My time as a prosecutor had prepared me to be a fighter. I had practiced law in what was essentially a war zone in Miami. This was a different kind of battle for survival, but it felt like a war nevertheless—one where I fought ongoing attacks from pain, fevers, blurred vision, poor digestion, and cognitive problems. I spent most days lying on the bed or couch, or even stretched out on the floor if it was especially hot. I couldn't go outside without being on oxygen; my only means of exercise was to walk back and forth along our long tiled hallway. On my best days I tried to do several laps in this tedious way. Sometimes I also forced myself to do push-ups and sit-ups on the floor. I had a sauna, meant to sweat out the toxins from my body on a daily basis.

All of these efforts got me exactly nowhere. I found no cure, just a lot of snake oil sold by medical "professionals" eager to take advantage of desperate patients. My time in Seagoville, Dallas, and Mexico had taught me that my illness was chronic. My immune and nervous systems were damaged beyond repair. Dr. Rea, Dr. Johnson, and the patients I'd met in the past year had given me the information I needed to survive in a bubble.

As a prosecutor, I had never given much thought to the victims of crimes. Back then, dealing with victims was simply a means to the end I sought: to incarcerate evildoers and prevent them from doing any more harm. I never identified with any victim's plight because it seemed like a pointless waste of energy and time. I was focused on beating the bad guys and putting them away, first and foremost.

Now that I had become a victim myself, my perspective changed. My heart suddenly filled with empathy for all of those people who had been injured or, in the worst instances, murdered. I had witnessed firsthand the tragedies inflicted upon them and their families. If I ever got out of here, I vowed, I would find some way to help those who didn't have the means, skills, or resources to help themselves.

I felt passionate but not overly optimistic about the possibility of my achieving this goal, given my current state. In many ways, my life resembled that of the stranded astronaut in the film *The Martian*. My only course of survival was to protect myself from the atmosphere all around me in this alien Arizona landscape. I couldn't emerge without my oxygen supply, and I had to be creative and resourceful to survive.

How long could I live this way? By some conservative estimates, I might last another five years if I was lucky. Many times, I thought of suicide. In fact, not a day passed without my having this persistent thought: it would be better for everyone if I just ended things. Why put my family through this hell? Why should I bother waking up every day, when all I desired was the ability to fall asleep and escape the agony of my own body?

Each morning, I'd open my eyes in bed, and the first thing I'd see was the ceiling spinning above me, as if I were on some horrible amusement park ride. I could no longer physically tolerate sleeping with Susan, so I was alone on a cotton mattress thrown on the floor in a room that was otherwise empty. No nightstand, no dresser, no lamp, no radio or TV, no chair: nothing but me on this pallet. And some nights even that was too much. I had to sleep out in the trailer, my little hospital on wheels parked beside the house.

Some days, I couldn't get out of bed because I was too weak or the vertigo was too extreme. And any time I was conscious, I was in pain: burning eyes, throat, and lungs; throbbing joints and muscles. I had no choice but to cope with the pain because I couldn't take any medications.

Whenever I could get out of bed, I'd sit in the portable sauna to sweat out toxins from my body, then gravitate to a chair in the kitchen and eat one of my five digestible foods: quinoa, almonds, cod, lentils, and mixed salad greens. I might shuffle into the war room, where I'd make phone calls to doctors and quacks, desperately searching for answers nobody could give me. I forced myself to exercise, though that meant walking back and forth along the hallway like a hamster on an exercise wheel, going nowhere. I felt like I was in my nineties instead of my thirties.

Still, I kept experimenting, especially that first year in Tucson. Since nobody could tell me what chemicals I could tolerate, I had to serve as my own lab rat, exposing myself to one substance at a time. I felt like a stroke victim, slowly learning to manage my body, one muscle at a time.

Everything that other people take for granted, I had to test, until I found things that worked for my impaired body. For starters, I had to figure out how to fulfill my most basic need: finding water to drink. Where do you get your water, if you can't drink it from the tap because of the chemicals, and you can't drink it from plastic bottles because of the chemicals in the plastic?

How do you brush your teeth or take a shower if you have a body like mine? I couldn't use toothpaste, shampoos, soaps, or shaving creams. I experimented with thousands of products, ultimately giving up on nearly all of them because my body wouldn't tolerate chemicals in even the mildest products.

Clothes, too, were a problem. That "new clothing" smell caused all hell to break loose in my body: my skin itched and burned, as if any place on my body that had touched the new clothing was on fire. Ultimately, I discovered I could only wear organic cottons. Even then, I had to wash the clothes multiple times. That meant finding detergents I could tolerate. I couldn't even handle residual detergents and fabric softeners previously used in a washer or dryer.

That one mattress I could sleep on was also hard to come by. I can't even count how many mattresses I bought and then threw away because the flame retardants and other chemicals caused me to have seizures. Whenever I lay down in bed, if my arms and feet started twitching, it was a sure sign that I'd better leap right up again.

Over time, I developed a regimented routine designed to keep me safely enclosed in my new bubble, learning partly through my own experimentation, and partly through the networks I'd built by phone and in Seagoville, where people were always counseling one another about what might—and might not—work for any individual body chemistry.

My fellow sufferers with multiple chemical sensitivities had, as I had, resorted to stripping everything out of their lives and starting over, piece by piece, reincorporating things gradually. We needed to expose ourselves to things one at a time, bit by bit, to see what we could tolerate.

Many drove ancient cars, as I did, thereby preventing reactions to chemicals found in new leather or fabric seats. They even stripped all fabrics and leather out of the cars and drove around in metal shells.

Like me, they threw their wardrobes away and started over with cotton fabrics. Before new clothing could be worn, the clothes had to be soaked in vinegar to neutralize the formaldehyde and then washed in baking soda to get rid of the vinegar.

I was lucky—if you can call it that—to be able to live in an actual house designed for someone with chemical sensitivities. I had family support and the financial resources to make that possible. However, along my journey to solve my own medical mystery, I encountered others who are far less fortunate. To escape chemicals found in ordinary dwellings and office buildings, they live in tents or sleep in cars, as I had in California, searching for any small measure of relief.

These people lose their jobs, incomes, homes, friends, and families because they are forced to live on the fringes of society. They often lack the support of anyone who believes in them and rarely have the education or resources I possess.

Some of these unfortunates actually do the unthinkable and end their own lives. One woman I met in Seagoville eventually shot herself. Another guy I knew—wealthy, educated—found a way to gas himself to death in his own living room.

But I couldn't do it. Each day, I looked at Ashlee, and knew I couldn't have her growing up in the chilly shadow of her father's suicide.

◆ ◆ ◆

A funny thing happened as I continued to survive: I became a celebrity.

It all began with an article that appeared on the front page of the *Tucson Citizen* on January 24, 1992, entitled, "Imprisoned by His Own Body: Tucsonan struggles to find cure for mysterious illness."

The features reporter interviewed me a few days before the article came out, and I was amused to see that the first lines of the piece were every bit as dramatic as the headline: "He is a 'universal reactor.' If that sounds like someone in the middle of a meltdown, you're right."

The article described my previous life: long workweeks, running, playing racquetball, and spending time with family. It recounted how I moved into a new house that was heavily treated with chlordane pesticides like many new homes in Florida, and also mentioned my move into 110 Tower. The photograph accompanying the article showed me standing behind the glass door of my environmentally safe bubble, so close to the outside world, yet unable to enter it.

Susan's quotes in the piece made me wince, as I read what kind of hell I was putting her through: "All you think about is how to live safely, how to find a safe place to sleep. We can't go out to dinner, we can't go visit anyone, we can't even go to a movie. It's the stress not only of being sick but of being an outcast."

In a cruel irony, my story shared the front page with an article describing how President George H. W. Bush wanted to increase the NASA budget and send humans to walk on the moon again and maybe on to Mars. The politicians were making plans to send humans into outer space, while I couldn't even walk out my front door. Something important was happening here on Earth, but nobody was telling the story.

After my profile ran in the *Tucson Citizen*, a number of other media outlets began contacting me. Jerry Brown, who hosted a national talk radio show between his terms as governor of California, interviewed me. In doing so, he not only showcased my plight but talked about how it reflected the widespread problem of environmental chemicals affecting human health. I credit him with being among the first to put my face on this issue. It would be a long time before I realized how important that would be.

♦ ♦ ♦

During this time, I received a phone call from an ex-girlfriend in Florida who had heard about my condition. She told me about a psychologist, Dr. Dan Baker, whom she'd met at Canyon Ranch, a Tucson health retreat. "He specializes in counseling families with chronic illnesses," she said. "Maybe you should see him."

I agreed at once. My relationship with Susan remained tenuous; we could certainly use some outside support.

There was just one problem: I couldn't leave the house. When I explained this to Dan on the phone, to my astonishment he said, "Well, I'll come see you at home, then."

A week later, Dan showed up at the door and went through the requisite steps of showering and putting on clothing washed in unscented detergent before entering the house. He was a very straightforward guy with the air of a strict college professor. At the time we met, he was writing what would become a series of bestselling books focused on teaching people how to live well in stressful situations. I immediately liked him. We arranged to meet for therapy sessions every week.

In the beginning, Dan met with us together as a family and also talked to Susan and me individually. His initial goal was to provide us with coping tools to help us navigate through my illness. Dan spoke with us about how important it was to recognize our feelings of loss, grief, anger, and depression as normal for our situation.

Working one-on-one, Dan helped me cope with being trapped in this safe yet isolating place by teaching me about the mind-body connection. He demonstrated visualization techniques I could use to separate my mind from the prison of my body. For instance, he taught me how to imagine a future I wanted to live—in essence, to create my own reality rather than live in the painful present.

On one occasion, he asked, "If you had a free pass for a day, what would be your wish?"

Immediately, I said, "I'd want to take Ashlee to Disneyland." Disneyland seemed like the gold standard of what every child would love.

"Okay," he said. "What would you do there? Tell me where you'd start in the park, what you'd eat, and what rides you'd go on." He encouraged me to imagine that trip to Disneyland with all the details.

At first, I was worried that such a visualization might make me sad. Why think about things I couldn't have?

But Dan coaxed me into it, explaining that having hope for a better future is the best way to live through difficult times. Once I got started, I had no trouble describing my fantasy, from the rides Ashlee and I would go on to the food we would eat. I almost felt like we were there.

When I'd finished fantasizing about that, Dan pushed me a little more. "Okay, if you could spend another day out, what would you do?" he asked. "Not for your child, but for you."

I thought for a minute. I was a University of Miami alumnus, to the point where I bled orange and green, our school colors. I nearly always wore my university sweatpants and shirts in the bubble, despite the fact that they'd been washed often enough to be tattered rags nearly falling off my frail body. I wore these team-themed clothes like a uniform because the clothing anchored me to my past—a time when I was healthy and athletic.

"I know exactly what I'd do," I told Dan. "I'd go to a national championship football game between my alma mater, University of Miami, and the University of Nebraska, because that's your team. We'd sit in the stands with a hundred thousand fans and watch the best team win. I'd be surrounded by perfumes, colognes, and fabric softeners, and nothing would bother me. I'd just cheer on my team like the good ol' days."

"Great," Dan said approvingly, though he looked a little surprised to be included in this visualization. "And who wins the game?"

I grinned. "Miami kicks Nebraska's ass!"

Another day, Dan asked me what I missed most about my old life. "Are there any memories of doing things that made you happy?"

"Playing music," I said wistfully. "I loved being in marching bands, jazz bands, and rock bands. I played the drums and wrote music. I'd listen to albums and transpose the music for all of the different instruments in my band. I really loved doing that."

"What about playing music again?" Dan suggested. "Think you could do that?"

I shook my head, grief-stricken. "I can't play drums anymore. I have too much pain in my joints and tendons."

He frowned for a minute, considering this. "What about your fingers? Are they okay?" he asked.

"Yeah, they're still pretty good."

"Okay," he said briskly. "Here's what I want you to do: I want you to start playing music again. Buy an electric keyboard and use it to play music from records you like, starting with the music you played in bands while you were growing up. Music can change your body chemistry, make you feel happier, and help you heal."

Although I was uncertain, I did as he said. I ordered an electric keyboard and started fumbling my way through music I remembered from the 1960s and '70s. Astonishingly, the music made me feel better than I had in a long time. I had forgotten the power music has to alter your psyche.

Playing music again helped anchor me to the life I once had, to happy times when I wasn't trapped alone in this body. I hungrily listened to one album after another, often long into the night, transposing the songs I heard so that I could recreate them on my keyboard. Two of my favorites were songs about the environment, "The Last Resort" by the Eagles and "Conviction of the Heart" by Kenny Loggins.

Occasionally, I'd have a sort of out-of-body experience while playing alone, especially late at night: I'd see this emaciated guy in this tiny house in the middle of the desert, illuminated by a dim light and surrounded by coyotes howling in the distance.

I'd imagine my music flowing out the windows, a stream of notes joining the desert's animal sounds beneath the bright, starlit sky. I felt less alone then, and believed, as Loggins sang in his lyrics, that I could be "at one with the earth and sky."

9 ⋅ Finding My Purpose on a Mountaintop

In late spring of 1993, I took Ashlee on a day trip to the peak of Mount Lemmon, the southernmost ski area in the United States. I had been seeing a naturopathic physician, Lance Morris, whose homeopathic injections of vitamins and minerals were helpful in cooling off my immune system and preventing a "landslide" or "free fall," as he described my acute reactions to many chemicals. He could not offer me a cure, but I am convinced he helped me survive. With Lance's gentle and gradual help in stabilizing my health, I could now make rare trips outdoors.

Mount Lemmon was a place I could tolerate because it was a snow-covered mountain high above the Arizona desert. The air was absolutely pristine.

We placed my oxygen tank on the front passenger seat of my retrofit Camry and Ashlee climbed into the back seat for the thirty-mile drive north to the Coronado National Forest. This trip into the Santa Catalina Mountains was one we both loved. For me, it was a thrill simply to be driving.

I loved the diverse microclimates along the Catalina Highway. We ascended from the desert floor through dense forests of saguaro cacti and paloverde bushes. That terrain then faded into open grasslands at about four thousand feet above sea level.

Above that altitude, we began seeing beautiful ponderosa, Arizona pines, and groves of aspen. Once we drove high enough to rise above the pollution, I could remove my oxygen mask, open the windows, and talk normally with Ashlee. It felt as if I were finally free of my body's prison.

Ashlee loved this trip, too. We usually stopped at a little park museum displaying natural history exhibits, including stuffed bears and mountain lions. There was also a Cookie Cabin where she got chocolate chip cookies as big as her red-haired head. We did both of those things on this particular day; because it was a weekday, Mount Lemmon was nearly deserted.

Since most of our travels together had to be imaginary given my physical limitations, this excursion felt almost exotic, as if we were passing through many different countries due to the rapid changes in terrain and climate as we climbed to higher elevations. The higher we climbed, the lower the temperature dropped. The desert floor could be forty degrees warmer than the mountain summit.

Whenever the desert grew too hot, ladybugs migrated upward to cluster in layers on the trees of Mount Lemmon. The trees almost looked frosted red with ladybugs. Ashlee absolutely loved those ladybugs! She especially identified with them because they were red like her hair, and she'd giggle as she let them crawl all over her. At home, she often drew pictures of ladybugs, which I hung on the walls of our home.

This particular day, we built a snowman at the base of the chair-lift. Then Ashlee and I threw ourselves onto the ground to make snow angels. The sky overhead was clear, crisp, and blue. I felt a rare moment of absolute joy as my daughter's laughter rang out over the hills.

Eventually, we finished playing in the snow and climbed onto the chairlift. Riding to the top of this nine thousand–foot summit was another favorite ritual.

I sat back and marveled, as I always did, at the pristine snow-covered mountains around us, the pine forests, the receding grass-covered hills, and the distant colors of the Arizona desert far below. Ashlee seemed equally transfixed by the natural splendor as we moved upward like silent ghosts, drinking in the panoramic views. We heard the wind whispering through the pines and occasional birdcalls. Otherwise, it was serene and silent.

Suddenly, Ashlee said, "Daddy, where is God?"

I was startled by her question. She was five years old and had never asked me anything like this before. Culturally, I am Jewish, but I've never been particularly devout. I don't believe that God should be defined by any specific organized religion. Rather, I look upon God as the same intelligent creator all major religions describe in different ways.

Yet something about being on that mountain with Ashlee led me to answer in a way that surprised even me. "I suppose He's everywhere, Ashlee," I said, realizing as I spoke that this was exactly what I believed: our Creator is everywhere and in everything.

"Is God in that rock?" she asked, pointing to an outcropping covered in lichen.

I laughed. "Yes, I think He is."

"Is He in that tree?" Ashlee pointed to a tree below us.

"Sure."

"Is He in you and me?"

"Yeah, honey, I believe He is."

At that instant, this little girl brought me to terms with my innermost beliefs, and perhaps my destiny. Her dialogue propelled me out of my body and into this altered dimension transcending the here-and-now. An odd sensation washed over my entire body as I felt a presence I couldn't see. The hairs on the back of my neck rose.

I didn't hear a voice, exactly, or see an image, but I sensed a command coming from both inside and outside of my body, as if the message were being infused into my every cell. It was a gentle but urgent plea: *You must do something to make a difference.*

I fell into a trance state, arguing silently with this internal voice: *Make a difference about what? How? What resources do I have?*

You need to make a difference. Make other people aware of what's happening to them.

By now, I was completely unaware that I was riding a chairlift up a mountain with my daughter. It was as though I went into another dimension, the way some people describe their souls leaving their bodies during near-death experiences, where they can see their bodies below them.

Ashlee must have seen a weird expression on my face because she started grabbing at my arm, saying, "Daddy? Daddy, Daddy, Daddy! Wake up! What are you doing?"

I couldn't snap out of my trance. My internal dialogue continued. *What do you mean?* I asked the voice. *Do what? What can I do?*

Just do it, it answered. *You need to make a difference. Start a movement. Make people aware of what's happening to them.*

Ashlee kept pleading with me and shaking my arm. I don't know how long I was out of it, but suddenly I returned to my body and looked at her. I could tell she was scared.

I was scared, too. It took me a few minutes to reconnect with my surroundings.

"Daddy, what's wrong?" Ashlee asked again. "Pay attention to me! I'm talking to you. What's wrong? What happened?"

Finally, I looked at her and said, "I don't know."

"What do you mean?" She cocked her head to one side and studied me closely.

I forced myself to smile. "Never mind, Ashlee. I'm fine. Really I am. Tell me what you were saying."

Thankfully, she was young enough to accept this. She started chattering again as we rode the rest of the way up the mountain, and we had our usual fun.

On the way home, however, as I was driving down that winding mountain road through all of those different elevations, I started thinking about the message again. I didn't understand what had happened, but I felt almost as if this message had been implanted in me. I continued thinking about it for days. The days turned into weeks. I kept mulling things over but always hit the same brick wall: what could I do to help other people when I was a sick guy trapped in a bubble and couldn't even help myself?

Yet I also realized the conversation with Ashlee had led me to connect to everything around me—the trees, the rocks, the birds, my daughter, the sky, you name it—in a way I never had before. I was an integral part of our planet at that moment, and I felt a deep sense of gratitude for that connection.

Perhaps this connection led me to a spiritual awakening of sorts, or maybe I'd just zoned out and reached a deeper part of my psyche. I really had no explanation. I only knew that the message kept gnawing at me.

Finally, acting out of instinct, I picked up the phone, dialed the University of Arizona's main number, and asked for the College of Medicine. When a secretary answered, I took the phone away from my ear and stared at it. I had no idea why I was calling or what I wanted to say.

"Hello? Hello?" called a voice from the receiver. "Are you still there?"

I put the phone back to my ear. "Um, yeah, okay, I'm here."

"May I help you?" the woman said.

"Um, yeah," I said. "Can you connect me to the Department of Environmental Health? Do you even have one of those?"

"Yes, we do," she said. "I'll connect you."

I was dumbfounded. There was actually a Department of Environmental Health? I'd just taken a wild guess and made it up. I couldn't go near a computer because using them made me sick, so I'd never been able to do any research online. I was a dinosaur stuck in a time warp.

When the next voice picked up the line and said, "Department of Environmental Health," again, I stumbled my way through the call, asking to speak to the chairman.

From that day onward, I began using my telephone, my only connection to the world, to work toward the purpose I was given. I felt my way through conversations with scientists and clinicians throughout the United States, asking each one how chemicals in our environment adversely impact human health.

And so my real education began.

◆ ◆ ◆

By the time Ashlee was five years old, she was spending her days in kindergarten at the synagogue. Susan was still in school and chipping away at the classes she needed to earn a college degree. With Ashlee and Susan gone much of every day, I spent many hours in painful isolation. Now I began spending those long, solitary hours cold-calling university medical schools, targeting specialists in different areas of environmental health. I made these phone calls from my war room, calling experts to talk not only about my own health, but also about global issues related to environmentally induced injuries and illnesses.

At first, I often didn't understand what they were talking about, especially when the researchers discussed various studies in immunology, endocrinology, and other areas of human health affected by environmental exposures. Bit by bit, piece by piece, I stumbled and fell, got up and fell again through this maze of information. But I kept asking questions and learning the lingo, until eventually I felt comfortable during these conversations. I still didn't know what I was going to do with all of this information. I only knew that I was driven to learn.

Why did doctors and scientists talk to me? Many were happy to do it out of pure generosity. Others were harder to reach, but I devised a strategy for getting through to just about anyone. When their secretaries answered the phone, I'd say, "This is Dr. Alan Bell. May I speak to . . ." Then I'd say I was calling to consult about a patient of mine.

Technically, this wasn't a lie, since my law degree is a *juris doctor,* or "doctor of law." My patient was me. As a strategy, it was practically foolproof. I even became adept at feigning impatience if I met resistance, saying, "Don't you think I have a room full of patients waiting for me, too? I'm taking valuable time to call, so please connect me."

Determinedly, I continued contacting any expert on the planet who had something to say about how toxic chemicals adversely affect human health. And at the end of each of these conversations, I asked the clinicians and researchers for names of other experts who might be willing to discuss this with me and followed those leads as well. Eventually, I developed a network of America's top scientists.

I realized that I couldn't wait for research to filter down through laboratories and governmental approvals to help me. I was in a race against time for my own survival, as well as for the survival of the human race.

During one of these thousands of conversations, I experienced another "aha!" moment. I was talking with a university scientist who said, "You know, your illness is really no different from cancer or heart disease."

"What do you mean by that?" I asked.

"Well, it's all connected to the environment," he said. "Other than accidents, war, or crime, all illness and premature human deaths are caused by only two factors: the genes we're born with and the harmful chemicals we're exposed to in our environment."

Cancer, heart disease, Parkinson's, Alzheimer's, autoimmune diseases, multiple chemical sensitivity, whatever—these are all different variations of the same global epidemic, he went on. "This epidemic is caused by our exposure to harmful chemicals found in our homes, schools, workplaces, and communities. Alan, your specific illness is the result of the environmental toxins you were exposed to, combined with the genes you were born with. Other occupants in that building exposed to those same toxins may have experienced a host of different diseases, depending upon each person's biochemical fingerprint."

Nobody, in all of my doctors' visits and networking, had ever connected the dots for me like that. I nearly dropped the phone as this stunning thought hit me: my plight was the tip of this huge iceberg.

I asked the scientist why there wasn't more research examining the links between disease and common environmental exposures, so more people would be aware of them.

"Because there's no funding for it," he said.

"Well, why not?" I pressed.

"Unless a pharmaceutical company can make money off a drug, nobody has the incentive to fund this kind of research."

"Are there any charities that raise money for research on human environmental health?" I asked.

"I don't know," he answered, sounding slightly irritated now. "Look it up."

So I did. I looked up environmental charities and found charities to save the whales, save the birds, and save the rain forest, but I couldn't find one devoted to saving the humans.

Next, I began calling all of the major charities raising money for research on different human diseases. When I got people on the phone, I'd ask if they knew about environmental risk factors related to the particular disease they were fighting, and of course they'd say yes.

"Well, do you fund any research on the biochemical mechanisms involved between environmental exposure and human disease?" I'd ask.

Every one of them said, "No, we don't study the biochemical mechanisms. We don't address causation. We raise money to treat the disease."

I was frustrated. Incredulous. And, most of all, angry. I could see this huge void in the collective research. Clinical researchers were experimenting with different treatment protocols for diseases. But they weren't focusing on the biochemical mechanisms linking environmental exposure to human disease; few were explaining how and why chemicals were making us sick.

Meanwhile, my plight was shared by people all over the world: millions and millions of people were getting sick and dying from various illnesses resulting from the intersection of genes and environmental exposure. This blew me away. Millions were dying; like me, many were disabled and imprisoned. And so much of this suffering could easily be prevented if people only knew about the harmful effects of ordinary chemicals that surround us and learned how to avoid them.

Nobody else seemed to be hitting this thing between the eyes. Maybe I was the one who had to do something. But what?

◆ ◆ ◆

I should have seen the end of my marriage coming. Susan had been spending less and less time with me and more nights at the apartment in Tucson. Yet I still felt blindsided when my wife finally left me. I suppose that was partly because it all happened so fast.

The year Ashlee turned six, Susan said, "I'd like to talk to you in the kitchen. I have something I need to tell you."

I could tell by the tone of her voice that whatever she needed to say wasn't good. Still, I sat with her and hoped it was something small—a dent in the car, maybe, or that she needed more money for school.

Instead, Susan said, "I'm leaving you."

"What do you mean, you're leaving?" I asked.

"I'm sorry, Alan. I have a new job. I'm leaving you. I want a divorce."

I stared at her with my mouth open. I didn't even know she'd been searching for jobs. "When is this going to happen?"

"The movers are coming tomorrow," she said. "I'm sorry. I just can't do this anymore."

Susan had planned everything in advance. I wanted her to wait so we could talk to Ashlee with a counselor, but Susan insisted on telling her that very night in the kitchen. I sat there stunned while this unfolded. I still couldn't believe my marriage was over for good.

But it was. The next day the movers came, and for the next few years Ashlee shuttled between us.

From the people I'd met at Seagoville, and from Dan Baker, too, I understood that chronic disease takes a severe toll not only on its victims but on the people around them. After watching me fall prey again and again to symptoms triggered by exposure to toxic chemicals, Susan still couldn't acknowledge that I suffered from a "real" illness caused by invisible but deadly assailants. She couldn't comprehend that I was vulnerable to environments that left many other people unaffected, and she simply had run out of patience for living with an invalid.

Every illness creates a zone of collateral damage around it. My marriage to Susan was part of that collateral damage.

I felt hurt, angry, betrayed, frustrated, helpless: you name it. However, what I felt more than anything was a steely resolve. I doubled down on my determination to beat my illness and vowed to do everything in my power to give Ashlee a happy, healthy childhood. Yes, her parents might be divorced, but she had a father who loved her and would always be in her corner.

10 ⋅ SAD GOOD-BYES

SUSAN LEFT THE DAY AFTER Christmas of 1993. The first week of January 1994, my family flew to the rescue and visited me. As we discussed ways I could care for myself and Ashlee now that I was truly on my own, my sister, Judi, began running a high fever.

My family was worried that Judi might be coming down with the flu; they knew it could be lethal if I caught it, too. Judi went to my internist to get checked out. He was worried enough to send her for x-rays, which revealed lesions on her lungs.

The doctor hospitalized her and ran more tests, including various biopsies. These revealed more bad news: lesions on her brain and liver, and a primary tumor in her colon. The doctors told us the cancer was terminal. My sister was thirty-three years old at the time.

Judi chose to be treated at the University of Arizona Cancer Center because it was renowned as one of the best cancer institutes nationwide and she wanted to stay near me. As the doctors did what they could, they warned us they could probably prolong her life a little, but nothing more. Thank God for Dan Baker, who arrived immediately to support my parents at the hospital.

While Judi spent the next few months in chemotherapy, I worked the phone from inside my war room, calling alternative health centers around the world in search of experimental treatments Judi could try. I'd make the calls each morning, then drag myself to the car with my oxygen tank for the drive to the hospital, where I sat by my sister's bedside.

One afternoon, I was sitting beside her when Judi turned to me with tears in her eyes. "I'm so sorry, Alan," she said.

"Sorry about what?" I asked.

"That I didn't understand before." Her voice was so weak that I could barely hear her. "But I understand better now. I get it."

"Understand what?"

She took a breath before continuing. "All those years you were sick, when this happened to you and you thought you were dying, you must have been so scared. I wasn't there for you, and I'm sorry. I couldn't understand what it was like for you. Now I do. I just wish it wasn't too late for me to do anything for you."

It was a heartrending moment. I didn't want Judi feeling guilty or sad. I only wanted her to get better. I swallowed hard and rolled my wheelchair closer to the bed, then took her hand in mine. "Don't worry about any of that," I said. "We're going to find a way to get you out of this. Then you can worry about whatever you want, okay? Promise me you'll just focus on getting well."

I knew my words were empty. The odds were against Judi beating the cancer that raged through her body. I think we both knew that. Still, I took comfort in saying this to her, and in trying to believe it myself. I felt worst of all for my mother. How terrible it must be for her, I thought, to watch her daughter die and to see her son so isolated and incapacitated.

From all of the research I'd been doing, I also couldn't help but wonder if Judi's cancer was partly triggered by whatever environmental toxins we'd been exposed to as kids, like the pesticides regularly sprayed to control mosquitoes. She and I shared similar genes, and those genes interacted with many of the same childhood chemical exposures.

Finally, after more phone calls than I could count, I found a place in Germany that was testing a new protocol for terminal cancer patients. My mother accompanied Judi there, and I talked to them by phone every day. Ultimately, however, the German doctors sent Judi back to the States, saying, "We've given you a little more time, but that's all we can do."

Judi and my mother flew back to Tucson and rented a house near mine. Judi wanted to stay in Arizona because she knew I was trapped there. In addition, she felt I could help her navigate through the medical labyrinth since I had so much experience in that strange, complex world.

I continued frantically phoning cancer clinics around the world. The next place I found was in Japan, where doctors were having some luck with advanced cancer patients. This time, Judi traveled with our cousin. She stayed in Japan a couple of weeks, but the doctors there couldn't help her, either.

Judi returned to Tucson and was admitted to a hospice near my home. Still tethered to an oxygen tank, I visited her whenever I could. We couldn't really speak much, since she was on a morphine drip and had a blockage in her throat that prevented her from talking. But she knew her big brother was there.

When Judi died, I was alone at home. My mother called to tell me that she'd passed, and I drove out to the hospice immediately. Judi's eyes were still open. I took her hand, but it was already cold.

I drove back to the bubble feeling more helpless and alone than ever because I hadn't been able to help Judi. I wasn't even well enough to travel to my sister's funeral.

I knew what time they were loading Judi's casket onto an airplane destined for Florida for the burial. I sat by the window in my bubble and watched her plane rise from the Tucson airport, a gleam of silver against the blue sky, and wept.

♦ ♦ ♦

I was already devastated by Susan leaving me. Now, I was gutted by my sister's death. Witnessing the grief on the faces of my parents and brother made me more determined than ever to survive. With Susan gone, my daily routines—so carefully crafted and thoroughly maintained—had to shift once again. I still woke up each morning in pain, and my activities were severely limited. Many days I couldn't even go out to the mailbox to collect the mail.

Clearly, I needed help. I found a sympathetic handyman willing to do odd jobs and clean the house using organic products. I also hired a woman who was happy to take Ashlee shopping for clothes when she needed them. Luckily, Ashlee had a mind of her own and a strong fashion sense; even as a young child, she had no trouble picking outfits that suited her taste.

Before she left me, Susan was doing the food shopping and cooking. I had no ability to do either, so I hired a young woman named Kristy who suffered a milder version of my illness and was sympathetic to my plight. She was healthy enough to shop and cook, and she understood my need to keep to a strict and simple diet of soy milk, spelt, quinoa, brown rice, carrots, sweet potatoes, red chard, kale, apples, and pears. Other than an occasional piece of steamed fish or skinless breast of chicken, that was it.

Ashlee adapted fairly quickly to the separation, since Susan had already been spending a lot of time in the apartment with her. She was in first grade by now and enjoying school. Since I wasn't well enough to drive, whenever Ashlee came to my home from Susan's apartment, I relied on a service called Kid Car to transport her between us.

Despite my physical limitations, I worked hard to be a good father. I put on a happy face any time Ashlee arrived at my place. I helped her learn to read using my reading box—she and I both loved books—or we played with toys that I bought from catalogs, with Ashlee's help in picking them out. We drew and colored together. I couldn't use felt or gel pens because those often contained toxic solvents. However, I discovered through trial-and-error that I could tolerate ballpoint pens with nontoxic, water-based ink.

Ashlee and I spent many hours simply talking. She was a profound thinker, even as a little girl. Our conversations were often deep philosophical musings.

We often engaged in imaginary play because I couldn't tolerate most activities that brought me into contact with chemical exposures. During one of Ashlee's favorite games, she sat on a kitchen chair while I stood about fifteen feet away next to a wall that protruded into the room. Behind the wall was a collection of her favorite toys—things I had already secretly removed from her bedroom.

I'd pretend to go into a trance, chanting, "Wish, wish, wish!" before reaching my hand behind the wall and producing one toy at a time, as if I had snatched them out of thin air. They were the same old toys. However, Ashlee was so ecstatic about the "magic" that she was mesmerized.

No matter what we were doing, I tried to turn the bubble into an enchanted castle of hopes and dreams in the eyes of this little girl. Sometimes, I made stories up for Ashlee instead of reading to her. Her favorite tale featured a magic pumpkin. The pumpkin was like a human; he walked and talked and was famous. To compensate for the fact that Ashlee and I couldn't have adventures on our own outside the bubble, I made up adventures for this pumpkin man that involved good deeds and always ended on a happy note.

It was tempting to do everything in my power to give Ashlee everything she wanted. After all, hadn't I cheated her in some way out of having a healthy father? However, every child needs discipline, and Ashlee was no different. I taught her how to use good manners, and creativity made discipline easier on both of us.

On one occasion, I read Ashlee a book that featured a main character named Margaret. Because Margaret was beautiful and older than my daughter, naturally she was the subject of Ashlee's adoration.

Occasionally, when Ashlee wouldn't do her homework or clean up her room, I pretended to speak with Margaret by phone, acknowledging Margaret's disappointment and assuring her that Ashlee would do better. This tactic worked like a charm. Ashlee didn't want to disappoint her idol, so she quickly turned herself around. She would then hear me call Margaret to praise Ashlee's hard work.

I also made up an imaginary person named Mrs. Butterfield, a stern authority figure who was closely following our lives. She was a handy person to call whenever Ashlee was being stubborn or disobedient. I had given Ashlee a guitar, and a music teacher came to the bubble; if Ashlee lapsed in practicing, I'd pretend to call Mrs. Butterfield on the phone and confide in her about it. I protested— loudly—when Mrs. Butterfield threatened to come over and scold Ashlee in person. Ashlee responded by quickly practicing her guitar.

Looking back on this time, I sometimes feel we were lucky, in a way. Ashlee and I had so much time together, uninterrupted by the usual things that typically fracture a parent's day. I had no job. I couldn't play sports. A social life was out of the question. When I was with Ashlee, I was all hers. How many parents really get that kind of blessed time with their children?

◆ ◆ ◆

Ashlee desperately wanted a pet, like most kids. But, for me, a dog or a cat would be a death sentence.

Finally, we came up with a solution: a hamster! Ashlee named her hamster Snowflake and kept his cage in her room. Unlike most kids, who beg for pets and then wiggle out of caring for them, she had to be completely responsible for the well-being of her hamster, since I couldn't go near it.

When the hamster was inside his sealed plastic exercise ball, the animal's fur didn't set me off. This plastic sphere allowed Snowflake to be in the main part of the house, running around on our bare floors. The floors were on two levels, with a few inches between them. The hamster would streak around in his ball, dropping or bouncing between the levels, and making Ashlee shriek with laughter. Eventually we got a second hamster, Squeaky, and the two went on to have ten pups.

I couldn't engage in normal outdoor activities with Ashlee—things like zoos, malls, and even trips to the park were out of the question—so I tried to bring the fun to her. On Ashlee's birthday, I rented a bouncy castle and popcorn machine and stood at the window of my bubble to watch through the glass as she played outside with her friends. I laughed at the fun they were having. Still, a small part of me wanted to curl up and weep because I couldn't join the others when it was time to sing "Happy Birthday" to my own daughter.

◆ ◆ ◆

I was feeling increasingly isolated as time passed. In addition to feeling deprived of one-on-one social contact, I realized that I was falling farther and farther behind on current events. Friends I talked with on the phone would sometimes mention a news story, and I would realize I had no idea what they were talking about; I often asked them to explain things. I might as well have been a castaway on some deserted island.

I eventually decided I'd had enough of feeling so completely cut off and decided to bring the world into my bubble via a television. This would be no easy task, since I reacted badly to EMFs—electromagnetic fields—emitted by televisions. But I had lots of time on my hands and a high degree of determination.

To find a creative solution, I tracked down a top researcher on EMFs in the University of Arizona's College of Engineering, Dr. Stuart Honeig. I introduced myself and explained my situation. He, in turn, called Ed Beebee, his trusted assistant. Ed agreed to visit me and see if he could help.

Ed was intrigued by my problem. He told me that people in today's world are exposed to millions of times more EMF radiation than our grandparents were, given the advent of things like cell phones, computers, and many other electronic devices. "Most of us just don't feel them," he said, "but you obviously detect dangerous frequencies other people can't."

I knew he was correct, though it had been a long process for me to figure this out. By now, I had become my own detective, always attuned to my environment as I tried to connect causes and effects when something triggered my body to react. With televisions, it was a simple matter of walking closer to one and then away; I could actually feel the invisible frequencies making me sick.

Ed had never seen anyone with my condition before, but he believed me 100 percent. He approached the problem as a scientist to help find a solution.

For starters, he hammered several 5/8-inch-diameter copper rods into the soil in my backyard, then ran cables from them into the house and connected these to anything that might generate an electric charge. Next, he and I concocted a plan for the television set, which essentially emitted the rays of a 15,000-volt electron gun. To a normal person, the rays weren't noticeably harmful, but they sent me into a tailspin of reactivity.

"I think I have an idea," I said, and pointed to the small, potbellied metal stove on the floor. The stove had a front opening. "What if we put a TV in that?"

Ed nodded, studying the stove. "If we do that, the TV will be shielded by metal on three sides, leaving only the open door for electromagnetic emissions."

"Right. And we could cover the opening with this." I showed him a clear Plexiglas shield I'd purchased. If you looked closely at it, you could see the Plexiglas was sprinkled with small pieces of thin lead foil that would block EMF.

Ed held it up. "Yeah, this could work," he said excitedly.

I handed Ed my credit card and asked him to go to the store and buy a decent television that would fit inside the stove. When he returned, he installed the TV in the stove, ran wires out to the ground rods in the yard, placed the Plexiglas sheet over the front of the screen, then handed me the remote control.

I sat down on the leather couch about eight feet from the television. "NASA control, ready to launch!" I said. "Prepare for countdown. Five, four, three, two, one!"

The television flickered to life. Ed kept his eyes fixed on me, watching for any sign of a reaction.

I looked over at him and grinned. "No reaction. I think this will work."

The first thing to appear on the television screen was a Time-Life infomercial advertising the greatest hits of rock and roll. I'd never seen an infomercial for the music I loved. I was mesmerized, especially because the collection featured so many songs by the Beatles. One of the few pieces of art in the bubble was my framed poster of John Lennon; I brought it with me wherever I lived.

"If you were to go out and collect all this music on your own," the TV announcer said, "it would cost you well over a thousand dollars, but we have arranged it all for you for $149!"

"That's amazing!" I said in disbelief. I glanced at Ed. "Did you know about this stuff?"

"Sure. Crap like this is on TV all of the time." He was laughing.

"Well, I haven't been able to watch anything for years, and I think this is great!" I hurried to the phone and ordered the collection.

My world was finally beginning to open up a little.

✦ ✦ ✦

When I first began living in Arizona, I thought, "Oh my God, give me the city! Give me the ocean!" I was spooked by the desert and hated being surrounded by so much sky and such absolute quiet. As the months passed, however, I began to appreciate how serene and spiritual Tucson and its surroundings were.

Other people must have felt the same way, because the area attracted an abundance of alternative healers. One day, Dan Baker suggested that I see one of them, a man named Dr. Andrew Weil. "I think he might be able to help you," he said.

"Sure. Great," I said, though by now I was skeptical not only of traditional medicine, but of many alternative medical practitioners, too. I was especially wary of anyone promising me a "cure."

A few days later, Dr. Weil called, saying he'd like to stop by and see me. "This week or next, if that's okay?" he suggested.

"Sure, it doesn't matter to me," I said. "My days are all pretty much the same."

A few days later, there was a knock on the door. Ashlee happened to be home; she was usually the one who answered the door, whether it was a delivery person or a visitor, whom she'd instruct to shower before entering the house.

This time she yelled, "Daddy, there's a hippie at the door! He says he wants to talk to you."

I had absolutely no idea who Dr. Andrew Weil was because this was long before it was easy to Google people. I didn't know he'd gone to Harvard Medical School, or that he had studied biology, concentrating on the ethnobotany of medicinal plants. Andy and I met behind the house, where we talked about his years with the Harvard Botanical Museum and his writings on the relationships between human consciousness, culture, healing, and drug experience, which led him to practice alternative medicine. Of course, I couldn't imagine at the time that he would later write bestselling books like *The Natural Mind: A New Way of Looking at Drugs and the Higher Consciousness*. From what I could see, this guy was just what Ashlee said he was: a hippie with ragged jeans, a T-shirt, and a beard.

"I'm sorry, but you can't come inside," I told him.

"That's all right," he said. "I'll sit out on the patio with you."

Andy asked questions about my life before and after I became ill. Though my case was certainly extreme, he acknowledged that the number of people afflicted with multiple chemical sensitivity is on the rise. "Certainly, the number of things in our environment that might be causing this has increased," he said.

At the end of our interview, he suggested that I allow myself to be tested by his colleague, Dr. Gary Schwartz, who was studying the impact of electromagnetic fields on human health. Then he said, "Listen, Alan, you know I've been studying how different cultures around the world treat medical problems using plants and herbs. I'm going to the rain forest. If I find something there that might help your symptoms, would you be open to taking it?"

"Andy," I said, "if you told me to jump off a cliff, and I felt like there was a reasonable chance I'd get better if I did it, I'd jump off the cliff."

"Great," he said. "See you soon."

At the time, Andy was traveling all over South America and Africa, researching how other cultures treat diseases using alternative medicines and remedies. He showed up at my door without warning about a month later, walked around to the back patio with me, and produced a small satchel tied with string. From this, he removed a vial containing a sparkling, iridescent liquid.

"Open it," he said. "I want you to smell it."

"Oh, I don't know, Andy. What is this stuff?"

"It's an herb from the rain forest in Brazil," he said. "Go on. Take a little whiff."

I did, and it smelled good. Very aromatic, although it didn't set me off the way perfumes did. Andy told me what it was—it had a long, weird name derived from a rare plant in the rain forest—and told me to open the bottle again and inhale the smell.

"Use it the way an asthmatic would use an inhaler," he suggested.

I didn't even bother asking what the herb was; by then, I was so disillusioned that I didn't really believe it would work anyway.

Still, I followed his instructions, then sat back for a second. Nothing happened.

He was watching me closely. "Alan, I want you to do this several times a day, and then I'll be back to check on you, all right?"

"All right," I said, because I could already tell this stuff, whatever it was, wouldn't kill me.

The herbal potion didn't help me, either. But I appreciated Andy's effort.

◆ ◆ ◆

Not long after that, Andy's colleague, Dr. Schwartz, visited me. Three vans pulled up to my bubble, stirring up a large cloud of desert dust. I waited for the dust to settle, then allowed Schwartz and his team to come inside after showering and changing their clothes.

Dr. Schwartz was another Harvard-trained physician at the University of Arizona. Like many scientists, he had never come across anyone with a condition as extreme as mine and viewed my condition with excitement. I felt like one of his lab rats, but I didn't particularly mind; I had little to lose, and if having scientists study the impact chemicals had on my body could contribute to the good of mankind, at least my illness would serve a greater purpose and give my life a deeper meaning.

Dr. Schwartz was researching how electromagnetic fields generated by televisions, cell phones, and other electronic devices adversely affect the human brain. He'd heard about my extreme sensitivity from Andy and wanted to test whether my brain waves would show any adverse response, including seizures, to EMFs.

"My team and I have tested ten people, but we haven't had any positive results yet," he said.

I agreed to be his guinea pig. If nothing else, this would provide another distraction, and my days were long without those.

The testing didn't begin well. Dr. Schwartz and his team had me take a seat, placed a blindfold over my eyes, attached electrodes to my head, and asked me to wear a headset to prevent me from hearing when the TV was turned on and off. I waited without knowing what was going on, feeling a little edgy as the moments passed.

After a few minutes, I felt the earphones being removed, then the blindfold. I looked around at their glum faces and said, "What happened?"

"Nothing," Schwartz said with a disappointed shrug. "There was no change in your EEG pattern when we turned the TV on and off."

Suddenly I realized something. "Wait, my television is shielded!" I pointed to the TV. "Didn't you see the special Plexiglas sheet covering the stove opening?"

Amazingly, they hadn't. Schwartz quickly turned to one of his research assistants and said, "Do we still have that extra TV in the van?"

"Yeah."

"Go get it."

They brought the TV inside and reattached the electrodes and blindfold. Then they slipped the headphones over my ears.

I waited for a few moments. I couldn't hear anything, but my body began to twitch involuntarily, and I knew it was corresponding to the television being switched on and off. Sure enough, when the earphones and blindfold were removed, the faces of the research team were all beaming. They looked like scientists who'd just successfully blasted a rocket into deep space. I had to smile, too.

"Oh, my God," Schwartz said. "This is incredible! Do you know how amazing this is? Every time we turned on the TV, we could actually see your brain reacting. You instantly started twitching. Your response was clear."

More importantly, he added, their machines had recorded small but measurable seizures in my brain that otherwise would have gone unnoticed. "This is a major breakthrough!"

According to Schwartz, I was the first human being he had tested who demonstrated a clinical response to an electromagnetic field, as measured by scientific equipment. While I was glad to have made these scientists happy, I didn't think my underlying health problems were being caused by electromagnetic radiation. I had no electronic devices anywhere near me during my stints in Elgin, Seagoville, and Cabo San Lucas, yet I was still sick.

Now, however, it was clear to me that my initial exposure to toxins in the 110 Tower must have injured my brain and central nervous system in a way that made me reactive to electromagnetic fields. This was one more clue I could use.

Schwartz was still speaking, growing more excited by the minute. "After this, nobody can ever scoff at the potential harm of EMFs again. It's at least a place to start addressing your condition."

I looked up at him and smiled, because the look on his face was one I hadn't seen in a long time: hope. It was the same look I'd seen years ago on the faces of my fellow prosecutors, whenever a case they thought had gone cold suddenly turned up a new lead. Although I eventually lost touch with Dr. Schwartz, other scientists and clinicians used his findings to further their own research.

Bit by bit, I was collecting information that linked disease to environmental factors.

11 ⋅ A Foundation Is Born

BY THE TIME I SAID good-bye to my marriage and my sister, I felt as though I'd been on an odyssey littered with countless obstacles. But there was a bright side: struggling to solve my own medical mystery enabled me to piece together a global view of environmental health.

Despite being trapped inside the bubble, I knew that I wasn't alone. Based on reading news articles and scientific journals, and on my conversations with top clinicians and other victims of toxic exposures worldwide, I knew with certainty that millions of people were being harmed every day by environmental poisons found in their homes, schools, workplaces, and neighborhoods. I was terrified.

My conversations with scientists taught me that all disease stems from interactions between our genes and environmental exposures. You could take a hundred people, pump them full of toxic chemicals, follow them for twenty years, and discover that each of them will acquire a different disease (or none at all), depending on each person's genetic predisposition. One easy example: a husband smokes three packs a day and never becomes ill, but his wife develops lung cancer from breathing in his secondhand smoke.

So far, few scientific studies have addressed this genetic-environmental axis. Pharmaceutical companies don't fund these studies because they haven't figured out how to make money by producing drugs to treat environmentally induced illnesses. Charities are raising money for scientific research aimed at studying various diseases, but they rarely address how such illnesses are linked to common environmental factors.

I was overwhelmed by this huge void. The only possible way to fill it was to start my own charity.

Soon after Judi's death, I placed a call to my brother, Bobby, and explained everything I'd learned. One thing I'd always respected about Bobby was his ability to turn an idea into a successful business—he had built the Banana Boat company into a corporate giant, with retail sales topping $95 million dollars in 1992.

"I want to start a charity to fight environmental illness through research and education," I told him. "We can fund scientific research to help treat and cure disease. We can also educate people about ways to modify their own environments to prevent illness and death. Nobody's doing anything about this, Bobby! Wouldn't it be great if we could take my misfortune and turn it into a benefit for others? What do you think? Would you be open to funding something like this?"

Bobby, bless him, said, "I'm in. Tell me what you need."

I set things in motion quickly from there. After so many painful losses, it felt good to have a new purpose that extended beyond my tiny, glass-enclosed life.

◆ ◆ ◆

By March 1995, Bobby and I had opened an office in Tucson for our new Environmental Health Foundation. In addition to funding the charity, Bobby brought in his top publicist from Banana Boat to get the media ball rolling. Meanwhile, I worked on everything else.

My long-term goal was to help prevent environmentally linked disease on a global level. I couldn't leave my bubble, but it's amazing what you can do with limited tools if you're driven by passion. I had only my phone, pads of paper, pens, and a fax machine to set up the foundation. That's it. Yet, I felt unstoppable.

I had kept up my law license by taking continuing education courses via videos and DVDs once I had my Plexiglas-shielded television set. That meant I could draw up and file complicated legal papers for the IRS, allowing Bobby and me to cofound the Environmental Health Foundation as a 501(c)(3) not-for-profit organization "dedicated to protecting mankind from environmental toxins."

In these registration papers, I made it clear that the Environmental Health Foundation wasn't like other organizations focused on cleaning up and protecting our planet. Instead, our group intended to save lives by empowering people with knowledge to modify their lifestyles in ways that would prevent environmentally linked disease. Our other major goal was to find treatments for people whose lives have become adversely affected by environmental toxin exposure. Or to put it more simply: our goal was to help "Save the Humans."

My immediate plan was to create a scientific summit that would emulate the Manhattan Project, which gathered great scientists in Los Alamos, New Mexico, and instructed them to produce a bomb that would end World War II and save American lives. I didn't want to destroy people, of course. I wanted to help heal them. But my strategy was the same: I intended to gather the greatest scientists and clinical researchers under one roof for a four-day Environmental Health Summit so they could collectively create a national blueprint to prevent and treat "the silent epidemic of the twenty-first century."

Basically, I wanted these experts to answer two fundamental questions: First, what are the biggest environmental risks humans face? And, second, how can we get the biggest bang for our buck in helping prevent, treat, and cure diseases caused by environmental poisoning?

Finding a venue for the first Environmental Health Summit of its kind in the United States was surprisingly easy: I realized immediately that we had the best place to do it right in Tucson, in the Biosphere 2. This is the world's most unique facility dedicated to researching our planet's environmental interaction with human health.

Located on forty acres, the Biosphere complex consisted of futuristic glass buildings housing the largest closed environmental system on Earth. The system included a rain forest, an ocean with a coral reef, mangrove wetlands, a fog desert, an agricultural system, a human habitat, and a subground infrastructure. One of the buildings resembled a giant glass pyramid, and several white geodesic domes nearby looked like they belonged on an enormous floating spaceship.

Biosphere 2 not only provided research laboratories, but also promoted interdisciplinary thinking and education about planet Earth and our future. The idea behind developing this fantastic complex was to learn how man might truly live in a self-contained environment in outer space.

Sure enough, the minute I explained the Environmental Health Foundation's summit plan to the Biosphere's management team, we had our location. Now all I needed was to find a way to convince scientists to participate.

One by one, I phoned every environmental health scientist and clinician I'd contacted in the past, as well as many I hadn't, and invited them to the summit. I started with the top university and government scientists, figuring that once I had a few big names, the rest would want to take part.

This proved to be true. Within a short time, I had assembled a founding Scientific Advisory Board consisting of our nation's top environmental health scientists and clinicians. The experts I assembled included over a dozen of the world's most important and influential scientists, clinicians, and leaders in environmental health.

Dr. Philip Landrigan, a Harvard Medical School graduate and chair of the Department of Preventive Medicine at Mount Sinai Hospital in New York, was one of the first scientists to join forces with us. His name was so well respected that others quickly agreed to participate, too. He agreed to serve as chairman of the Environmental Health Summit. Dr. Landrigan had a long-standing interest in the effects of chemicals on human health and was deeply moved by my story.

Trained as a pediatrician, he had a strong interest in neurology. He believed that many chemicals widely used today are wreaking havoc on all of us, particularly on young children whose brains, immune systems, reproductive systems, and lungs are growing rapidly.

"We have abundant evidence that toxic chemicals cause diseases in children," he said. "We know that air pollution causes asthma and other respiratory diseases. We know that these chemicals cause loss in IQ, shortened attention spans, and behavioral problems, all of which plays out in school and in the workplace as they get older."

Dr. Landrigan is also concerned that chemicals are "innocent until proven guilty." It's true: we're constantly introducing new chemicals into our environment, extolling their virtues until finding out later—too late, in my case—about the harm they might cause.

Dr. Landrigan applauded me for setting out on this crusade to educate the American public about chemical hazards. We agreed that US laws are inadequate and fail to regulate chemical usage in ways to protect human health. "We're conducting a massive toxicological assault on the American population," he said. "Our children and grandchildren are the experimental animals."

Bobby and I were so impressed by Dr. Landrigan that we funded his newest research on genetic susceptibility to lead exposure. This was our way of honoring Dr. Rea and Dr. Johnson for their gallant and lonely battle on behalf of victims and survivors like me. Years later, as I watched the news unfold about the 2015 lead crisis due to contaminated water supplies in Flint, Michigan, and in various cities around New Jersey, I winced at the widespread scale of injury. Despite all of the research focusing on environmental toxins and their impact upon human health, this silent epidemic is still with us, and growing every day.

＊ ＊ ＊

With the Environmental Health Summit scheduled for June 1995, the media momentum escalated rapidly both among local publications, like *Phoenix Magazine*, and national outlets, like the *Los Angeles Times*. I also appeared on CBS, NBC, and PBS talk shows, though I always had to be interviewed on camera just outside of the bubble, because I was too ill to tolerate being inside radio or television stations.

Before long, our first-of-a-kind spectacle drew cosponsors, including the National Institute of Environmental Health Services, the Agency for Toxic Substances and Disease Registry, the Centers for Disease Control and Prevention, and the University of Arizona Health Sciences Center. Vice President Al Gore provided a written endorsement of the summit, praising our long-term agenda and public-private approach to fund-raising and policy making.

Our foundation rapidly gained traction partly because environmental poisoning seemed to be making daily news headlines. For instance, the issue of the *Tucson Lifestyle* magazine that covered my story in 1994 also reported the Tucson City Hall's closure due to suspected asbestos contamination. In another disaster, a railway tank car valve failed in Richmond, California, sending hundreds of residents to hospital emergency rooms, where they were treated for sulfuric acid inhalation.

A *New York Times* story reported that tiny particles of soot, though falling within current legal limits, posed unexpected health risks. A study conducted by the Environmental Protection Agency and Harvard's School of Public Health suggested that up to sixty thousand deaths a year were caused by particle pollution—a far larger number than any other form of pollution, and one that rivaled the death toll from some cancers. This was like having a Vietnam War every single year. Where were the protests about *that*, I wondered?

As word spread about our foundation, I received more calls and letters from people expressing their support.

Congressman Joe Kennedy called to express his support for our upcoming summit. Actress and singer Olivia Newton-John, who believed her breast cancer was partly caused by environmental factors, also applauded our efforts, as did Ross Perot, who met with our foundation president. Kenny Loggins offered his endorsement, along with actors Matthew Perry and Alan Thicke.

As Bobby and I finalized plans for the summit in 1995, I realized we needed a promotional video to capture the essence and goals of the Environmental Health Foundation. Although I couldn't leave the bubble most of the time, I called people, did paperwork, and even managed to find a videographer.

I asked Ralph Colwell, who owned a video production company, to do the job. He visited me, probably trying to figure out if I was for real or just another nut in Tucson. We stood outside on my patio so his cologne wouldn't set off any hypersensitive reactions.

Ralph cared a great deal about our environment. He was convinced that our cause was worth his time. He offered to attend the Biosphere 2 conference and videotape the scientists and physicians meeting under one roof.

After I'd hired Ralph, we agreed that we'd need a famous spokesperson to host the video. "Maybe an American folk hero sort of celebrity," I mused.

"I might know somebody," Ralph said, but he left still holding his cards close to his vest.

Not long afterward, Ralph called me. "Listen, Alan," he said. "I know Gene Cernan, the commander of Apollo 17 and the last American to walk on the moon. I think he'd do the video."

How fitting, I thought with a grin. As a freshman at the University of Miami, I had driven with my father to Cape Kennedy for the launch of Apollo 17 with Cernan as command module captain. I told Ralph this, adding, "I can't think of a better spokesperson."

Sure enough, Ralph asked him, and Gene signed on immediately. The pieces were in place.

◆ ◆ ◆

The only person missing from the summit was me. Although I had created, planned, and organized the event, I was too ill to attend it.

Still, I was determined to make my voice heard. Ralph filmed my introductory speech so that I could address the conference participants via a video feed. As I began speaking, I presented the same cheerful, hopeful facade my father had adopted years earlier while selling Florida real estate.

"On behalf of the Environmental Health Foundation, I'd like to welcome each and every one of you here today," I began. "This summit brings together some of America's finest scientists under one roof for the purpose of putting together a national blueprint for the direction of environmental research in the twenty-first century. Millions of American lives are dependent on what we do here today."

I went on from there, describing what led us to establish the foundation and stating our goals. Then Dr. Kenneth Olden, the director of the National Institute of Environmental Health Services, gave the keynote address, congratulating the Environmental Health Foundation for bringing together people "from academia, the private sector, government, and industry to map out and plan an environmental health science research agenda for the year 2000 and beyond."

In his address, Dr. Olden expressed his interest in having a private-public partnership between our foundation and the National Institutes of Health. Can you imagine? Here was a director of the all-powerful NIH—a George Bush appointee—excited about a "partnership" with my fledgling brainchild. Wow!

The summit's priorities were divided into five categories of environmental impact: children's health, the respiratory system, the immune system, the nervous system, and the reproductive system. As the scientists worked through the next few days, I thought of them constantly.

I felt like a star football player sidelined for a busted knee, watching the game unfold without me: I was yearning to be called onto the field and frustrated I couldn't take a more active role. Although I was aware that my life was taking on a deeper meaning, I was too sick to be truly excited or joyful.

While on some level I was thinking, "Oh, wow, this is actually happening. This is really cool," my emotional highs and lows were gone. No matter how good the news was in my life—or how horrible—I had learned to cope with things I couldn't change by flatlining emotionally.

Remember the movie *Rocky?* How he gets hit and hit and hit, to the point where the pummeling doesn't even hurt him anymore? It was like that for me. I would always get up. I knew that much. But I couldn't feel much joy in my accomplishments.

Bobby attended every day of the conference, as did Ashlee and my parents, who were glad to have a positive event to focus on after Judi's death. While my image was projected on the screen, Ashlee—who was only seven years old—walked around the auditorium, staring up at these white-coated doctors and scientists.

As young as she was, Ashlee understood two things: Her daddy was sick enough to be trapped in a cage, but he was the one who had gotten these people together. She also knew that the summit participants were scientists trying to understand and cure illnesses like mine.

At some point, Ashlee must have thought, "Wait a minute. These doctors are helping other people. Why can't they help my dad?"

The very first day of the summit, she began asking scientists that very question, going up to each one in turn and saying, "Excuse me, I'm Ashlee Bell. You know my daddy. Can you help him?"

One of the scientists—to this day, I have no idea who it was—finally scrawled a name—*Dr. Jay Seastrunk*—and a phone number on a piece of paper. He handed it to Ashlee, saying, "Here. This guy might be able to help your daddy."

Ashlee hung on to that scrap of paper all day. When Bobby brought her back to my bubble that night, she handed it to me. "Here, Daddy," she said. "You go see this doctor. He's going to help you."

I stared at the paper dully. "How? What kind of doctor is he?"

"I don't know," Ashlee said. "But a scientist said he's the one who can help you, Daddy. You have to go!"

I took the piece of paper out of her hand and mustered a smile. "I've heard this a million times, sweetie," I said tenderly. "All these doctors do is take my money and make me sicker."

There were few people in the world more stubborn than this redheaded, seven-year-old girl. Ashlee wasn't about to let me off the hook. Throughout her short life, she had simply accepted my condition because, to her, that's the way I always was. Now, though, she had started to notice how radically different the lives of other people were from ours. She was also painfully aware that her father could die at any time.

"You've got to fight, Daddy," she begged. "You can't give up."

I took a deep breath and shook my head. "Ashlee, I'm stuck in this bubble and that's the best I can hope for, but I'm not giving up. I'm fighting for others. You know that!"

"You think you're really helping people, stuck in here?" she demanded. "Think how many people you could help if you got out!"

I sighed. Clearly, she wasn't going to let this go. And what did I have to lose, really? One more doctor or one more quack, what did it matter? I would be no better off than before if I saw this guy, but at least I could make Ashlee happy.

"All right, honey. You want to know what this doctor's treatment can do? Fine. I'll check it out."

❖ ❖ ❖

Months passed before I called Dr. Seastrunk, however. Despite my ongoing health issues and isolation in the bubble, I remained driven to do whatever I could to focus on our newborn Environmental Health Foundation. Bobby and I had determined that our research priorities would be long-term, low-level toxic exposures including sick building syndrome and Gulf War syndrome, which had affected thousands of veterans returning home with chronic illness.

Bobby gave seed money to launch the foundation. Beyond that, we pursued grants from corporate and governmental entities. Our aim was to support unbiased medical institutions through fund-raising activities and private donations, without having to align ourselves with specific political or special-interest groups. We also continued building awareness of the foundation through direct mail and a grassroots effort similar to the Muscular Dystrophy Association's campaigns.

One day, I spoke to a woman on the phone who also suffered from multiple chemical sensitivity. I respected her because she was an attorney who had graduated from Harvard Law School. She claimed she was cured now and swore that the reason she'd beaten her illness was a Baptist minister in Atlanta, Georgia, who called upon Jesus to heal people with environmental poisoning.

I was skeptical, naturally. But, oh, how I wanted to escape that bubble. I was tired of living like a Martian, especially when that meant not being able to go out and about with my daughter. Before she left me, Susan made videos of Ashlee's important moments, like her school performances. But watching them only sent me deeper into a dark place within myself. I ached to support Ashlee's big accomplishments in person.

So off I went to Georgia, embarking on what would turn out to be my most outlandish cure quest yet. My trailer—the hospital on wheels—was hauled down to Atlanta ahead of my flight so that I could sleep in it. Once I arrived, I was disheartened to hear the preacher tell his religious leper colony that demonic forces caused environmental illness and that we could only be cured by accepting Jesus into our hearts.

For the next few weeks, I tried to swallow all of the stuff this guy was trying to sell us, but I just couldn't do it. The nail in that particular coffin was hammered in by Hurricane Opal, which charged into Atlanta in October 1995 as I was sleeping in my hospital on wheels. The preacher's biggest claim to fame was that he once used the power of Jesus to turn away a hurricane while living in Tampa, Florida, saving his whole congregation from destruction.

Now, Hurricane Opal's raging winds and punishing rain made it clear how puny this man's powers actually were. While I rattled around in my tin can, I thought, "Enough! That's it. I'm out of here." I wasn't surprised that the guy was a fraud—in fact, I'd been saying that to other people there—but I was definitely surprised that, for the first time ever, a hurricane hit the Atlanta area. In my most cynical moments, I've wondered if this was God's little joke, and a way of exposing the preacher's fraud to others. Whatever the explanation might be, it was spooky.

I'm embarrassed that I fell for this charlatan, but that experience highlighted just how lost and desperate I was. I wasn't thinking very clearly. Despite my intense preoccupation with researching hard science and gathering facts about environmentally induced illnesses, I was too exhausted and debilitated to always be completely rational. Fortunately, I had Ashlee and the Environmental Health Foundation to focus on, or I might not have made it through this darkness.

In December 1995, two months after I returned from Georgia, I threw myself into the next fund-raising effort: a celebrity hockey event we put on at the Tucson Convention Center. It was held on a Saturday evening, featuring actors Alan Thicke, Matthew Perry, and Cuba Gooding Jr., as well as supermodel Kim Alexis, playing against a team of University of Arizona alumni skaters. The event packed the Convention Center, and its success gave me the energy boost I needed to think about my next move.

12 ◆ My Daughter Saves My Life

Maybe Ashlee was right, I decided: I should consider seeing Dr. Seastrunk in Dallas. Through my network of fellow patients—which was vast by now—I found the name of a woman who was a patient of his. She gave him a rave review and assured me that he was a well-qualified neuropsychiatrist affiliated with a major hospital.

Dr. Seastrunk was also a researcher who devoted much of his career to topics close to my heart. For instance, he'd studied the links between chemical exposures and a person's susceptibility to electromagnetic frequencies, and he'd investigated ways to control subclinical seizures in Gulf War veterans. His research proved that repeated exposures of animal brains to either chemical or electrical irritants produced changes in both brain activity and behavior; he also discovered that repeated brain stimulation eventually produces intense seizure discharges. He called this repeated brain stimulation a "chronic irritant," or a "kindling effect."

Once I read his work, I remembered that Dr. Iris Bell, one of the experts on our scientific advisory board for the Environmental Health Foundation, had applied this same "kindling effect" concept to chemical sensitivity. She had pointed out to me that the olfactory system in humans allows environmental chemicals direct access to the brain via the nasal passages. When solvents, perfumes, aromatic hydrocarbons, or any other chemical molecules pass the "olfactory bulb" (the entry point of the smell system), they continue traveling directly into the brain, progressing neuron by neuron into the brain's limbic system. This is important because the limbic system serves as the location of our emotions; it's also the place in our brain where we organize information.

Again, I recalled the smells in my office at 110 Tower and winced as I thought about how those smells must have emanated from toxic chemicals. By breathing them in, I'd given those toxins a direct highway into my brain. Eventually, I'd suffered that "kindling effect."

I wasn't expecting Dr. Seastrunk to actually help me. How could he succeed when so many others had failed? But I owed it to Ashlee to try him.

✦ ✦ ✦

It was an incredible ordeal to fly the two hours from Tucson to Dallas. I found a friend to drive Ashlee and me to the airport and push my wheelchair to the gate while I held my oxygen tank on my lap.

It was hard work for me to stay calm on the plane, knowing I was being assaulted by chemicals that could prove lethal to me. I hoped that the oxygen tank and mask would afford me enough protection to make it through; once again, I felt like an astronaut visiting an unexplored planet with countless hidden dangers.

Naturally, I was worried that something might happen to me on this trip, and Ashlee would then blame herself. Yet a part of me was exhilarated. At least Ashlee was seeing me as a man who courageously ventured out into a dangerous world. I longed for my daughter to learn the value of taking risks in life. I didn't want my illness to be a reason for Ashlee to curb her own life adventures.

From the moment I met him at Tri-City Hospital in Dallas, I knew that Dr. Seastrunk was markedly different from other physicians I'd seen. He had a strong Texas accent, and he was built like "Poppin' Fresh," the Pillsbury Doughboy.

Despite his stout build, Dr. Seastrunk exuded energy. I felt his intense intellectual curiosity at work as he questioned me and examined my medical records. He also had the warmest, kindest eyes of any doctor I'd ever seen. You could tell by looking into this man's eyes that he was humble and spiritual, almost angelic. Unlike many of the other physicians I'd seen, he didn't treat me as a number or a statistic, but as a human being who deserved dignity. Dr. Seastrunk wasn't practicing medicine as a business. He was a healer.

My body had deteriorated significantly by that time. I was 6 feet 2 inches tall, but my weight had diminished to a near-skeletal 140 pounds. I looked like I was at death's door. Everything was spinning around me, and I couldn't concentrate or think. I had to force myself to focus minute by minute, or I'd forget where I was and what I was doing.

Dr. Seastrunk put me through a battery of tests, one of which was magnetic resonance spectroscopy (MRS). This procedure is often used to complement the more traditional magnetic resonance imaging (MRI) and requires a technician to inject dye into your blood as a means of determining the concentration of brain metabolites. Doctors typically use this test to evaluate disorders of the central nervous system and low-grade brain tumors.

I went into a small exam room and changed from my street clothes into a hospital gown. A technician wheeled me on a gurney into a plain white room with a large machine. The MRS machine looked like the MRI machine I was already familiar with; it was shaped like a big white plastic doughnut. I was inserted into the machine like a torpedo into a submarine.

I heard the *whir* and *clunk* of the machine as it began working and tried to stay still. After a few minutes, I heard Dr. Seastrunk say, "See these lesions on the right side of his brain? I think that's part of the problem."

From the reading I'd done on chemical exposures, I already knew that I had lesions on my brain. These were essentially scars on my gray matter. Nothing new there.

Once I was back in the exam room, Dr. Seastrunk told me he had all the information he needed, and said the MRS showed that my liver also had lesions. "Those lesions on your liver might indicate that your liver was injured and can't detoxify your body properly," he said, pointing out the white marks on the scan.

"How did I get those?" I asked.

"We're not sure," he said. "They could be caused by a virus, but I think in your case it was chemical exposure. The lesions on your liver suggest that you were poisoned, because it's the liver's job to detoxify poison. Your liver had to work so hard, the detoxification pathways in your body have become compromised."

I had been poisoned. I shook my head a little, remembering Dr. Kirkpatrick, the doctor who had theorized that I might have been poisoned by one of the criminals I prosecuted. I had been poisoned all right, but by a building, not a person!

"Have you ever seen anybody like me before?" I asked dully. "And, if so, did you help cure that person?" Of course I expected the answer to be "No."

Or, worse, maybe Dr. Seastrunk would promise me a cure, like some of the other doctors who said they'd be able to help me, adding, "It'll get worse before it gets better" as they prescribed this or that "miracle" treatment.

What Dr. Seastrunk said next floored me: "Absolutely, I've seen people like you before, and I've been fortunate enough to be able to help a lot of them."

He told me about his work with Gulf War veterans suffering from exposure to toxins causing symptoms similar to mine. He also talked to me about the kindling effect, which he described as a "cascade effect" in my nervous system caused by my neurons becoming hypersensitive after an initial environmental insult.

"In your case," he said, "the lesions on the frontal right lobe of your brain were most likely caused by environmental exposure to toxins. Plus, because your liver is compromised, it can no longer totally remove toxins you're exposed to. I'm going to give you a medication that will almost certainly help you."

I couldn't believe it. This man wasn't boasting. He seemed sincere. "But now you're going to tell me that the pills I take will make me worse before I get better, right?"

He laughed. "No. If this drug works, you'll feel better right away."

The medication Dr. Seastrunk prescribed for me was called Neurontin—the brand name for gabapentin—a synthetic amino acid that had originally been developed by the Japanese.

"Neurontin was developed as an anticonvulsant and analgesic," he explained. "Physicians typically prescribe it to help control epileptic seizures and treat neuropathic pain. For people who have experienced brain injuries, this drug helps stabilize injured brain cells and stops them from misfiring."

The drug basically acts like a Band-Aid for brain cells, he added, giving them time to heal by protecting them. "Your brain is constantly in a state of fight or flight, misfiring continuously in response to things in the environment that most people don't even feel," he said. "The Neurontin may help prevent that from happening."

"What about my immune system?"

"If we treat your brain and it heals, your immune abnormalities should also improve."

Suddenly remembering an earlier, very different, diagnosis, I asked, "Why did my doctor at the Cleveland Clinic tell me that I had a prolapsed heart valve?"

"I believe his diagnosis was incorrect. Your abnormal heart test results were caused by the misfiring of your brain cells that mimicked a false positive for a 'prolapsed valve.' You don't have any structural abnormalities in your heart."

"How long will I have to be on it?" I asked, still doubtful.

"That depends on the result," he said. "Everybody's different."

"Yes, but are you talking about weeks? Months? Years?"

"Years," Dr. Seastrunk said. "But our goal is to eventually help your brain heal to the point where we can wean you off the drug." He disappeared for a moment, then came back with a pill bottle. "Here."

"Wait. You want me to start the drug right row?"

"Yes. That way I can monitor you," he said. "I'm going to start you on a low dose and titrate you up slowly. If I started you on the therapeutic dose, there's a chance it would blow you away."

"What about side effects?" I asked.

He listed a number of possible side effects, including fever, dizziness, viral infections, migraine headaches, lethargy, and fatigue. None of those worried me, since I was already battling with those symptoms—and more.

"It's not going to work, you know," I said.

"I think you're wrong," Dr. Seastrunk insisted. "The lesions we see in your brain are similar to what we've found in other victims of environmental illness. They've responded well to this medication. You will, too."

"Fine," I said, too tired to keep arguing. "Tell you what. Give me a prescription and I'll take Neurontin at home." I explained it would be impossible for me to stay in this hospital, with all of the chemicals in the air. "You're not set up for me. Just being here might kill me, and you know that."

To his credit, Dr. Seastrunk agreed that my approach made sense, provided I agreed to be in touch with him regularly by phone so that he could monitor my reaction to the drug. He wrote me a prescription.

As we seated ourselves on the plane for the flight back to Arizona, Ashlee was giddy, nearly beside herself with joy. "I told you this doctor was going to do something to help you. I told you!"

I smiled down at my little girl. Like me, she was a fighter, and that made me proud. The hardships in her life hadn't robbed her of enthusiasm and resilience. In fact, facing up to adversities had strengthened her character.

At the same time, I couldn't share her enthusiasm.

As the plane rose above the tarmac, I glanced at Ashlee again. For her sake, I had to act like I believed better days lay ahead of us.

◆ ◆ ◆

The bottle of Neurontin capsules sat on my counter for two weeks. When Ashlee was at Susan's place, she'd call to ask if I'd started taking them yet. When she came over, she pestered me about beginning the medication.

"I know you're afraid, Daddy," she said, "but you have to try."

One night, after she'd left my house and returned to her mother's, I picked up the bottle, studied it for a moment, and unscrewed the cap. It was filled with orange capsules.

I tipped the bottle and let one of the pills fall into my hand. I had to suppress a laugh as I looked around my barren Tucson home. As if I were dying, my life flashed before my eyes, an unlikely chain of events that had landed me here, with this orange capsule in my palm: prosecuting gangsters and drug lords in Florida, holing up in the high desert in Elgin, surviving the leper colony of Seagoville, languishing at the castle in Cabo, barricading myself in my Tucson bubble, and pushing for the Environmental Health Foundation's first summit.

Through all of those events, Ashlee was there. Ashlee wanted me to take this pill. I did not for one second believe this drug would work. But Ashlee did, so I owed it to her to try it. I went to the refrigerator, took out a bottle of water, popped a capsule into my mouth, and washed it down.

The deed was done. What would the morning bring? If this was going to be the end for me, at least people could say I'd gone down fighting.

+ + +

I woke up the next morning, relieved that the medication hadn't killed me. But the bigger surprise was that I'd slept through the night.

Ironically, despite my fatigue, pain typically prevented me from resting. Had the Neurontin allowed me to sleep?

I was well aware of the placebo effect. Unfortunately, no matter what treatments I'd tried over the past few years, not one of them had ever tricked my body into feeling better.

I immediately telephoned Ashlee, who'd spent the night at her mother's house. Before I could tell her about my marvelous sleep, she said, "Did you take the medicine?"

"Yes, I did."

"And?"

"Nothing bad happened. In fact, it was kind of strange. I actually slept all night."

"So it's working?"

I could hear the excitement in her voice. My first impulse was to temper it. No way would this medication work. Nothing ever had.

"I don't know," I said cautiously. "Maybe. At least it's not causing any negative reactions."

"Isn't it pretty good for you to be able to sleep through the night?" she insisted.

"Well," I hedged. "It's not like I'm dancing on the table or anything."

"Did you dance on tables before I was born?"

I laughed. "No."

"So this is it, Daddy. I know it is! I love you. I've got to go to school now. Bye."

I lay in bed for a few more minutes, allowing a spark of optimism to bloom in my chest.

♦ ♦ ♦

I continued taking the Neurontin under Dr. Seastrunk's supervision by phone, gradually ramping up the dose over a period of weeks. It was astonishing: I could actually feel my body healing in ways that were small but significant.

My pain was beginning to dull into a background ache instead of something incapacitating. The vertigo had lessened. I continued to sleep well and began feeling stronger and more energetic.

Still, I stuck to my careful routines. I didn't want to risk a crash. If this drug was really doing its job, there would be time for everything.

I waited a week. Two. Three. Finally, when I'd been on the pills a month, I made a momentous decision: I was going to try walking out the front door without my oxygen tank and stroll through my neighborhood. I was going to pretend to be normal.

On the day of my big adventure, I rose early to go outside while it was still cool, and before people filled the air with hydrocarbons from their cars. I felt as nervous as I imagined athletes must feel before the Olympics, even though I was only planning to take a short walk.

I showered and put on my reliably comfortable University of Miami Hurricanes tracksuit. To the outside world, I would probably look like any scruffy, suburban Dad.

At the entrance to my fortress, I opened the air-lock door and stepped outside. As I hovered on the front step, all of my alarm bells went off. Panic struck. I had no idea what to expect.

Should I take a deep breath, or just experiment with shallow ones?

I took several short breaths and tried to force my mind to stop racing. My body seemed to be fine. My head was clearer than it had been in years, and the cool morning air felt luxurious against my face, especially around my mouth and nose, which were so often covered by the oxygen mask.

After a few minutes of hesitation on the landing, I put one foot in front of the other and began slowly walking toward the street.

I could feel my face breaking into a smile as I tipped my face to the sun and walked toward the edge of my property. When I reached the street, I turned around and looked back at the bubble, imagining my abandoned oxygen tank inside the door. Again, I couldn't shake that image of me as an astronaut, only now I was free from the mother ship and drifting in space.

Which way should I go? Right or left? I'd never made this choice before. Who would ever imagine that simply being able to choose your own direction could inspire such momentous feelings of joy and freedom?

I turned left, wondering if I could walk as far as the next house. I set that as my goal and proceeded cautiously. All that lay between me and my neighbor's front door was air! How splendid was that?

Suppressing a laugh, I imagined walking up and knocking on the door, saying, "Hi, I'm your neighbor, Alan. I've been stuck inside my house for years, but I can go outside now. I hope to see you around!"

Naturally, my neighbor—whom I'd never met—might call the cops, thinking I must be some psych patient who'd gone off his meds.

That first day, I stayed outside for ten glorious minutes before retreating back to the house—not because I was feeling bad, but because I was afraid to push my luck.

I was bursting with excitement. I had cursed, hoped, prayed, researched, and seen one doctor after another in an attempt to regain my former life. I no longer cared about achieving anything that grand. Not anymore. To me, just being able to step foot outside my home without an oxygen tank was a huge deal.

Over the next few days, I extended my outdoor excursions bit by bit, until finally I decided I was ready to spend half a day walking in the Tucson foothills. For a man who'd grown up among the flat green marshes of southern Florida, then had been confined to a bubble for years, the experience of being outside in the dry Arizona air was amazing. Being surrounded by mountains, deserts, flowers, cacti, and exotic wildlife that included coyotes and tarantulas presented a sensory overload.

Each creature I saw, from a lowly lizard to a gorgeous butterfly, filled me with delight. As I walked, breathed, and took in the sights and smells around me, I realized that my body had not only been protected by the bubble; it had also been severely deprived. I'd been on a sensory retreat as well as a chemical one.

The environment I'd been living in was gray and lifeless. I'd chalked that up to depression. Now that I was on the Neurontin, I understood that my illness had dampened my senses. Possibly, that was my body's way of shutting down unnecessary functions to conserve energy and protect me. Now, like Rip Van Winkle waking up from his coma, my senses were miraculously restored.

♦ ♦ ♦

By the second month on the Neurontin, Ashlee began accompanying me on my walks around the neighborhood. Being outside with me was such a novelty that she eyed the landscape with the same childlike wonder I did, exclaiming over everything from the lizards skittering in the underbrush to the birds winging overhead.

In the past, Ashlee had to leave the bubble alone because I was trapped inside. She'd explored the limits of our three-acre property like a junior geologist, scavenging different kinds of rocks. She also loved building forts and playing imaginary games in them.

Now she stayed close to me, holding my hand whenever she wasn't darting ahead to investigate something or collect some natural wonder to show me, chattering excitedly as we walked.

Whenever Ashlee was at her mother's house, I'd take my walks and then call to talk with her after school, describing what I'd seen.

"It makes me so happy that you can go outside now," Ashlee said during one of these conversations.

"Me too." I was glad to hear her sound so joyful over the phone, but I was hatching a plan to make my daughter even happier. I knew the next thing I said was going to blow her mind: "Ashlee, I want to take you shopping. Let's make a date. I think I'm ready for the mall."

I was grinning as I spoke. Until that moment, I had nearly given up imagining being able to say these words. In an ironic twist of fate, the daughter I fought to stay alive for—so she wouldn't be fatherless—had saved my life.

13 ✦ REENTERING THE WORLD

PEOPLE WATCHING ME WITH ASHLEE on that first excursion to the Tucson Mall must have noticed something curious: while most children excitedly drag their parents by the hand around stores, begging Mom and Dad to buy things for them, in our case, I was the excited one. I stopped every few minutes to exclaim over displays in the shopping center as if I were in a museum examining artifacts of a foreign culture.

I had retreated from the world in 1989. Now it was 1996. Between those years, there had been innumerable technological advances. Why were people talking on cell phones at the mall? What were computers doing in the shops? Why was everyone wearing such bizarre clothing?

"Come on, Daddy," Ashlee kept laughing. "Don't you know about that? Let's keep moving."

Ashlee knew exactly which stores she wanted to show me. For my part, I was too keyed up by the vivid smells and sights around me to care about our exact destinations, despite my daughter's heat-seeking agenda.

She had always chosen her own clothes. Now that Ashlee had gotten me to the mall, she was determined to make the most of it. My daughter led me through Dillard's, Macy's, Claire's, and other stores that were just a blur to me. Ashlee's biggest thrill, though, was visiting the food court with me. Even though I still didn't trust my body to digest anything other than the careful roster of safe organic foods, I happily watched her devour a pastry from Cinnabon.

I'd started with 300 mg of Neurontin three times a day. Over the next few months, I ramped up to 4,800 mg of the drug per day. My health continued to improve. I wasn't cured—certain things still set me off—but I was far less sensitive to everyday chemicals, and many of my symptoms had abated.

When I told my primary physician how much Neurontin I was taking, his eyes nearly popped out of his head. "That's enough to kill a horse," he said.

I shrugged. "It's not killing me."

I could only hope that was true. Far more important to me, though, was the fact that my life with Ashlee was beginning to assume a shape familiar to most parents: we took walks, went to the mall, and eventually started seeing movies together. The first time I felt the rumble of a THX movie system, I nearly jumped out of my skin.

I also took her to a Go-Kart track in Tucson, remembering Ashlee's love of speed as a toddler, back when I'd race around with her in our Florida neighborhood. The faster we drove around the track, the more she loved it. I could hear my daughter's laughter even over the roar of the engines as Ashlee's little helmet bobbed around while she was sitting next to me.

The world was coming at me fast and loud, but I was welcoming it with open arms. I'd been away far too long.

◆ ◆ ◆

My release from the bubble granted me an unexpected gift: a sixth sense. I could now determine with some accuracy when toxic chemicals were around me. I was like a drug-sniffing dog able to detect low levels of toxins that other people couldn't sense.

This was a wonderful gift because if I could channel it, I could call upon this new superpower to alert others to danger. However, it was also a great responsibility because I constantly felt obligated to help prevent others from poisonous toxic exposures—and I knew many of them wouldn't believe these poisons were in their environment. Alarm bells went off in my body whenever I was around toxins, even though the Neurontin kept me from reacting to them. Yet nobody else seemed to sense what I did. How could I convince them that these poisons really did exist in our everyday environments?

My sense of smell was heightened. In the shopping mall with Ashlee, for instance, I picked up things coming at me from all directions: perfume, fabric softener, hair spray, cologne. I'd been terrified by this discovery at first. I was afraid something would set me off and I'd experience the symptoms that had disabled me before: headaches, eye irritation, tightened muscles, congested breathing, or seizures. What if I had such a severe reaction that I wouldn't recover, even on the Neurontin? Fortunately, my body held up well, despite all of my warning bells clanging at once.

I soon learned that I could walk into any restaurant, store, business, or house, and determine immediately if my surroundings were clean or not—the same way you might be aware of the popcorn smell in a movie theater as you enter through the cinema doors and the odor of fake butter hits you. I could even sense where a chemical concentration was higher as I walked toward it or away from it, sort of like that "you're getting warmer and colder" game my siblings and I played as children. As Dr. Seastrunk had suggested, Neurontin was acting like a Band-Aid on my brain: I still sensed these chemicals around me, but, like touching a cut on your finger that's now covered by a bandage, the sensations of those chemicals assaulting my body were lessened to a degree that I could tolerate them.

I began gradually testing my abilities here and there. For instance, if I smelled fabric softener in someone's home, I'd follow the scent until I found the stuff in a cupboard. Once, I walked into a friend's house and immediately said, "Hey, you got a new mattress!" The shock on his face confirmed that I was correct.

"How could you possibly know that?" he asked. Usually, it took some convincing before people believed me.

Over time, I began to appreciate this gift. Previously, I'd gotten sick when exposed to something without knowing what triggered my body to react. Whenever that happened, because I was too sensitive, I felt hit from all directions, not knowing where the assaults originated. Now that my sensitivity was dialed down, I was able to distinguish the origins of specific harmful exposures. I was better equipped and more experienced. With luck, maybe someday I could use this gift to help others protect themselves.

◆ ◆ ◆

Even in the spring of 1996, nearly a year after the Neurontin kicked in, I still had to pinch myself occasionally to make myself believe my new life was real. Because half of me expected my improved health to be yanked away, I was determined to make the most of every moment.

For instance, that spring I drove with Ashlee from Arizona to the Grand Canyon, torturing her all the way there by playing Eagles songs until she'd lie in the back seat with her hands over her ears. I still didn't trust my condition to remain stable in a hotel room, where I'd be subjected to many chemicals, so we pitched our tent and camped out.

Ashlee was miserable. She had no trouble telling me she hated every minute of that trip—even when we were tucked into our cozy sleeping bags, or during our exciting helicopter ride over the Grand Canyon, where the majesty of the views took my breath away.

"Look at this? Don't you love the view?" I chided her, shouting over the noise of the helicopter's blades. "It's better than the chairlift to the top of Mount Lemmon, right?"

"Nope," Ashlee said, crossing her arms stubbornly. "I hate this. And I hate camping!"

Ashlee had always been opinionated, smart, and strong willed. When she was younger, I could manage her defiant behavior with a little creative discipline and coaxing. Moreover, her concerns about my health would prevail over her need to defy me. However, as I became healthier, she took opportunities to argue with me, knowing I could physically withstand her adolescent challenges. Our relationship was changing. I no longer looked like I was on death's door, and Ashlee was getting older. She began to rebel against me the way many preteens and teenagers do when their parents try to force them to do something they don't necessarily want to do. Surprisingly, this was comforting to me. Ashlee's life was becoming normal despite everything we'd been through together.

◆ ◆ ◆

It was important for me to continue building awareness about our environment's impact on our health. In 1997, a group of people in Tucson asked me to be one of their keynote speakers at their Natural Choices Expo. I enthusiastically agreed, despite knowing that it would take a toll on me physically.

The Natural Choices Expo '97 was billed as the first convention on alternative medicine in the United States. It signaled our country's growing interest in alternative health and eco-friendly living.

"Who else will be speaking?" I asked the person who called to invite me.

"Dr. Andrew Weil," she replied. "Perhaps you've heard of him?"

She told me that Andy had recently published another book on natural health and explained that Andy's Integrative Medicine Program at the University of Arizona was opening a month before the expo. In addition to Andy and me, another keynote speaker was actor Dennis Weaver, who had built his own house out of recycled tires while campaigning in the anti-hunger movement.

What could I do but laugh and say, "Are you kidding? Of course I've heard of Dr. Weil. We've actually met. But, look, do me a favor. Please don't tell him I'm coming, okay?"

The woman agreed.

On the day of the speech, I walked up to the head table at the event and grinned when I spotted Andy. He was talking to someone and didn't see me right away. Andy looked exactly the same: bearded, slightly disheveled, very casually dressed.

Finally, he glanced up and saw me. Andy's face paled and his eyes widened. He looked like he'd seen a ghost. All I could do was look at him with a big smile and say, "Hello, Andy. We meet again."

"*Alan?* What are you doing here? How did you get out?"

"I'm taking Neurontin," I said.

"You're kidding me," he said, shaking his head in disbelief. "Seriously. How did you get out?"

I repeated my answer. "How are you?" I asked him then. "It's good to see you."

"It's good to see you, too!" Andy said. "But I can't believe this. I can't believe what I'm seeing, that you're out of the bubble. And you're the keynote speaker sitting next to me! I thought for sure it had to be a different Alan Bell on the program."

I was introduced to the audience to speak before Andy. It was my first public appearance outside the bubble. I was nervous, but I had thought carefully about what I wanted to say. I put all of my heart and passion into telling the crowd that we had a duty to spread the word that what we breathe, eat, and drink can sustain and promote our health—or literally destroy it, even killing us.

In some ways, because this was a Tucson crowd that was already committed to living a more organic, natural lifestyle, I was preaching mostly to the converted. But I didn't care. If I could reach even one more person and convince him or her of the importance of avoiding harmful substances being poured into our environment, I was determined to do it.

I talked about the millions of Americans becoming ill each year because of air pollution, and how outdoor air pollution causes one out of every twenty city deaths. I spoke about the rising incidence of cancer, and how the National Institutes of Health had recently reported that 70 percent of all cancers can be linked to environmental pollutants.

"Many scientists predict that, unless we act now, environmental illness will be the epidemic of the twenty-first century," I went on. Then I reminded the crowd that, once upon a time, we had a polio epidemic that crippled and killed many children.

"Back then, researchers and doctors told us that very little could be done about that polio epidemic, but a small group of parents believed otherwise," I told the audience. "They believed that, if they could help spread the word, something could be done. So this small group of parents, with cups in their hands, began knocking door-to-door, collecting one dime at a time. And because they spread the word, they found the answer: the Salk vaccine."

My message emphasized that we can make a difference in the fate of humanity—but only if all of us work together. At the same time, I urged my listeners to convince legislators to enact laws that better regulate *all* chemicals, not just those in foods or medicines.

The cost of inaction is too high, I reminded them. "I've seen firsthand what a poisonous environment can do to a human life. I've seen the illness, the suffering, and the death. I'm here to tell you that everybody is at risk. Nobody is immune. This silent epidemic knows no borders. Its victims are rich and poor, black and white, Christian and Jewish, young and old. We're all in the same boat . . . and this boat is *sinking*."

After the applause died down, Andy stood up and spoke easily, without notes. He began by talking about how he and I had first met, and how he still couldn't believe that I'd managed to walk out of that bubble.

"I saw this guy when he was on death's door," Andy said, "and I've got to tell you, Alan Bell knows firsthand what it's like to be poisoned by environmental toxins. I'm absolutely amazed and blown away to see him standing here with us today. You have no idea how happy I am."

Andy went on with the rest of his speech. When he was finished, people in the audience rose to their feet and applauded loudly, probably thinking Andy and I had planned to speak together in this way. We had delivered our message, loud and clear. They'd heard us and believed our message.

Now I just had to figure out how to reach an even bigger audience. But how?

◆ ◆ ◆

Although Dr. Johnson in Dallas was still my primary physician, Dr. Seastrunk wanted to examine me again. He had opened up a satellite office in Southern California—a quicker flight from Tucson than his main office in Dallas—so I decided that was doable.

Dr. Seastrunk's office was located in Dana Point, a city of just over thirty thousand people in Orange County, California. It's one of the few places in Orange County with a harbor, and it's a popular place for surfing.

I fell in love with the area immediately. The harbor was stunning, and my overall impression of Dana Point was that of a little seaside Italian village. Seeing it made me remember how I'd always escaped to the beach in Miami whenever I was feeling ill. Maybe the combination of being near the ocean and taking Neurontin would cure me for good. I decided to rent a place in Dana Point and see if it suited me.

It did. The Pacific air here felt good to me—so good, in fact, that I felt my recovery take another giant step forward soon after making the move. I also kept my bubble in Tucson because Ashlee was shuttling between that house and her mother's, spending two weeks of each month with me and the other two with her mother. I lived in Southern California during my off weeks.

As it turned out, that plan didn't last long. Susan soon married again, and, in a shocking move, without any explanation or warning, suddenly surrendered custody and all parental rights. I became Ashlee's sole guardian.

How do you tell your little girl her mommy doesn't want her anymore? Susan has not spoken to or seen Ashlee since.

Life goes on, and we do the best we can with the cards we are dealt. I brought Ashlee to Capistrano Beach in California and bought a house. This was a painful transition for her, but I did my best, continuing to make up for the time we'd lost by redoubling my efforts to bond with her through activities we both enjoyed.

I was starting over yet again. This time it felt good.

◆ ◆ ◆

That year, Ashlee turned eleven and I made good on the fantasy I'd crafted with Dan Baker in my Arizona bubble: I took my daughter to Disneyland.

I was nervous about the idea of spending an entire day at an amusement park, so I took some precautions. I asked my parents to accompany us and brought my oxygen tank and an electric scooter. I also ordered a special meal to meet my strict dietary needs.

We started with Space Mountain, the giant indoor roller coaster designed to simulate a rocket ship blasting through the universe. During my years of confinement, even the thought of venturing outside my bubble was akin to a space journey because I required so much protective gear. I couldn't believe I was flying through the stars with my daughter, both of us breathless with laughter and excitement.

Next, Ashlee and I tackled Futurama, where kids drive their own cars around a track while their parents sit in the passenger seat—Ashlee was in heaven, as always, sitting behind the steering wheel—and then the Matterhorn, where we zipped through a snowy mountain landscape before coming face-to-face with the Abominable Snowman.

Ironically, the gentlest ride of them all—It's a Small World—was nearly my undoing. As the scent of the chlorinated water hit my nose, I experienced an immediate sensory overload. I backed out of the line of people waiting to board the ride, saying, "It's the chlorine, honey. I'm sorry. It's too much. I can't do it." My sixth sense had kicked in once again to save me from harm.

I could see the alarm on the faces of Ashlee and my parents, and felt their worries, even though they didn't dare share them with me: *Is Alan going to have a seizure? Is this all going to end badly? Have we pushed things too fast?*

Then Ashlee spoke up. "Dad, are you okay if I go on the ride by myself?"

I stared at her in wonder, impressed by the fact that she was now comfortable enough with the state of my health to leave me on my own—something she wouldn't have done even a year or two ago.

"Sure," I replied, though I suggested my parents accompany her.

My father shook his head. "I'd rather do Space Mountain again than this ride."

"Me too," my mother said. "What about you, Ashlee?"

They didn't have to ask her twice. The three of them went to take another turn on Space Mountain, while I rested on a bench far from the scent of chlorine. When they returned, still flushed with excitement, I grinned up at them. "Ready to keep going?"

"Are you sure you're okay, Alan?" my father asked, his face creased with concern.

"I'm fine, Dad. I just need to stay away from chlorine."

And so we did. We made the most of that magical day, and I never once had to use the oxygen tank. As for my electric scooter, I never got a chance to use it. A certain red-haired little girl was having too much fun driving it; Ashlee used the scooter to travel from one food stand to the next, loading its basket with every kind of fast food the park offered.

Late in the afternoon, I looked around at my little family: my father, the World War II veteran who'd stayed by my side through the horrors of Mexico and Seagoville; my mother, who gave me such an idyllic childhood and the values I still live by; and Ashlee, who'd been responsible for pushing me until I finally found freedom outside a bubble.

It was all too much for me. I started sobbing uncontrollably and finally had to sit on the electric wheelchair. Immediately, my family gathered around, drawing close like a human fortress, as if they could surround and protect me.

"What is it?" my father asked. "What's wrong? Are you sick, son?"

I shook my head, struggling to put into words everything I was feeling. "No, no. I'm fine. But I thought this day would never come. I love you all so much, and I'm just so glad to be alive."

We stayed at the park until the fireworks show, cheering as the rockets exploded over Sleeping Beauty's castle, marveling at the colors sparkling bright in the sky.

◆ ◆ ◆

I also took Ashlee to Six Flags and Knott's Berry Farm, where I introduced her to the daredevil thrill of riding roller coasters. I knew my speed demon would love them, and she did. We also enjoyed the thrill of jet skiing in Dana Point Harbor, where we'd crash into the waves and fall off the jet skis into the cold Pacific Ocean, only to climb back on and do it again.

I introduced Ashlee to the music I loved and took her to concerts with the Beach Boys, Paul McCartney, Kenny Loggins, The Monkees, Chicago, and more. And because I wanted to share Ashlee's music, I bought her tickets to see the Backstreet Boys and other groups she loved. On another memorable night, we sat in the audience for a taping of *The Tonight Show* with Jay Leno.

One of our favorite activities was to take the aerial tramway to the top of Mount San Jacinto in Palm Springs. The saucer-shaped, rotating tram starts in the dry desert at about 2,700 feet and ascends through several different climate zones to the summit, an alpine forest at just over 8,500 feet.

I loved this outing partly because it reminded me of our trips to the top of Mount Lemmon when Ashlee was much younger—only now there was a big difference because I felt as good at the lower elevations as I did at the higher ones.

When we visited my parents in Miami, Ashlee and I often rented a boat in the Florida Keys and went snorkeling on their amazing reefs. The reefs had essentially been my backyard while I was growing up. Now I introduced Ashlee to ocean life and taught her about the different fish. This was a chance for me to recapture one of the many experiences I didn't expect to ever have again. I had every reason now to believe that we'd share many more special experiences together soon, and I was humbled by my good fortune.

14 ✦ From Survivor to Advocate

In 1999, I was flying home from Florida to California with Ashlee when, while standing at the baggage claim in Los Angeles, I overheard a conversation between two men standing nearby. They were discussing a "toxic tort" case—that's a legal case involving a plaintiff claiming injury after exposure to environmental toxins.

Naturally, my ears perked up. I introduced myself to the men and told them I was an attorney who had founded the Environmental Health Foundation. We began discussing their case, and the men introduced themselves as Attorney Ed Masry and his office manager, Jim Hira, of the law firm Masry and Vititoe.

I'd heard of the firm, of course. In environmental health circles, Ed Masry was famous. He and his law clerk, Erin Brockovich, successfully built a legal case against the Pacific Gas and Electric Company in 1993. The case proved how the gas company's Hinkley compressor station, which served as part of the natural-gas pipeline connecting to the San Francisco Bay area, used the toxic chemical hexavalent chromium to fight corrosion in their cooling tower. This chemical was discharged to unlined ponds at the site through wastewater, and some of it percolated into the groundwater, contaminating it. The lawsuit alleged the chemical was responsible for many people being diagnosed with cancer in the area.

The case was eventually settled in 1996 for $333 million, the largest settlement ever paid in a direct-action lawsuit in US history. The case became the subject of a major motion picture, *Erin Brockovich*. Ed Masry, who was portrayed in the film by Albert Finney; Erin Brockovich, who was played by Julia Roberts; and their law firm rocketed into the spotlight after the movie was released. They were flooded with worldwide requests for representation from victims of environmental poisoning.

As we were leaving the airport, Hira said, "Hey, Alan, why don't you come up and have lunch with us sometime? We're just north of Los Angeles. Maybe you could help us out on some cases."

"I'm retired," I said. "I don't practice law anymore."

"Yeah? That's too bad," he said. "We could really use a guy with your knowledge. Well, come have lunch anyway. I'd love to talk over a few cases with you, maybe get your input on them."

That sounded easy enough. I agreed, and we parted ways.

I drove up to the offices of Masry and Vititoe in West Lake Village a few weeks later. Ed was a generous man, active in his local community and government. He was also on kidney dialysis during the time I collaborated with him. He often came to work in sweatpants after going through a couple of hours of dialysis—a solemn reminder that, not long ago, I'd been trapped in my bubble, wearing only my University of Miami sweatpants and unable to leave my house. I admired his determination to live as normal and full a life as possible given his illness.

I admired Jim, too, and we began a friendship based on common interests. We met occasionally for lunch or dinner. Eventually, he began giving me cases to review. "We can't handle all this stuff," Jim admitted. "Ed's sick, and we're just a two-man law firm. We could use your help, Alan."

I agreed to look at some of the cases, but only as a favor, and in an unofficial capacity.

◆ ◆ ◆

Up to that point, I had never handled a toxic tort case. However, as I began reading through files Jim gave me, I realized that I had the medical knowledge and legal skills to assist the law firm.

In the beginning, I limited my involvement to making phone calls. I called victims on behalf of the law firm of Masry and Vititoe to determine if their cases could potentially yield some kind of positive, tangible result in court. Most did not, for a million different reasons.

A toxic tort case isn't worth putting hours into if the defendant—the company, individual, or organization being sued—doesn't have insurance or deep pockets. Moreover, unless we could clearly prove the defendant was negligent, we couldn't help these victims. And even if we *could* prove negligence, it was still necessary to link the victim's illness to a particular toxic exposure.

The cause-and-effect of a toxic tort case is often an elusive thing to prove. An environmental injury is never as clear-cut as, say, an automobile accident where you walk across the street, get hit, and boom! You're down! In that situation, witnesses can clearly describe what happened, there might be evidence like blood on the curb, and somebody probably caught a cell phone video of the event.

In the case of environmental injury, on the other hand, the cause-and-effect is tricky to prove. We're exposed to many different chemicals in our daily lives. In addition, victims of such exposures often don't experience symptoms until many years later, so it's difficult to link the symptoms back to a specific exposure as the cause. The defense can successfully argue that an intervening event may have caused the injury, creating room for doubt. In addition, since each person has an individual biochemical fingerprint, the defense can argue that the illness or injury—the "effect"—might be due to genetic factors, independent of any environmental exposure.

To complicate matters, in 1991, this was an emerging area of law. The medical establishment was only beginning to agree that environmental chemicals were potentially harmful to human health. Proving personal injury lawsuits depends upon solid science. Each claimant must demonstrate, through expert testimony, that a toxic exposure caused their illness. If there aren't any doctors or scientists willing to testify that certain chemicals are definitely linked to specific illnesses or injuries, then you can't build a legal case. Hard science must support each expert witness's testimony.

I became increasingly involved with Masry and Vititoe over the next few years, moving from simple phone calls into analyzing and developing various toxic tort cases. I began very slowly, dipping my foot in these legal waters by helping out here and there, offering my advice about which cases might be worth pursuing.

In addition, I spoke regularly with victims, either those referred to me by Masry and Vititoe or people who found me on their own. They came to me out of desperation, usually, because they were in the same place I'd once been, feeling as if they were alone and howling in the wilderness, unable to find doctors who could help them—or even people who believed them.

As time passed, it became increasingly apparent to me that an awful lot of these people weren't going to get help unless I rolled up my sleeves and helped them myself, so that's what I did.

Whenever Masry referred a case to me that I thought had promise, I'd start by calling these clients on the phone. I'd listen to them describe how they'd been injured by some kind of chemical exposure and do my best to refer them to the right medical specialists. If legal action was called for that might bring them some kind of monetary compensation, I'd pursue it, but not until I first addressed their medical issues.

This kind of work felt meaningful. I was grateful to be physically able to help. At the same time, it was difficult for me to witness how the lives of these families were ripped apart through no fault of their own.

Toxic tort law is a highly specialized legal area that is still emerging. About 99 percent of the top US trial lawyers have absolutely no experience in the field. I was in a unique position to advocate as a former victim, survivor, medical proponent, and legal avenger all wrapped into one person.

I participated in most of these cases pro bono because I was fortunate to be financially independent and have the opportunity to help those who lacked the money to pay for legal assistance. Knowing that I was helping victims who had nowhere else to turn infused my life with new purpose and meaning. That was gratification enough.

I went about my work systematically. For instance, if a nurse claimed she'd contracted a respiratory illness after being exposed to harmful chemicals while working in a hospital, I'd ask for her medical records proving her claim. If her medical records confirmed a respiratory ailment, I would then find out if anyone had tested the air in the hospital. If not, I'd help locate a certified industrial hygienist to test the air for the presence of toxic chemicals known to cause respiratory disease.

I had no trouble finding environmental health experts. I'd spoken with plenty of environmentally ill patients about how they got sick and which professionals had helped them. I also had a long list of scientists who served on the Scientific Advisory Board of my Environmental Health Foundation. Previously, these scientists had advised us on what research project proposals to fund, offering us insights into what studies were legitimate and relevant to global environmental health. They also recommended public awareness programs designed to help prevent disease, by providing people with the knowledge they need to modify their lifestyles and minimize their risk of environmental illness. My past relationships with the professionals on our board served as a springboard to secure top environmental scientists as expert witnesses in the courtroom.

It wasn't long before my fax machine was spitting out pages in the middle of the night. I'd wake up, and they'd be all over my floor: frantic pleas for help from victims all over America.

◆ ◆ ◆

Over time, I had investigated many heartrending toxic tort cases. Eventually, I realized I had no choice but to take further action.

I became an advocate.

I am probably the least likely advocate for environmental health you'd expect to find: a conservatively dressed former prosecutor, not a liberal with long hair or hippie sandals—no turquoise rings, no pierced anything. Yet talking to victim after victim eventually got to me. I became their voice.

For local cases, I sometimes met with victims in person. Looking into their eyes was like looking into a mirror because I could see the same fear I had felt when I couldn't understand what was causing my symptoms or how to treat them. They were scared, struggling to understand what had happened to them, but they simply couldn't put the pieces together. They were just beginning the long and difficult medical odyssey I'd been on since giving up my legal career in Florida.

My sixth sense kicked into high gear as I began helping people fight against those who'd poisoned them. I'd practiced long enough that I could determine with one sniff if there was mold, new carpeting, new paint, or other chemicals present in an area.

I was able to start relying on my hypersensitivity to alert and divert others. This was an admittedly unorthodox approach. To some, it appeared too good to be true, but I was able to save victims thousands of dollars and unnecessary delays caused by hiring experts who would conduct lab tests and arrive at the same conclusions I did—only I did it faster and free of charge.

Unorthodox or not, my ability to sniff out or "feel" the presence of toxins was actually pretty straightforward and simple. Some victims would call me to say they thought their workplace or home was making them sick, but they weren't sure why. I'd go on site to help them figure out the likely source of their illness. If there was black mold or another toxic chemical in their environment, I could sense it. My lungs would immediately seize up, or I'd feel an intense sinus pain. If it was really bad, my vision would blur and I'd feel a swelling sensation in my brain.

Often, I could even determine the class of chemical hidden in a particular environment by my body's response. Whether I was in the presence of formaldehyde, chlorine, mold, pesticides, or flame retardants, my body had instantaneous neurological and inflammatory responses to the poison. This was my secret weapon.

One woman, for instance, was a single mother renting a Newport Beach condo. She and her baby were both sick, and she was certain it had something to do with their living quarters. She just couldn't prove it. I arrived and sat with her at the dining room table. We chatted for a few minutes while I sniffed the air.

"I know what's wrong," I said.

"What do you mean?" She gave me a startled look.

"There's mold in here. Do you mind if I look around your place?"

She shook her head. "No. Please do."

The woman trailed after me from room to room as I followed the scent of the mold, until I located its source behind a wall.

I tapped the wall and said, "There's mold behind here."

The woman stared at me like I was crazy. "But how do you know that? I can't smell anything. And we can't see the mold, right?" She looked around as if the mold might suddenly pop out of the walls.

"No," I said. "Trust me, though, it's there behind the wall. That's your problem."

"What do I do about it?" she asked.

I felt sorry for her, because she was a single mother in her early thirties, a woman obviously without many options. I thought back to all of the cases I'd handled as a prosecutor, and how often the powerless people were handed the worst attorneys and sentences: power is often in the hands of those with money and position. This woman had neither.

"Tell you what. I'll bring in a certified industrial hygienist,"
I said.

"But I can't afford that!" She looked panicked.

"Don't worry. I'll pay for it."

I did, and sure enough, when I met the hygienist in the condo,
he found mold behind that wall and under the sink, where I had
also sensed it. I told him right where to look for the mold and take
samples. That was a good thing because it costs less to take samples
if you know right where to look for the toxin.

The hygienist examined the mold under the microscope and
said, "Yup. You were right, Alan. It's black mold."

Black mold is toxic to humans. Sometimes it's even lethal. The
woman was watching us like we'd beamed down from another
planet. She looked really scared now. "What do I do? Is that dangerous? Can I sue my landlord?"

"You could," I said, "but it would be a lot of aggravation and
money, and the court costs would have to come out of your pocket.
It probably wouldn't be worth it for you financially. Look, both you
and your kid can recover simply by moving out. Do yourself a favor
and forget about the lawsuit. Just get the hell out of this place."

"But how will I get out of my lease?"

"Let me take care of it."

There aren't many lawyers willing to walk away from a lawsuit, but I knew how taxing a court case would be. Although
the woman was experiencing symptoms, I also knew it would be
tough to prove that the mold in the condo was actually *causing* her
symptoms. Not all people react to mold. Her landlord could claim
something else had caused the illness. I had no intention of taking
advantage of her.

However, I was certain that, having found evidence of the mold,
I could scare the landlord with the prospect of a lawsuit, and that's
what I did: I sat down with him and said, "Look, she's sick, her kid's
sick, and here are the test results showing you have black mold in

that condo. Do everyone a favor and cut her loose. She'll be on her way, and you won't have a lawsuit on your hands."

Not surprisingly, he agreed. He also followed my advice to have the apartment cleared of mold—not to protect his next tenants, but rather to insulate himself from potential future lawsuits.

I assisted victims in over a hundred cases for Masry and Vititoe. In addition, countless others began contacting me for personal and legal advice through the Environmental Health Foundation.

Although I was finally able to live outside the bubble, my health was still fragile. Even as I took more active roles in some cases, I had to do the work from behind the scenes rather than travel, since I didn't want my clients to suffer if my health took a turn for the worse. I brought in other lawyers to do the heavy lifting, always careful to choose only attorneys I trusted, lawyers who kept me intimately involved in the cases. I provided advice, guidance, and support both to my colleagues and especially to the victims.

By becoming an environmental health advocate—a legal avenger fighting to give victims a voice and seeking justice—I came full circle. I was now back in the dynamic legal arena, this time fighting for a cause I believed in with my whole heart, mind, and soul.

I was no longer prosecuting one crime at a time by putting bad guys in jail. Instead, I was going after the biggest, most powerful villains of all: chemical manufacturers, pharmaceutical corporations, and other entities that refuse to admit they are heedlessly spewing toxins into our environment and killing people.

And I was determined to win.

15 · Chemicals Take Down a Football Coach

Dan Allen was a beloved head football coach at Holy Cross College in Worcester, Massachusetts. His wife, Laura, contacted me through my Environmental Health Foundation. She reached out to me because her husband suffered from multiple chemical sensitivity and they were searching for treatments.

"Dan's been coaching from a wheelchair on the sidelines, but now they've fired him because he can't do it anymore," Laura said, obviously near tears as she told me her husband's story.

Dan was working in his office, located inside the gymnasium at Holy Cross College, in early 2001 when he saw men wearing white suits and gas masks working on the gym floor. The coach left his office, walked over to the gym, and asked what was going on. The workers told him they were resurfacing the floor.

"Do I need to leave?" Dan asked.

They assured him he would be fine in his office.

Dan's health problems began shortly afterward. He developed a headache first. Then a toe went mysteriously limp. Within eighteen months, he was confined to a wheelchair with a lifeless right arm and had to rely on his family to feed and bathe him. Hearing this made me wince in sympathy; my own days of confinement in a wheelchair and dependency on others hadn't been that long ago.

Laura, a registered nurse, was trying to find answers for him. They'd been to many medical specialists. She said, "I'm convinced he developed MCS when they resurfaced the floor of the gym, but his doctors won't make the connection to the chemicals. I was hoping you could recommend a doctor who might have some experience with this kind of injury."

"If he has MCS, the best place you can go is to Dallas," I told her.

"What about stem cell treatments in the Bahamas?" she asked desperately.

"No, don't go there. That's quackery."

"Okay. Thanks," she said.

The next time she called, Laura told me they had gone to the Bahamas and spent a hundred grand on stem cell treatments to no avail. I suggested that she take Dan to Dallas to see Dr. Seastrunk because he'd helped me.

"No," she said. "That's too far."

As we continued to talk and I heard more about how the company had resurfaced the gym floor knowing Dan was in his office, I realized Dan had a solid legal case against the company. Despite the fact that Laura had already consulted several lawyers who refused to represent him because they said he had no case, I was convinced otherwise. "Let me send you to a doctor I know," I said. "She can evaluate your husband."

I wanted Dan to visit her primarily to help him medically. If her evaluation also helped his legal claim, that would be a bonus. However, when I said the doctor was at Boston University, near where Dan and Laura were living, Laura balked, saying Dan had already been there.

"You don't understand," I argued. "It's not the university that matters. It's the particular scientist. You need to see Dr. Marcia Ratner at Boston University. She's an internationally recognized neurotoxicologist."

I knew Dr. Ratner from the Scientific Advisory Board of the Environmental Health Foundation; I had brought her on board when we were planning the summit. When she examined Dan, Dr. Ratner came up with a shocking diagnosis: Dan had amyotrophic lateral sclerosis (ALS), also known as Lou Gehrig's disease. We both wondered if the coach's chemical exposure triggered his early onset of ALS. Was that possible?

I called Laura after Dr. Ratner had seen Dan. "Look, this is serious," I said, after saying how sorry I was about her husband's diagnosis. "Holy Cross College isn't paying your husband anything, right?"

"Right," she said. "Nothing."

"Let me talk to your husband."

When she put him on the phone, I said, "Okay, Dan, here's what we're going to do. I'm going to get a lawyer for you, so you can sue Holy Cross College for terminating you without giving you workers' compensation for injury on the job. Is that all right with you?"

"Yes," Dan said.

"Okay, great. Mind if I talk to your wife again?"

When Laura came back on the line, I told her I was going to arrange for a colleague to work up the workers' compensation claim. "Can you find out what exact product was used on that floor?"

"Sure," she said. "I'll talk to the maintenance guy. He has the stuff in the shed."

Once I knew what the resurfacing product was, I obtained its material safety data sheet (MSDS)—an itemized list of chemicals it contains. I was shocked to discover that these chemicals included benzene, toluene, and isocyanates, all of which are classified as ultra-hazardous substances in Massachusetts.

Slowly and meticulously, I proceeded to build two lawsuits on behalf of Dan Allen. The first was against his employer, Holy Cross College, seeking workers' compensation because he had been injured on the job. The second was a lawsuit against the manufacturer of the resurfacing compound.

I arranged for a workers' compensation expert to file a claim. Next, I contacted a dosing expert I knew at Harvard University, who calculated the chemical dose Dan had been exposed to. Based on our data—including the square footage of the area, the cubic feet of air in the space where the compound was applied, the location of Dan's office, the doors and windows, and so on—we calculated the exact chemical dose Dan inhaled as a result of the floor resurfacing.

We now had the right pieces in place to prove that Dan's injury was caused by his exposure to the chemicals used in resurfacing the floor. We knew Dan was in the building when the floor was being refinished with chemicals known to be neurotoxic—in fact, the floor refinishers were required by their employer and Occupational Safety and Health Administration (OSHA) regulations to wear respirators. They had sealed off the area where they were doing the work, but somehow Dan's office, adjacent to the gymnasium, became part of the sealed area instead of being sealed *off*. He was therefore working without a respirator in the same area as the toxic chemicals.

Dr. Ratner told me that Dan's initial symptoms—nausea, headaches, dizziness—made a great deal of sense to her. "We have an area of our brain, called the *area postrema*, that alerts us to something poisonous," she said. When toxic chemicals penetrate the nervous system, this part of the brain signals the body to get rid of it by triggering the vomiting reflex. "That's one of the reasons why people inhaling these chemicals inside buildings report feeling nausea and vomiting as well as dizziness, headaches, and other symptoms."

✦ ✦ ✦

Once Dr. Ratner diagnosed Dan Allen with ALS and the dosing expert from Harvard had calculated the exact dose of the isocyanates Dan was exposed to, I recruited Dr. Mohammed Bahie Abou-Donia of Duke University, a world expert on isocyanates, as a medical expert on Dan's legal case. Dr. Abou-Donia had conducted research studies exposing mice to the same chemicals used in the flooring compound that caused Dan to fall ill. Like humans, some mice are born with a gene that predisposes them to developing ALS after exposure to certain chemicals.

The result? Basically, his studies proved that mice with the gene developed ALS after chemical exposure, while the animals without the gene stayed healthy. Dr. Abou-Donia concluded that it wasn't the coach's fate to develop his fatal disease. Like Dr. Ratner and me, he believed that Dan's exposure to isocyanates triggered his onset of ALS.

Like all diseases, whether you get ALS depends on a combination of your genetic predisposition toward the condition combined with environmental triggers, including chemical exposure. ALS usually affects older people, he explained. "Although you can see it in younger people in their forties and fifties, it's rare." Dan was only in his mid-forties.

"We know chemical exposure can alter the DNA of a human being," Dr. Abou-Donia said, "and make people more susceptible to disease, causing up-regulation and down-regulation of many genes that cause disease."

What does this mean in layman's terms? Each of us begins life with a particular set of genes—about twenty thousand to twenty-five thousand of them. Scientists are gathering evidence proving pollutants and chemicals are altering our genes—not by mutating them but by sending signals that switch them on when they otherwise might remain dormant, or even "silence" the genes altogether. Exposure to gene-altering substances can lead to disease long after the toxic exposure is gone, permanently injuring glands, organs, and cells throughout your body. Animal studies show that some environmental chemicals cause epigenetic changes that trigger breast and prostate cancer, obesity, diabetes, heart disease, asthma, Alzheimer's, Parkinson's disease, learning disabilities—and ALS.

When genes are turned off due to chemical exposure, they can't direct the manufacture of proteins essential for healthy cell function. Chemicals can also cause chromosomes to uncoil and genes to "express" or be "turned on," when they otherwise might have remained dormant. Dan's brain chemistry had been altered on a cellular level by his exposure to the toxins used to resurface the gym floor, causing his onset of ALS at a tragically young age.

Dr. Abou-Donia believes that chemical exposure is one of the primary causes of today's chronic diseases like asthma, autism, birth defects, cancers, developmental disabilities, diabetes, endometriosis, infertility, Parkinson's, Alzheimer's, and others. In his 2015 textbook, *Mammalian Toxicology*, he cites statistics that should terrify us all, like this one: "In 1900, US chemical consumption was less than 100 million metric tons, but by 2000 this had increased to more than 3.3 billion metric tons."

In his estimation, there are over five million man-made chemicals, of which only seventy thousand are in commercial use today, with many more to come. The methyl isocyanate that Dan was exposed to was also linked to thousands of human deaths in 1984 after the explosion of a chemical plant in Bhopal, India, owned by the Union Carbide Company. Yet somehow this chemical is still finding its way into our everyday products.

◆ ◆ ◆

With my experts on board, I had the scientific support necessary to prove this case. Next, I needed legal boots on the ground in Massachusetts to walk the case into the courtroom. I recruited Michael Hugo, a well-known attorney who had been a partner in the law firm of Schlichtmann, Conway, Crowley, and Hugo.

This firm had successfully won compensation for victims of a toxic chemical spill in Woburn, Massachusetts. The case was dramatized in the bestselling book and film *A Civil Action*, with

John Travolta, Robert Duvall, and James Gandolfini starring in the movie. The case eventually bankrupted the lead attorney, Jan Schlichtmann. In the eyes of many, this outcome served as a cautionary tale depicting the risks inherent in pursuing complex environmental injury cases. To some, Schlichtmann was a hero, a noble lawyer willing to risk it all for a worthy cause. To others, Schlichtmann was a crazy man.

I didn't care either way, because Schlichtmann had won, and I would, too.

During the trial, my team presented solid evidence that most human disease and death is the result of the interaction between our genes and environmental exposures. In Dan's case, the disease was a horrific one that vastly reduced his life span.

Dr. Ratner believes Dan had a predisposition to develop ALS, which made him more sensitive to chemicals. She noted, "Genetic predispositions and past insults to the body, including previous chemical exposures, can make a person hypersensitive to future chemical exposures, which in turn can exacerbate or unmask latent liver, kidney, or neurological disorders like ALS."

When filing a toxic tort lawsuit, case law requires that the claim be based on science generally accepted by the scientific community. This is called the "Daubert Standard," the standard used by trial judges to determine whether an expert's testimony is based upon scientifically valid reasoning or methodology. This standard has been the subject of intense criticism over the years. Plaintiffs' attorneys claim this restriction bars many worthy claims by disallowing juries to hear cases and denying victims their day in court.

The legal team representing the chemical manufacturing company tried to get Dan Allen's case thrown out of federal court using the Daubert standard, claiming our case wasn't based on "sound science." Dr. Ratner's testimony was critical to our case because it logically connected the dots.

Up until that point in the legal arena, ALS was thought to be purely genetic. Now, together with my local legal counsel and experts, we were attempting to prove in court for the first time that chemical exposure can trigger the onset of ALS. The Dan Allen case would potentially break new ground.

◆ ◆ ◆

On September 24, 2008, United States District Judge F. Dennis Saylor handed down his decision regarding whether the testimony of Dr. Marcia Ratner and other experts could be heard by a jury. The testimony of Dr. Ratner was allowed, as well as that of Dr. Christine Oliver, an assistant clinical professor of medicine at Harvard Medical School, who concluded that Dan Allen had sporadic ALS.

When the judge ruled in our favor, saying we could proceed to a jury trial based on the science involved, the chemical company panicked. They knew the floodgates were open, not only to our lawsuit, but for many more to follow. We had shown in court that chemicals can trigger the onset of a previously dormant disease.

Sadly, by then, Dan had died of the disease, causing heartbreak for Laura and a deep sorrow among all of those who knew and loved this amazing man. The only thing we could say to comfort his family was that we had won the decision, which meant the defense knew their chances of winning at trial were dismal. Testimony from a sympathetic widow, combined with powerful evidence that the chemicals Dan was exposed to caused him to die long before his time, would smash their case to bits. The defense opted to seek a settlement. The case settled in 2009.

For the Allen family, and for us, too, it was a bittersweet victory. While the case broke new legal ground and exposed the truth behind what had really happened to Dan Allen, it couldn't erase the pain and suffering he and his family had endured.

I was left feeling both triumphant and grief-stricken, but I vowed to keep fighting for those who needed me.

✦ ✦ ✦

After the Dan Allen case concluded, Dr. Ratner asked me to lecture her medical school class in forensic neuropsychology at Boston University. I taught them how scientists can help lawyers bring legal justice to victims of chemical injury.

I had no medical degree. But I was able to act as a conduit of sorts. I explained to these young physicians that I was a bridge between their world and the legal arena, and encouraged them to consider environmental exposures when listening to their patients describe symptoms. I called my lecture "The Anatomy of a Toxic Tort Case," and instructed them that, in toxic tort cases, the two opposing sides are very different.

On one side of a toxic tort case is a defendant, I told them, typically a wealthy individual or corporation interested in the financial bottom line. "These types of defendants can usually afford the best lawyers money can buy," I said, "and their goal is to prevent a flood of similar claims and protect the finances and good name of the company."

On the opposite side is the plaintiff, "usually a single victim, or a cluster of victims, who have experienced chemical injury or illness," I said.

I explained that victims come from a wide variety of racial, economic, political, and cultural backgrounds. "They often know their illness is the result of a chemical exposure, but they usually have little or no proof, because the medical and legal specialists they've consulted offer no guidance. Doctors often can't provide help because they typically have only about six credit hours of training in environmental illnesses throughout their medical education."

Lawyers, I added, are often poorly trained in this area, and are wary of taking risky and expensive cases.

I also told these medical students that if they did encounter such a patient, they should consider a standard series of questions to probe the truth: Did any aspect of the victim's environment change near the time of onset of illness? What are the victim's symptoms? When did they appear? Could any other independent factors have caused the symptoms? Are there any environmental clues? Were any other people in the victim's life—especially in the victim's family—also ill with similar symptoms?

Once I'd finished, Dr. Ratner told me she appreciated me talking to her medical students, because my personal story put a face on this massive silent epidemic that all physicians struggle with.

"As scientists, we can't reject victims of environmentally linked disease," she said. "You can't say it's not happening when we know it is. If we can better appreciate these patients and help them recover, that's huge."

In her view, chemicals are an essential part of our society because many enhance our quality of life. However, we must innovate ways to live with chemicals more safely, she said, harnessing their benefits while minimizing the risks they pose to human health.

It was a surreal experience: in the past, as a patient, I had gone all over the United States, desperately trying to find help from various doctors. Now, I was standing in a classroom and teaching physicians how to help other victims. For me, the opportunity to address medical students provided a new kind of high.

I was an ordinary guy, but I'd been thrown into an extraordinary fight. I relished the challenge.

16 ◆ Black Mold Breaks a Mother's Heart

Ashlee was deeply wounded when her mother abandoned her. As Dan Allen's case wound its way through the legal system, I was doing my best to raise my daughter as a single parent.

After making the permanent move to my home in California, Ashlee started attending a public middle school in our neighborhood. When she had trouble reading, I found her a tutor and her grades soared. When she began eating to comfort herself and told me how unhappy she was about this problem, I found her a therapist and a personal trainer.

Probably the biggest challenge we faced together, though, happened when Ashlee started ninth grade. I sent her to the local high school, and some of the students there were skinheads, the children of soldiers stationed at the nearby military base. When they found out Ashlee was Jewish, some of these kids began threatening to put her in an oven "and burn you like Hitler fried those other Jews."

Ashlee was terrified, understandably—she had never experienced anything like this—and I was furious. I went to the principal, who suggested that I transfer my daughter to a different public high school. "Maybe she'd fit in better there," he suggested.

"Wait a minute," I said. "My daughter's the victim here. You know who the perpetrators are. Yet you're telling me you're not throwing those kids out of school? You want to punish the victim instead?"

I was livid. But with Ashlee begging me every day to send her to a different school, I knew the best thing for my kid was to get her out of there. Ashlee had enough to deal with already. She was very fragile, and I was worried about her.

We began touring all of the private schools in the area. Finally, Ashlee chose a small, private school where she immediately felt comfortable. This was a warm and loving community that felt like a safe nest.

I saw the metamorphosis take place in Ashlee almost immediately. Before, she was unable to excel at her studies in public school because she was being bullied. Now she could relax, focus, and be herself. Her new school highlighted the importance of an independent mind, empathy for others, and thinking "outside the box." By sophomore year, she started to view the world with a much broader, deeper perspective. It was as if I'd put her in a place where her wounds could heal and melt away.

The next legal case I became enmeshed in really hit home because of my devotion to Ashlee's well-being: it involved a parent's broken heart.

♦ ♦ ♦

In 2003, two-year-old Neveah Lair was hospitalized several times near her home in Bakersfield, California, for flu-like symptoms. Before then, Neveah had been a happy, healthy child. Doctors couldn't find any cause for the little girl's recurring illness.

Her mother, Jessica, believed Neveah's problems sprang from the black mold that plagued their apartment complex. Jessica told the complex's property manager about her concerns several times, but the management company refused to address the problem. On the morning of February 29, 2004, Jessica walked into her daughter's room to get her ready for the day. Neveah was dead.

The coroner listed the little girl's cause of death as pneumonia. Jessica, however, didn't believe that was true. She vowed to prove that the mold in the apartment was responsible.

Jessica found me through the Environmental Health Foundation in late 2004. She was devastated by her daughter's death and wanted to know if I would help her and other tenants of the apartment complex prove their management company was negligent by ignoring their complaints about black mold.

"All the doctors I've seen tell me mold is natural, there's nothing wrong with it, and it doesn't hurt anybody," she said. "They're telling me my kid didn't die from mold. But I have another kid who's sick now. Can you help me and the other tenants?"

"I'm not sure," I said. "How many moms and kids are involved?"

"A lot," she said.

"Okay. Why don't you have some of the others give me a call."

Some of the tenants followed through and called me. The more I talked to them, the more convinced I became that Jessica was right: black mold was making these people sick.

By then, if the right case walked in the door, I knew exactly what to do. My own health was still fragile enough that I often didn't position myself as the attorney on the front lines. With the Dan Allen case and others, I learned that I could efficiently participate long distance.

However, Jessica was living in Bakersfield, California, close enough that I decided to meet her in person. I also wanted to talk with the other sick tenants in her apartment complex.

Bakersfield is in California's central valley, just over a hundred miles north of Los Angeles. It's a flat, featureless landscape with a desert climate. The main industries are oil and agriculture. The population of Bakersfield is extremely diverse, with about 375,000 residents.

During that first visit to the apartment complex, I met Jessica and many other tenants in a community room. The whole place was full. It felt like a town hall meeting, with everyone trying to be heard.

Most of the people in attendance were single mothers with young children. They were hardworking and lived on modest means. Many lived in the apartments under Section 8 housing (legislation that allows tenants to pay only 30 percent of their incomes for rent). In short, they lived in those particular apartments not by choice, necessarily, but because they lacked the resources to go anywhere else, despite their worries about adverse health effects.

The residents told me their stories about respiratory problems, strange flu-like symptoms, and skin lesions. Previously, they had contacted a number of doctors and attorneys in their search for answers and relief, but nobody was willing to take on their case or offer advice. There had been a curious lack of interest in their plight by the city's doctors. I suspected this was partly because the victims had lousy health insurance, if any.

After my meeting with the residents, I called a certified industrial hygienist and asked him to check for mold in the apartment buildings. My hygienist worked like a crime-solving detective on a TV show, taking swab samples from surfaces inside the apartments, the ventilation systems, and the air to determine what antigens were floating around. He cultured whatever was on the swabs, examined the cultures under a microscope, and had them genetically analyzed.

It didn't take long for the hygienist to confirm the residents' fears. He identified the culprit responsible for making these people sick as *Stachybotrys chartarum,* more commonly known as "black mold," also called "greenish black mold" by the Centers for Disease Control and Prevention (CDC).

Stachybotrys is a unique kind of mold. There are many kinds of common molds, and they're everywhere we work and live. Most aren't pathogenic; ordinary molds may be allergenic and cause you to sneeze and cough, but they won't cause you to become seriously ill.

Stachybotrys, though, is a different story. It grows only in damp, dark areas where there's no UV light. This mold lives behind walls, under floors, and above ceilings. Drywall is the perfect food for it because it's made from cellulose. That's essentially wood, which serves as food for this kind of pathogenic mold. *Stachybotrys* commonly grows in buildings that have experienced water damage, excessive humidity, water leaks, water infiltration, or flooding.

In 2004, the Institute of Medicine linked black mold exposure to a host of health problems. Otherwise healthy individuals suffered from upper respiratory tract symptoms, coughs, and wheezing when exposed to this kind of mold. In individuals with asthma or compromised immune systems, this mold exposure triggered pneumonia. The CDC labels *Stachybotrys* mold as "toxigenic" because this mold produces trichothecene mycotoxin, a mycotoxin that has been shown to cause neurotoxicity and brain inflammation in laboratory animals.

I now had my smoking gun: proof that toxic black mold existed in the apartment complex where Neveah had died and where many others became sick.

The next thing I needed was a reputable physician who could help me prove to a jury that the residents of the apartment complex sustained injuries *caused* by the bullets fired by that gun.

I contacted one of the leading mold experts in the country, Dr. Eckart Johanning, in Albany, New York. He had trained at Mount Sinai Medical School and was board certified as an environmental and occupational physician, as well as a family practitioner. More importantly, he had already logged twenty years of experience in the field of indoor air pollution and mold.

I told him about the case and asked if he'd be willing to serve as an expert. Dr. Johanning was intrigued enough to fly out to Southern California and examine the residents and the apartment building himself.

The doctor's visit was like something out of a film. By the time I brought him to Bakersfield, we had seventy mothers and children lined up, waiting to be examined, including Jessica and her two surviving children. Dr. Johanning brought his medical bag and various examination equipment. He sat at a desk and, one by one, thoroughly examined all of the residents. He also carefully looked over the mold-laden apartments they had to call "home."

Dr. Johanning's conclusion? The victims' horrifying symptoms were consistent with exposure to the black mold in their apartments. I now had my expert for a toxic tort case.

Later, the doctor told me that the Bakersfield case reminded him of an investigation he'd made of basement offices at a Boston museum that had experienced periodic flooding. "The sheet rock got wet and retained the moisture for a long time, causing mold growth," he said, adding that the museum employees had also developed severe health problems.

Black mold was also implicated in a Cleveland case, where several children developed hemorrhagic lung disease—bleeding of the lungs—causing some of them to die. "*Stachybotrys* was one of the key molds implicated in that outcome," he said. "Mycotoxins produced by toxic mold can adversely affect the blood and immune system, making people much sicker than your typical allergic reaction."

As my investigation proceeded, I developed a road map for the judge to follow that linked the mold to the victims' illnesses. My map began at the point where the deadly mold first developed in the apartment complex and led directly to little Neveah's tragic death.

On the first floor, the outside sprinklers threw water onto the building. The water then seeped into the wall cavities, allowing the walls to remain damp. In addition, broken pipes and roof leaks caused water to drip into the ceilings and walls of the apartments. Drywall, water, and a dark environment with no UV light made this place the perfect breeding ground for pathogenic black mold.

During one of my visits to Bakersfield, I asked Ashlee to accompany me. I wanted her to see how I built a legal case. I also thought it would be good for her to observe firsthand that not everyone is fortunate enough to live as we do. She was extremely quiet as we walked around the apartments, talking to the tenants and inspecting the mold.

As we were leaving, Ashlee finally spoke up. "How can they let people live like that, Dad? Everything in the buildings is broken and leaking."

I wished there were a better reason to give her than pure greed, but I couldn't think of one.

+ + +

As the investigation progressed, I discovered that many of the tenants at this apartment complex had moved from a different apartment complex, The Village at Bakersfield, after complaints of mold infestation. That complex was also the subject of a wrongful death claim brought by the family of Steven Raina, claiming he died as a result of a fungal infection caused by conditions in their building. Both apartment complexes were managed by the same company.

Luckily, a woman who had formerly worked for that company as a property manager, Marlene Medina, had kept a daily journal of tenants' complaints about maintenance problems and her correspondence with the company's top officials. The complaints and concerns she passed along were largely ignored. Marlene became so frustrated by her employer's negligence, she eventually quit her job. She became a whistle-blower and one of our key witnesses.

"Look," she told me. "The management company knew what was going on. I told them all these people were sick, but all they did was tell me to cover it up."

The deeper I dug into my investigation, the more rot I uncovered and the more incensed I became. In my mind, the death of two-year-old Neveah Lair was nothing less than a homicide.

Although Neveah died in 2004, my team found evidence that the management company had known about the mold problem since 1999. We found evidence of toxic mold in sixteen of the eighteen apartments. We also learned that whenever a family requested a move to a safe apartment because one or more family members fell ill, the management company moved them, but then stuck a brand-new family into the same toxic apartment that had just been vacated without telling the unsuspecting incoming family anything.

By February 2005, we filed the lawsuit.

There were a lot of moving parts to this complex case. We had to communicate with all of the doctors who'd examined Neveah and the other tenants, then review the necessary medical records and all hospitalizations. Most importantly, we needed to prove the presence of mold in Neveah's lung tissue in order to positively link the cause of her illness with its effect—her tragic death.

The tissues were being held by the coroner who had performed the autopsy on Neveah. He refused to willingly turn over the samples for testing, so we had to subpoena him. When Dr. Johanning finally was able to test the lung samples, he confirmed that they matched positive to the same black mold found inside Neveah's apartment.

Meanwhile, the defense—composed of the management company and the owners of the apartment complex—pushed back. The attorneys for their insurance companies were determined to bury us in paperwork. They get paid by the hour, so for them cases like this can be a legal bonanza.

The defendants deposed every single one of our victims and doctors—a process that took months. They put up roadblocks at every turn. One common tactic was to make their witnesses unavailable for deposition, which delayed the entire process. They also asked for extensions of time to turn over documents we requested and resisted showing them to us. They sought continuances of hearings on motions, and asked for postponements of the trial date. The longer it took to go to court, the longer the management company kept its money. That was their game.

In response, we launched a media campaign. I was ready to play hardball. On the courthouse steps at a press conference, we spoke about our lawsuit and answered media questions. We attracted coverage not only by local newspapers but also by CBS's *Early Show*, a national weekly television program. The program highlighted Neveah Lair's death as a clear demonstration of black mold's global danger. The piece aired on the *CBS Evening News* as well.

Jennifer Lair made a powerful TV presence, weeping and wiping her eyes as she told her story on camera. Then I took my turn, calling black mold "an insidious cancer that grew from within this complex."

The end of the broadcast must have made it difficult for anyone with a heart to ignore what had happened. The reporter mentioned that the Lair family had to live in a hotel because they'd moved to a different apartment in the same complex only to have the mold reappear. Now, Jessica's youngest child was seriously ill. He also suffered from severe respiratory problems; he was on albuterol sulfate, an inhaled drug that treats and prevents the bronchial spasms experienced by asthma sufferers, and prednisone, a powerful anti-inflammatory drug prescribed to treat inflamed lungs, sinuses, and systemic inflammation. Respiratory inflammation is often caused by exposure to environmental toxins and allergies.

"A week and a half ago, my son turned completely blue—stopped breathing," Lair said into the television camera. The reporter then talked about how Lair's family's contaminated possessions remained inside the mold-infested apartment; they included the urn with Neveah's ashes.

♦ ♦ ♦

The media coverage was successful in pressuring the defendants to settle. They wanted the case to go away without facing a jury. Now it was a question of how much money the "bad guys" were going to pay.

With multiple defendants, they're all responsible for kicking in a piece of the pie. The costs were massive in this case. Both sides had hired many experts and doctors disputing the amount of damages sustained by the plaintiffs.

Our legal team representing the fifteen families argued against counsel for the apartment complex and the management company. Finally, on May 26, 2006, the case was settled.

At that time, it was the largest settlement in the county for the wrongful death of a child. But had justice been done? Jessica Lair had walked into Neveah's room and found the child dead. This case didn't bring her little girl back.

Yes, I had shown these tenants that somebody would stand up and fight for them, and yes, they had been financially compensated. But the question of justice is deeper than simply getting insurance companies to write checks to injured people.

This case touched me deeply, not only because a parent had lost her little girl and I was the father of a daughter, but because it brought me face-to-face with evil. The real estate management company knew about the mold. They knew it had possibly caused the death of Steven Reina in 2002, *two whole years* before Neveah died. They also knew a number of tenants were getting ill. Yet they did nothing.

Back when I was hunting down criminals in Florida, I prosecuted some horrific crimes, including murders among family members. But somehow this case seems even worse, because it illustrates how corporations can poison unsuspecting victims with invisible toxins for financial gain. And, if they are caught, the wrongdoers simply move on with a different name and commit similar crimes again and again.

I had to wonder if our willful blindness to the deadly consequences of these poisons would eventually spell the end of humanity. Or would science and humanity right itself by acknowledging our mistakes and choosing a better path?

I still have no idea. The jury's still out on that one.

17 ✦ Pesticides Poison a Postal Worker

During my visualization sessions with Dan Baker in Arizona, one of my fantasies had been to attend a national championship football game if the University of Miami ever played the University of Nebraska. On January 3, 2002, my wish came true when the Cornhuskers faced off against the Hurricanes in the 88th Rose Bowl Game in Pasadena, California.

I rented a limo and, accompanied by Dan; Ashlee; my brother, Bobby; and my high school friend Tiny, I fulfilled that long-ago, impossible-seeming fantasy: I sat in a stadium with about ninety-three thousand other fans and watched the University of Miami pummel the University of Nebraska, winning the national championship.

If this were a Hollywood movie, that might make a great end to my story. It was a day I will truly never forget. In truth, though, my real healing was only beginning.

✦ ✦ ✦

The next case that touched my heart involved Judilyn Knight, a woman who loved her job for the postal service. She delivered mail to the rural parts of Cumberland County, North Carolina, an area of about 660 square miles that is home to Fort Bragg and the Pope Army Air Field.

Originally settled between 1729 and 1736 by Highland Scots, much of this fertile green land is devoted to agriculture, with farms devoted to corn, cotton, tobacco, and soybean crops. There are a number of large lakes, rivers, and creeks in this area, making boating a popular recreational pastime.

Judilyn delivered mail using her own car. She loved driving along the rural roads, often stopping to say hello and chat with people she knew along her route. She had a solid work record and was innovative, too, often coming up with routes that made more sense than those assigned by some distant bureaucrat. She was married, with a young daughter in elementary school, and often worked as a parent volunteer in her class.

On the morning of October 18, 2002, Judilyn was delivering mail along Bethel Road, one of her regular routes. She wasn't surprised to hear the sound of a crop duster buzzing over the fields. It was humid that morning, and Judilyn had her windows rolled down to enjoy the breeze as she drove. There were no other vehicles on this quiet road at the time, just Judilyn in her car and, above her, the plane flown by Edward L. Owens Jr.

Judilyn spotted the plane flying toward her and saw immediately that Owens was still releasing chemicals, even though he wasn't over any crop fields. Surely he knew that, she thought, as he flew over her. The pesticide hit the windshield and front of her car.

She tried to roll up her windows in time, but failed. Judilyn instantly smelled the chemical fumes and felt the spray settle on her arm and on the lower parts of her legs, which were exposed in shorts. She also drew the fumes in through her nostrils and tasted the spray in her mouth. She didn't know it at the time, of course, but the crop duster's spray contained three chemicals that day: tribufos, a cotton defoliant; ethephon, an organophosphate; and carentrazone, an herbicide.

Within thirty minutes, Judilyn's skin on her arms and legs began itching and burning. She immediately drove to the farm where the crop duster had just sprayed and told the farmers about the incident. They assured her that the pesticides wouldn't hurt her.

As Judilyn continued working that day, however, she developed a cough. Her throat swelled and she began producing mucus and running a fever. Over the next few days, she experienced additional health problems. She often felt nauseous and suffered from diarrhea and piercing headaches. Acute pain in her neck and abdomen sometimes made her double over in agony.

Judilyn filed a complaint with the North Carolina Department of Agriculture. The claim was investigated five days after the incident by a State pesticide investigator who took six swabs from Judilyn's car and from the road where the spray hit. Based on these swabs, the State concluded that Owens, the pilot, had unlawfully sprayed the area and charged him with a violation. This claim was settled on April 10, 2003, and Owens agreed to pay a $1,500 fine.

During the next few months, Judilyn continued to suffer flu-like symptoms. She was also having increasing difficulties with her concentration. Then, on August 16, 2003, less than ten months after her first exposure, Judilyn was delivering mail on Highway 401 when once again she spotted a crop duster flying overhead.

It was Owens again, and this time he was spraying a mixture of the insecticide Mustang Max (zeta-cypermethrin) and Mepex (mepiquat chloride), a plant growth regulator. The moment Judilyn saw the crop duster approaching, she tried to quickly roll up her windows and close the car's vents.

Again, she ran out of time. The plane zoomed over her, dousing her car with chemicals in a direct hit. As the chemicals poured through the windows and vents, Judilyn felt that same painful burning sensation on her bare skin and in her nostrils, as well as a chemical taste in her mouth. Her eyes grew teary and her vision blurred.

Panicked, Judilyn immediately drove to a nearby house, explained the situation to the owners, and asked to use a bathroom to wash herself off and rinse out her mouth. Despite these measures, she experienced greater memory loss and more trouble concentrating. She also suffered from numbness in her limbs and dryness in her mouth and throat. Her ongoing health problems caused her to become too incapacitated to continue working at the job she loved.

To Judilyn, it was clear that the pesticides caused her symptoms. She saw several doctors, but none of them would definitively link her chemical exposures to her health problems. The same thing happened when she contacted various lawyers: not one was willing to take her case, even though she had abundant documentation.

Then Judilyn remembered seeing the movie *Erin Brockovich* and how the character played by Julia Roberts was, in fact, a real woman who worked in Ed Masry's law firm, helping victims of environmental injury. She decided to call the firm for help.

Masry and Vititoe continued to be swamped with more requests for representation than they could handle and were regularly faxing cases over to me for review and analysis. They faxed Judilyn's case notes over to me. "We don't know what to do with this one," Jim admitted when I called to talk to him about it. "What do you think? Is it worth pursuing?"

"It's very interesting," I said. "I've never seen anything like this before." I told him I'd give Judilyn a call and do some digging.

Judilyn was thrilled when she got my call. "Oh my God!" she cried. "I can't believe it. You mean Erin Brockovich really wants to take my case?" She sounded like she'd just won the lottery.

"Well, I'm helping Erin Brockovich," I explained, attempting to calm her down. I didn't want to get her hopes up until I knew more facts. "My name is Alan Bell. I'm an attorney, and I'm just calling as part of a preliminary interview to see if we can help you. Why don't you start by telling me exactly what happened."

Judilyn proceeded to tell me her story, starting with the first time she was sprayed, and detailing her various medical symptoms.

Next, I spoke with her husband and daughter. "She can't think anymore," her husband said. "She's walking into walls and having seizures. It's almost like she's got Parkinson's. She used to be fun-loving, perky, and lively, but now she can hardly function. She slurs her speech and all that stuff."

My heart ached for this woman and her family. I could relate, especially as I listened to them describe their frustration with the doctors and lawyers they'd seen. Not one of them was willing to confirm that Judilyn was suffering from pesticide exposure. Taking her history was horrible for me because I was filled with dread about her dismal future.

The first thing I did after talking to the family was contact two specialists by phone. One of them, Dr. Mohamed Abou-Donia from Duke University, had helped me on the Dan Allen case. He had worked extensively with organophosphates, particularly with sarin, the nerve gas many soldiers were exposed to during the First Gulf War (Operation Desert Shield). Like many pesticides, sarin kills at higher doses. At lower doses, it causes nervous system damage, leading to symptoms such as memory difficulties, fatigue, weakness, pain, and gastrointestinal problems.

Dr. Abou-Donia's research had shown that organophosphates cause nervous system damage by inhibiting acetylcholinesterase, an important enzyme that protects the nervous system. Without that protection, neurotoxicity and nerve cell degeneration occur. He had already testified about these findings in a congressional subcommittee and before the British House of Commons.

I explained the case to him and got the answer I was hoping to hear. Because Judilyn sustained two direct hits from aerial pesticide spraying and her symptoms began immediately afterward, Dr. Abou-Donia concluded that her symptoms were caused by the pesticide exposure.

Money wasn't my primary focus in this case. Before we sued the pesticide sprayer, I needed to help Judilyn find the right medical help. I called her and said, "Look, you need to get healthy before we tackle the legal stuff. Are you willing to let me help you do that?"

"I'll go anywhere and do anything," she said.

"Great," I said.

I called Dr. William Meggs, an emergency room doctor and a professor at the University of East Carolina with expertise in chemical exposures. Dr. Meggs had also served on the advisory board of my Environmental Health Foundation. More importantly, he was close enough to Judilyn for her to drive over and see him.

Following an extensive examination, Dr. Meggs called me to say that Judilyn's symptoms were consistent with organophosphate exposure. As he began treating her symptoms, I could see that the legal evidence against the crop duster was piling up. But we needed at least one more expert opinion before I would be willing to put Judilyn through a lengthy courtroom battle.

I called Judilyn again. "Okay, now I want you to see Dr. Kaye Kilburn at the University of Southern California in Los Angeles," I said. "He'll do more tests and evaluate you. I'd like to meet you, too, if you're interested."

She agreed. Judilyn flew to Los Angeles and I met her at the airport. I was immediately impressed with her. She stood about five foot nine and had long auburn hair, milky white skin, big blue eyes, and a wonderful smile. She had a nice, fun-loving personality despite her health problems, and chatted easily as we drove to Dr. Kilburn's office, telling me how much she loved camping, hiking, canoeing, and gardening in her backyard. It was important for her to be a good wife to her husband, Thomas, and a good mother to their daughter. My heart went out to her.

Dr. Kilburn was also on the advisory board for my Environmental Health Foundation; in 1998, he published *Chemical Brain Injury*, a book based on his research explaining how certain chemicals abundant in our environment adversely affect human brain activity. I knew he would run the necessary tests to determine whether Judilyn's cognitive difficulties were due to her chemical exposure; he would also serve as a convincing expert witness in the courtroom if the case got that far.

After spending the day with Judilyn, reviewing records and performing various tests, Dr. Kilburn agreed that she was suffering from the effects of pesticide exposure. Like Dr. Meggs, he diagnosed Judilyn with a chemical brain injury. That clinched it for me: we had a solid case, and I intended to pull out all the stops to win it for Judilyn.

I still wasn't well enough to travel much. I remained vigilant about my health, eating only organic foods, taking vitamins, exercising, and sitting in the sauna every day to excrete toxins. These careful routines helped stabilize my health, but I still had to be extremely careful to limit the places I went, restricting my exposure to chemicals that had the potential to set off a domino effect of symptoms.

Logistically, that posed a problem—I couldn't travel to North Carolina to represent Judilyn. Although I could develop the case from my home, ultimately I'd need a local attorney to represent the case in court.

I contacted several lawyers who specialized in toxic tort litigation and eventually settled on Bryan Brice. He was a young, enthusiastic lawyer who had clerked for a justice of the North Carolina Supreme Court before becoming a staff attorney for the Environmental Protection Agency in Washington, DC. He now had his own environmental law practice.

When I spoke with Bryan about joining me on the Judilyn Knight case, he was immediately intrigued both by Judilyn's story and by my personal experiences. He said he'd be honored to jump on board. We had a team.

Bryan and his new associate, Cathy Crawley-Jones, drove to Judilyn's home to meet with her and her husband. Bryan confirmed my view of Judilyn as an energetic, hardworking woman whose life had been irrevocably changed. "She has trouble walking and remembering things," he reported, "and it's hard for her to get out her thoughts in a cogent manner, which is frustrating for her. She's sad about being disabled."

I led Brian through the steps of putting together a chemical exposure case. He was a fast learner and didn't seem to mind as I kept pushing him with questions: "How are we going to present this to a jury? What are the things we want to show about Judilyn's work history? What's important about her family history? What are the key facts about this crop duster, his violations, and his attitude?" I also brainstormed with Bryan about courtroom strategies, like how to pick jury members who would be most sympathetic to this woman's plight.

There was a large community of retired military personnel in the area, I pointed out. Although Judilyn didn't have a military background, I thought her service to the US government would appeal to jurors with military connections. She was the type of person who was dedicated to her government job and was passionate about completing her daily responsibilities no matter what the circumstances.

◆ ◆ ◆

While working on Judilyn's case, I came face-to-face with a new sorrow of my own: Dr. Jay Seastrunk, the man who had essentially rescued me from life in a bubble, was dying from cancer. I had no idea he was ill until a fellow patient of his called to say, "He's about ready to go, Alan. You need to see him."

I discussed the situation with Ashlee. She was the one who had found Dr. Seastrunk, and she and I often talked openly about death and the afterlife. Ashlee was in high school now, old enough to understand my conflicted feelings.

"It's going to be difficult for me to see my doctor in such a precarious physical state," I said, "but I feel a strong sense of loyalty. I want Dr. Seastrunk to understand that I accept my improved health as a gift, and that I'm using this second chance at life as a call to help others. He made that possible."

"Can I come with you, Daddy?" Ashlee asked.

I shook my head. I knew what terminal cancer looked like, having been through it with my own sister, and I didn't want to expose Ashlee to that. "It's probably better if I go alone," I said, "but I'll tell you about it when I get back."

I drove from our home in Capistrano Beach to Seastrunk's ranch in the hills above San Luis Obispo. As I wound my way up through the golden California hills filled with brush and oak trees, I thought about how much the landscape reminded me of certain parts of Texas, where Dr. Seastrunk had lived most of his life.

When I arrived, I was met by Dr. Seastrunk's wife, who led me into the room where the doctor was lying in a hospital bed tethered to an oxygen tank. His face was gaunt. The cheerful Pillsbury Doughboy look was gone. But he managed to crack a smile when I walked in, as he gently perched on the edge of his bed.

"Dr. Seastrunk, I wanted to come and thank you for everything you did for me," I managed to say, my throat tight with emotion. "Because of you, I've been able to make a difference in the lives of other people. Here. Let me show you."

I had brought newspaper clippings of my various cases. As I handed the articles to Dr. Seastrunk one by one, he took them between his shaking hands and began reading, peering down at the newsprint through his glasses. Within minutes, his chest began heaving up and down as he started to weep. Dr. Seastrunk handed the articles back to me and lowered himself back onto the pillows.

Alarmed, I said, "Is there anything I can do for you? Anything at all? Just name it!"

To my surprise, a visible wave of energy swept through the bed-ridden man as he looked up at me with a gaze that pierced my very soul. "Go get 'em!" he said. "Go get 'em!" His voice was hardly above a whisper, but it was defiant and strong just the same.

I started crying and reached across the hospital bed to hug the man who had brought me back from a hellish existence. "I will," I promised.

The next day, I got the call that Dr. Seastrunk had died.

◆ ◆ ◆

My own health wasn't stable enough for me to travel to North Carolina to be present in person for Judilyn's case. Instead, I attended the depositions via Skype and stayed in contact with Bryan.

As the first deposition was taken of Judilyn Knight, the case nearly erupted in violence. Judilyn's husband, Thomas, was extremely protective and wanted to sit in on the proceedings with her. But the defense attorney, a man as large as Thomas, refused to let him be present during the deposition.

The two men began arguing. As their voices escalated, they pushed their faces close together and the threat of violence permeated the air. Bryan had to physically place himself between the two men for fear that one would throw a punch at the other.

Other depositions for that case also turned surreal. The crop duster, Edward Owens Jr., had been cited eighteen times for violations by the North Carolina Department of Agriculture, more than any other crop duster in the state. Observing that the man was mentally slow, Bryan wondered whether Owens himself had been adversely affected by the pesticides he had used through the years. Owens admitted outright that he oversprayed occasionally, which resulted in chemical drippings, but insisted that he'd never done anything intentionally wrong despite his many citations.

"If Owens has been cited eighteen times by the State Department of Agriculture, how many times do you suppose he's done it without getting caught?" Bryan asked me.

"I had the same thought," I told him, "and it's a scary one."

One of the farmers, an older Southern gentleman wearing overalls, stated during his deposition that he often stood in the middle of his fields while they were being sprayed. "They fly right over me and drop them chemicals!" he said. "I breathe them in with no problem. It's like rain, it's so refreshing!"

"You mean you stand out there in the middle of your field and just breathe it in?" Bryan asked in astonishment.

The farmer continued to assert this was true.

After several depositions and significant discovery had occurred, we scheduled mediation, hoping to avoid a trial. Both sides present evidence during mediation, with the idea of giving a sneak peek at what would likely be revealed during a trial. This open exchange of evidence is meant to encourage both sides to settle the case.

At the mediation, the crop duster's lawyer initially lowballed his settlement offer to Judilyn. Bryan thought there was space to start negotiating. However, Thomas was concerned about the additional stress being put on his wife by the lawsuit, since Judilyn's health was already fragile.

"I just want the case to be over," Judilyn said.

"I know," I told her, "but if you fast-forward yourself years from now, you may not be happy if you agree to what they're offering at this moment."

"What would you do?" Judilyn asked.

"I wouldn't settle this case," I replied. "Not for the amount they're offering. Let's try the case."

Judilyn's husband, Thomas, spoke with me privately. "Alan, I don't think you understand," he said urgently. "She's going backwards. She's a mess. I don't know if she can survive this. The stress is killing her."

I urged him to look at the situation long term. "I realize she's fragile," I said, and meant it: I comprehended Judilyn's weakened physical state better than anyone else involved in the case, since I had gone through the same rapid health decline.

When Judilyn first contacted me and flew to California, she was strong and sturdy despite her cognitive issues. Back then, she had expressed a willingness to do whatever it took to get justice for what happened to her, saying she wanted to "bring those people down."

I was ready to do just that. But the Judilyn at mediation was not the same woman I'd met in California. Her physical condition had deteriorated drastically after she was belittled and beaten down by the crop duster's legal team. She was physically and mentally exhausted and just wanted the pain to end.

Even so, I continued to urge Thomas to look at what might take place in the future and push for more compensation. "If something happened to you, and you were unable to support your family, how would your wife and daughter survive financially?" I asked.

The mediation broke up that day without coming to an agreement, though the defense did agree that Edward Owens Jr. would surrender his crop-dusting license. The defense also tried to sweeten the pot with the offer of a bigger cash settlement.

I continued to recommend to both Judilyn and Thomas that a trial was worth the effort, since it would net them more money. But to avoid the stress of the trial, the couple opted to settle.

Despite the fact that Judilyn and her husband were the ones who ultimately made the decision to settle the case, I couldn't help feeling yet again that justice had not been adequately served. What happened to this woman was a tragedy, and it was only a microcosm of the tragedies taking place worldwide. Big companies throw pennies to the people they're hurting—people who are too badly injured to fight, even when their lawyers are ready to do battle.

Bryan shared my frustration. "No amount of money would compensate them fully for this level of injury," he fumed later. "Even a billion dollars wouldn't be enough to compensate this woman for having her life taken away."

He was right. It was an unfair outcome. It's a travesty of justice that insurance companies have almost unlimited legal budgets to spend on wearing victims down, hiring numerous experts who will say and do whatever it takes to screw the little guy. I sighed as I reflected on my own career prosecuting guilty people who were found innocent or innocent people who had been found guilty, and representing a top insurance company with deep pockets crammed with cash they doled out on lawsuits to defend their interests.

Judilyn, however, was mostly satisfied with the outcome. She said she hadn't had much hope at all until getting in touch with me. On the larger question of pesticides and environmental poisoning, she said, "It's really bad that people don't know about chemical exposures and how sick they can make you. I'd like to see them be a lot more careful when they're spraying pesticides. It really did ruin my life."

I could only hope she'd find peace somehow. For my part, at least, the case provided me with the opportunity to educate a few more people about the harmful chemicals in our everyday environment. As I was working on Judilyn's case, for instance, I was also researching a case involving bisphenol A (BPA). BPA is an industrial chemical that has been used in plastics since the 1960s. I told Bryan that research studies showed BPA had damaging effects on the human brain, behavior, and prostate glands of fetuses, infants, and children.

Based on my information, Bryan and his wife stopped boiling their baby's milk in plastic bottles—a year before the results of these studies made major news headlines. "Man has reached the point where we're destroying ourselves and our environment," Bryan said during one of our last conversations. "If we don't take care of our planet, our environment, and each other, what are we going to leave for the next generation?"

What, indeed? This is the question that plagues me.

18 · A Toxic Waste Dump Destroys a Neighborhood

IN 2005, A CASE LANDED on my desk that again demonstrated the kind of hell environmental chemicals can create for people—especially those without resources. This case hit me especially hard because it took place near my office in Fort Lauderdale, Florida, where I first became ill.

Even decades ago, when little was understood about the toxic effects of chemicals from burned waste, the wealthy and powerful didn't want an incinerator burning city trash and polluting the air around their homes. From the late 1920s through the mid-1950s, the City of Fort Lauderdale incinerated the area's household and industrial waste in a municipal facility they built inland, in an area called Lincoln Park.

In 1938, Florida officially designated this same area as a "Negro" district; it would eventually include the communities of Lincoln Park and Wingate Road. Though never stated outright, the plan was designed to allow white people to live by the ocean, where sea breezes break the sweltering humidity, while relegating blacks to living inland. If you were black, you had no choice but to live close to the incinerator; blacks couldn't even visit the white areas of town past curfew without obtaining a permit based on a specific purpose for being there, such as a landscaping job or maid service.

This was true even during natural disasters. For instance, when the powerful 1926 Miami hurricane struck, white members of the community were advised to go to public shelters set up by the government. The blacks were forbidden to use these shelters and were instead advised to seek refuge at the incinerator site.

In 1954, the United States Supreme Court's decision of *Brown v. Board of Education* banned segregated schools. Around the same time, the Lincoln Park incinerator was deemed no longer efficient in accommodating the city's waste. It was shut down and razed. A brand-new elementary school and community park were built on land that was originally part of this incinerator site.

The school and park were literally sitting on top of piles of ash. Children often played on the ash piles, sliding down on them and building forts from the debris they found. It was the only place to play in the neighborhood. Later, it was discovered that the layer of ash beneath the community park was ten feet deep. The ash was often placed into large dugout pits and covered up. After the school was built, students were often instructed to pick up trash and debris in the playground.

A new city dump and incinerator were built a mile away, still in the City of Fort Lauderdale's designated "Negro" district. This time the trash was burning in the community of Wingate Road. From 1954 until its closure in 1978, this incinerator burned about 480 tons of household and industrial waste every single day.

The Wingate Road incinerator's closure was the result of its violation of the Clean Air Act regulations. Hot ash was being dumped into a cooling pond at the site until the bottom of the pond eventually became impermeable. During heavy rains, the polluted pond overflowed into the backyards of the homes surrounding the site. The locals nicknamed the pond "Lake Stupid."

As a solution, city leaders decided to build a trench that drained the water into Rock Pit Lake. This was an especially unfortunate decision, given that many of the area's most impoverished families caught fish in that lake to supplement the food they could afford on their meager incomes.

Leola McCoy, a community leader, uncovered alarming documents proving chemical contamination at the Wingate Road site in 1984. The incinerator ash and the ground around it—where children had been playing for decades—was toxic. She pestered government officials until Wingate Road and Lincoln Park were both designated US government "Superfund" sites in 1989. This designation amounted to an acknowledgment by the government that the site was tainted with harmful chemicals and a promise to clean it up.

That never happened. In 1996, the US Department of Health and Human Services reviewed census data from 1981 to 1990 and found that Wingate area residents suffered from a higher incidence of pancreatic, prostate, kidney, breast, and eye cancers than other Florida residents statewide.

"Environmental remediation" is a governmental phrase used to describe the process of cleaning up waste and pollution from toxic areas and making those areas safe for human habitation. The community park at Lincoln Park had supposedly been environmentally "remediated" by placing a plastic cap over the Wingate Road incinerator site. However, many residents, as well as lawyers and scientists who later examined the area, were convinced that the area was unsafe for human health because the ground was still poisoned.

◆ ◆ ◆

In 2005, I received a call from a real estate lawyer in my old stomping grounds, Broward County, about the situation in Lincoln Park and Wingate Road. This attorney didn't do toxic tort litigation, and when a group of area residents contacted him about it, he thought of me. He knew I'd been working with Masry and Vititoe.

"I don't know what to do with this case, Alan," he said. "Can you help out with it?"

I listened to his account of events and, after I hung up, began doing a little investigating of my own. I was infuriated that, once again, the people most at risk were those who had so few resources. People were getting sick and dying in that neighborhood, and nobody was doing a thing about it.

One of the most damning pieces of evidence I uncovered was a report issued in October 2005 by the US Department of Health and Human Services. Their Agency for Toxic Substances and Disease Registry disclosed that, around Lincoln Park's incinerator site, "both non-yard and yard soils (0 to 3 inches deep) contained arsenic and carcinogenic congeners of polynuclear aromatic hydrocarbons (PAHs) and dioxins above the residential Soil Cleanup Target Levels." What's more, ash from the incinerator contained metals and by-products of burning.

"On-site soil samples from 6-24 inches and below 24 inches showed higher chemical levels," the report went on. "Therefore, past exposure to the ash itself or the ash layers before they were covered (especially if exposures occurred daily, over long periods) caused adverse non-cancer health effects from ingestion of arsenic, copper, and lead."

Despite this evidence, the government concluded that "the health hazards are indeterminate because we do not know if, or for how long, people were exposed to this ash, or at what levels the exposures could have occurred."

Translation: the government claimed not to know how dangerous the Lincoln Park incinerator site was to the families who lived around it, despite the poisons that were visibly spewing out of those smokestacks for years.

"Hey, Ashlee," I said after digesting the report. "How would you like to take a trip to Florida with me?"

"Sure, Dad," she said.

Ashlee was seventeen by then and a high school junior. She was beautiful inside and out, with an exceptional social conscience and a genuine concern for other people. As she began thinking about college applications, I discussed the possibility of law school with her. I thought she'd make an excellent lawyer.

"I don't want to be a lawyer, Dad," Ashlee said. "I don't like fighting."

"Lawyers don't just fight," I said, though naturally I understood how she might have that impression after living with me. "We write contracts, do appeals, and even put together deals for movie stars. Most of us never even set foot in a courtroom."

She wouldn't budge on the subject. I hoped that bringing Ashlee with me to Florida and involving her in this case might help her reconsider a career in law.

♦ ♦ ♦

Community resident Leola McCoy had been fighting to clean up the areas around Lincoln Park and Wingate Road for twenty years by the time I met her. Meanwhile, a new generation of community activists had risen to join her. One couple I worked with, Mickey Hinton and his wife, Joan, attended Lincoln Park Elementary School and grew up playing on those toxic ash piles. Their personal backgrounds, combined with their leadership skills, made them committed and trusted community advocates.

As Mickey toured us around the Lincoln Park and Wingate Road neighborhood, I watched Ashlee closely. These struggling neighborhoods were a far cry from my parents' Miami Beach condo and our own home in upscale Capistrano Beach, California. She seemed deeply affected by the evident poverty.

At one point, Ashlee turned to me and whispered, "In school, we read about the Civil Rights era in the 1960s. They say segregation doesn't happen anymore, but that's not true, is it, Dad?"

"Yeah, it's still going on, honey," I said.

I'd been thinking the same thing. Growing up in South Florida in the 1960s, I had seen the sunny side of the American dream. Yet, I couldn't forget how my own mother had driven my brother, sister, and me around at Christmas to look at the decorations, always making a point of driving past the country clubs with signs reading "No Jews or Negroes Allowed." Now that I was older and had been through so much, I understood the injustices experienced by people in impoverished neighborhoods not only intellectually but also viscerally: I *felt* them.

As Ashlee said, you might be told such places and prejudices no longer exist, but once you see this stuff with your own eyes, you cannot unsee it. Environmental health is the new civil rights issue because it so often violates the rights of low-income people—often people of color—more than the rights of any other population.

After our tour, Mickey led us to the local Baptist church to meet with other community leaders and residents. They talked with us about the diseases they suffered from, including rare types of cancer and numerous reproductive issues. They also told us about the illnesses and injuries afflicting their aunts, uncles, mothers, fathers, sons, and daughters. Many family members had fallen ill and died tragically young. There was an epidemic in this neighborhood, all right, and its source was that incinerator. These people were getting screwed because they had no voice.

Mickey also led us around the neighborhood to knock on doors. We asked the residents to speak with us about their family's health for a few minutes. They trusted Mickey, so they invited us inside their simple, rundown homes while they bared their souls.

♦ ♦ ♦

It turned out I wasn't the only environmental attorney interested in the case at this time: Jan Schlichtman was also trying to move it forward. I met Schlictmann in Florida in 2005 for the first time, but I had heard about him years earlier.

While I was in Florida investigating how to file suit against the City of Fort Lauderdale, Jan was also there, giving a speech. The director of the neighborhood health services shared the story of Lincoln Park and Wingate Road with him afterward.

Jan and I began collaborating on the case. Unfortunately, neither he nor I had the deep pockets to fund a lawsuit against the government, but we were both eager to do the heavy lifting necessary to build the case legally. Once that was done, we hoped to package the case in a way that would tempt a wealthy law firm to take it on, even though Florida law limited the amount of recovery to peanuts when suing the government.

"It was a known contaminated site, a known neighboring community, and clearly a very high water table and flooding," Jan said. "A whole different mixture of contaminants, a lot of metals, and other unknown materials were present in the ground." We had lots of questions and very few answers. How could we find those answers? It takes time, money, and resources used in a certain way to do that.

We did our best to help the community approach the problem. We counseled them on how to gather information, especially neighborhood demographics, health statistics, and a history of site violations. Much of this information was in the public domain; it was just a matter of digging for it.

♦ ♦ ♦

There was trouble here of all kinds. However, as much as I wanted to help these people, I was stymied by the Florida laws governing their legal remedies. Florida's sovereign immunity statutes made it difficult for these people to bring a legal case.

Subsection 5 of Florida sovereign immunity statute 768.28 stated, "neither the State nor the agencies or subdivisions shall be liable to pay a claim or judgment by any one person which exceeds the sum of $200,000, or any claim or portion thereof, which when totaled with all other claims or judgments, arising out of the same incident, exceeding the sum of $300,000." In other words, no matter how egregious the City's actions had been, the limit of its liability was $300,000 *in total* for all victims combined. The amount of expenses involved to sue the city would far exceed that amount, leaving the victims with less money than before. To make matters worse, attorney fees were capped at 25 percent of any damages recovered. This meant no law firm would earn over $75,000 for bringing the case to court.

We went to work anyway, trying hard to convince various local law firms to take the case for this amount, or even pro bono. No one was willing to do it. I understood why: these local lawyers were hitting the same brick wall. It was one thing for them not to be paid enough to cover the cost of the case, but when you factor in the injured residents not getting any compensation, there was no way to justify pursuing the claim.

By 2006, we had exhausted every avenue. I had to inform Mickey and the community that we couldn't see any way to help them.

In the end, it wasn't Schlichtmann or me who got the City to take notice of this community's problems. It was Louise Caro, a young law student, who began working on this case before she even took the bar exam.

◆ ◆ ◆

Louise Caro never meant to become a lawyer. She was drawn to study science by a strong desire to make a difference in the quality of people's lives. She earned a bachelor's degree in environmental studies and went to work for a medical device company.

Her tasks involved working on endocrinology and thyroid assays used in hospitals, typically after patients suffered heart attacks.

Before long, however, it seemed to Louise that her scientific work was leading nowhere. Her work seemed to vanish into the ether. That's when it hit her that maybe she should become a lawyer; she could use her scientific background in combination with the law to help people.

During law school, Louise took a job at the local Legal Aid office—a group of attorneys representing indigent clients who can't afford to pay their own legal fees. As she worked with the residents of Lincoln Park and Wingate Road, it quickly became clear to her that they desperately needed help.

"There were a lot of multigenerational families in that neighborhood," she observed. "A lot of people in that community stayed because this was their home."

The residents wanted to "deal with their health problems, clean up their neighborhood, and make it a better place to live," she added. "That was the right thing to do."

Louise's work with the Lincoln Park and Wingate Road communities overlapped with my own involvement. Her resolve to help the residents never wavered. She also had advantages I lacked, because she lived in the neighborhood. She wasn't going anywhere. This was her home. People trusted her.

Eventually, Louise graduated from law school, earning the Outstanding Local Government Law School Student award from the Florida Bar. She continued working with the Legal Aid office and, as she helped various residents untangle their legal problems, she kept an eye on the neighborhood health issues.

Legal Aid functions as a private attorney general for low-income individuals, protecting the community with the full force of law. In her capacity as a representative for various residents, Louise was able to obtain relevant reports generated on the area by the Department of Health and the Environmental Protection Agency.

In 2007, just as Louise was contemplating her next career move, a report by the Florida Department of Health landed on her desk.

This report—funded by the Agency for Toxic Substances and Disease Registry—addressed the Lincoln Park incinerator site. Based on the chemicals in the soil samples they'd taken, and the amount of time that had passed, the report concluded that everyone living near the incinerator site was at risk for serious health problems.

While most people assume the government releases all relevant information to those who request it, this is far from the truth. What Louise discovered in this report was something nobody else had been alerted to: the fact that, in 1997, the City of Fort Lauderdale considered selling off the Wingate Road incinerator site. In doing so, they were required to perform environmental testing on the soil. The report concluded the ground was contaminated. The City decided against selling the property because the report would have been disclosed during the sale, raising too many red flags.

The implication of this report was abundantly clear to Louise: the City of Fort Lauderdale had known since 1997—a full *ten years*—that the Wingate Road site was poisoned. Yet they had failed to warn the residents. To avoid detection, the City had ceased all testing in the area. They didn't want to attract any undue attention to the problem.

This report galvanized Louise into action. She began barnstorming the neighborhood, giving talks to anyone who would listen, from homeowners' associations to Bible study groups, attempting to alert the community to the problem. She also joined forces with Mickey Hinton and other residents to petition the Department of Environmental Protection to do further testing. Maddeningly, the test results were always the same: the results were deemed "inconclusive," with the suggestion that "further testing was needed."

Louise attempted to enlist the help of Randy Merchant, the Director of Environmental Health for the Florida Department of Health. She thought he was underplaying the potential health hazards of the site. When Randy met with the residents at her request, he told them they would "need to eat a lot of the dirt" for them to be harmed by contaminants at the site.

This didn't go over well. Louise encouraged community members to ask productive and challenging questions to Randy about their concerns.

In an attempt to break the impasse between Randy and the community, Louise suggested that his department use the health information from the 2000 US Census tracking cancer rates to determine if the area's rates were elevated. Tracking significant types of cancer wasn't a perfect approach; "cancer" isn't always listed as a cause of death on a death certificate if a patient dies of some other ailment, like pneumonia. However, it was her best shot, and this might at least provide them with more accurate information about what was going on.

Randy agreed to her proposal, then produced a report showing no increase in cancers in the area based on the 2000 Census data. Louise didn't believe him and asked for the raw data, which he agreed to provide.

Weeks passed without Louise receiving the information. Fuming, she finally called Merchant and said, "If I don't get that information, I'm going to call a press conference, and it won't be pretty."

The data arrived a few days later. As she reviewed it, Louise saw major flaws in how the data was analyzed for Lincoln Park and Wingate Road. She sent the information off to Dr. Richard Clapp, a professor at Boston University who had received numerous awards for ethics in science.

Dr. Clapp's initial review revealed that the Florida Department of Health hadn't taken certain variables into account when analyzing their data. Since the toxic region was inhabited mostly by black residents, the study should have compared the incidence of cancers in blacks living in the affected areas to the incidence of cancers in black residents living in different neighborhoods not impacted by the toxic waste site. Instead, the Department of Health had compared cancer rates of blacks in the neighborhood with the rates among whites in the neighborhood. The problem with that approach was the paucity of white residents living in the affected area. In his opinion, the State had used a statistically questionable method deliberately designed to disguise any potential cancer uptick.

When Dr. Clapp used a different methodology, the results were starkly different. While the Florida Department of Health had reported no difference in the rates of lung and respiratory cancers, Dr. Clapp found that, among blacks living near the former Wingate incinerator site, there was a 7 percent increase in Kaposi's sarcoma (a soft tissue cancer), a 22 percent increase in kidney cancer, and a 30 percent increase in lung cancer.

The rise in women's reproductive illnesses was another issue that became apparent. On many occasions, Louise met with a group of women from the neighborhood, and they'd talk about how they'd played together as kids. Many of these women suffered from reproductive problems; a disproportionate number were undergoing hysterectomies despite being only in their twenties. In fact, by Louise's estimates, a shocking 85 percent of her Legal Aid clients were women with reproductive issues.

While at Legal Aid, Louise partnered up with another lawyer, Reggie Klein, who had successfully sued the City of Fort Lauderdale for racial discrimination in employment practices. Klein joined the law firm of Napoli, Bern, Ripka, and Shkolnik, and in 2011 Louise followed him and became managing partner in their Miami office. She was finally in a position to get top-level help in obtaining justice for the residents of Lincoln Park and Wingate Road.

Louise decided their best chance was to file a claim for continued medical monitoring in the community, as well as diminution in the property value of the residents. Jan and I had considered this same approach years earlier.

As she continued putting the case together, there were two low points for Louise. The first was in 2009, when she was having trouble with the judge handling the case. He had long-standing ties to the attorneys representing the City of Fort Lauderdale; in Louise's view, this spelled doom for her case. She worried that the judge would eventually rule against the community of victims as a result of his connections.

Then, in 2010, Louise lost a good friend. She had become close to Mickey Hinton's daughter, Gale Martin, who was every bit as passionate a community activist as her father had been. Gale developed breast cancer twice and then uterine cancer; she died in January of that year.

Gale was close to the chief investigative television reporter for the local CBS affiliate, Michele Gilen. Michele produced eleven pieces on Lincoln Park. One of these, a three-part series entitled *Secrets of the Soil,* included Gale getting back in touch with a childhood friend who had moved away from the area, but who also suffered from health problems, including a brain tumor that kept returning despite eleven surgeries to remove it. The series won an Emmy award; Michele gave the Emmy to Gale before she died.

Louise told me that, on the day of Gale's funeral, she was feeling despondent both about the loss of her friend and about the judge she expected to dismiss the case. Michele took Louise aside that day and led her to an elevated area above Lincoln Park. From there, they had a view of a local housing unit, the Olive Garden Apartments, and the house where Gale had grown up with Mickey and Joan Hinton.

Michele encouraged Louise not to give up, as they observed two little girls playing on the jungle gym in front of the apartment building. The girls were hanging on the monkey bars; every so often, they'd drop to the dirt (contaminated with lead and arsenic), brush off their hands, and start climbing the bars again.

Louise told me that was the moment she felt a renewed determination to fight for the people in her community. They had to keep fighting to clean up this neighborhood, Louise said, because these victims lacked the resources to fight for their own health. I imagine she felt something similar to what I experienced with Ashlee at the top of Mount Lemmon.

She intends to keep fighting for this neighborhood until she wins compensation for the people who have been poisoned by the City's negligence. The battle continues.

Louise is an inspiration for me, as she should be for all of us. As I've seen time and again, the justice system is flawed, but that shouldn't stop us from storming the courtrooms and shouting from rooftops to make people aware of the danger they're in every day. We can't depend on our government to keep us safe and healthy.

You and I have important work to do if we're going to protect ourselves and our families.

Epilogue: Now What?

"How's your health now, Alan?" people often ask after hearing my story.

I use the word *stable* as my standard answer, even though that isn't completely true. The reality is that I'm still on the Neurontin, though I've managed to taper the dose down, and I do have relapses. A couple of them have been serious—one in 2008 and the other in 2014.

What happens when I relapse? My chemical sensitivity becomes worse, and I experience extreme pain and flu-like symptoms. My brain once again misfires.

These relapses scare me. As I fall down that same black rabbit hole again, I can't help worrying that the Neurontin might have stopped working.

I've found that the best treatment in the case of a serious relapse is to rein in my activities, rest, and go for hyperbaric oxygen chamber treatments. These treatments involve lying in a sealed chamber where the air is pressurized up to three times higher than normal, or the equivalent of diving fifty feet below the ocean's surface. In the chamber, I'm breathing 100 percent oxygen, which infuses oxygen deep into the tissues of my body, allowing healing to occur at a cellular level. I'm healthy enough now to follow a daily exercise routine of walking, swimming, and doing core exercises at a gym. I can eat out at health restaurants, see concerts, and conquer increasingly difficult challenges.

As I have resumed a more normal life, I'm happy to report that Ashlee took her old man's advice about pursuing higher education. She did well in high school, became a class leader, and spoke at graduation. I was proud and grateful to be there, wiping my eyes along with the rest of the proud parents.

Ashlee was then accepted into the University of Southern California. I was filled with joy on her first day, as I helped her move into her dormitory. When she joined a sorority, they held a father-daughter event, which I enthusiastically attended. I also showed up for events arranged for mothers and daughters, since I was playing both roles in her life.

After graduating with a bachelor's degree in communications, Ashlee went on to earn her MBA from Pepperdine University. I had the honor of sitting there and cheering for her during yet another graduation. And then, astoundingly, I had the opportunity to applaud her at one more ceremony, as Ashlee graduated from flight school with her wings, pursuing her dream of traveling the world as a flight attendant for a major airline.

My legal advocacy for victims of environmental poisoning continues to motivate Ashlee to support our fight. She understands the plight of victims who have been poisoned by the environment better than most, having helped save me as I struggled to survive.

◆ ◆ ◆

I hope my shared journey highlights how essential it is to count our blessings. We are all mere humans, fragile and vulnerable, and our existence on this earth is a temporary radiance. We should all strive to leave our planet a better place than when we first arrived.

Escaping my bubble taught me that being alive is a gift. We honor that gift by loving our families, and by finding purpose and meaning in making a difference in the lives of others. Learning how to embrace moments of joy and wonder by walking barefoot on a beach, marveling at clouds racing across the sky, is far more valuable than growing the size of your house or bank account.

A number of people have had near-death experiences and written about them. They describe what it's like to "see the light," go to heaven, and come back. My situation was the reverse: I went to hell and was lucky enough to return to this sunlit heaven we all live in.

◆ ◆ ◆

I'm grateful for the second chance I was given to move forward in my life. First on my wish list was to return to Fort Lauderdale, Florida, where I became a prosecutor and learned how to fight for justice while making so many friends among my colleagues. It's where I fell in love, got married, bought my first house, and had my daughter. Returning to Fort Lauderdale, specifically to the places where I'd spent my young adulthood, was my way of reclaiming who I was back then, and merging that young man with the older, wiser man I am today.

Most important, I wanted to confront my nemesis, 110 Tower. That building represents my own Ground Zero. Like many victims of violent crimes, I was determined to revisit the site where I was injured and conquer my fears by reminding myself that I'm a survivor.

My first stop in Fort Lauderdale was the house in Coral Springs, where Susan and I were living when Ashlee was born. Ashlee and I stopped by and introduced ourselves to the residents, who were nice enough to invite us inside. I showed Ashlee her bedroom and the living room where we'd taken videos of her as a baby.

Next, I went to the Broward County Courthouse. I hesitated on the steps before going inside, thinking about the nineteen current and former employees of the Broward County Courthouse who ended up suing the County, claiming the building made them sick because it was infested with toxic mold. In addition, they alleged that tiny asbestos fibers were floating through the air, exposing them to further health risks.

In court documents, the County denied the presence of floating asbestos fibers and toxic mold, and argued that Florida's sovereign immunity law—the same law I ran up against in the incinerator case—protects the government from hefty damages. The County also rejected allegations that it was negligent in failing to test for the toxins and not warning its occupants properly. The government falsely assured employees and the public that the mold and flooding problems were being addressed as they occurred.

The ninth floor—where Circuit Judge Cheryl Aleman, who died of an aggressive form of lung cancer, had her courtroom—was stripped and the ceiling tiles were ripped out. Other offices had also been redone after various flooding incidents.

Finally, in October 2013, the first employee lawsuit was settled, with a $166,500 out-of-court settlement to a former prosecutor who claimed the facility caused her severe sinus damage. In Stefanie Krathen Ginnis's case, a tissue sample taken during sinus surgery revealed that the mold in her nose was identical to mold spores found in the courthouse, where she worked from 2003 to 2010. This was the first solid proof the building posed health hazards to the public.

A few years ago, the County agreed to replace the half-century-old courthouse with a new $328 million building and parking complex. They never tore the whole courthouse down, just the old part of the building that was deemed toxic, and they didn't do that until they'd added on the new part of the building. Meanwhile, clerks, lawyers, judges, and other staff were working—and being poisoned—there every day.

I was already extremely sick before I learned about any of this. And, although I felt vindicated in some way by the lawsuits finally being filed, I felt extremely sorry for the people who had to suffer before county officials finally owned up and took responsibility.

After a moment's hesitation, I walked inside and visited courtrooms where I'd spent many hours as a young lawyer. I saw judges whose campaigns I'd managed, too; some of them hadn't seen me in years, and they were shocked when I suddenly appeared.

Rumors had been circulating, some of them suggesting that I had died; a few people looked at me as if I were a ghost. One judge rapped his gavel on the bench at the sight of me and asked for a brief adjournment of the case he was hearing, calling me into chambers to look me over and hear my story.

"Want your old job back?" asked my former prosecuting chief, only half joking.

I shook my head. "No, thanks. I'm fighting a bigger crime," I said, and explained my situation.

For my part, however, the dragon I really needed to slay wasn't the courthouse, since that's not where I got sick—I didn't work long in the mold-infested part of the old building. It was 110 Tower. That was my nemesis: I needed to walk into that building and prove to myself that I had survived against all odds.

As I hesitated in front of the doors of 110 Tower, I was flooded with conflicting feelings. This was the building where I had, in my youth, felt at the height of my physical, professional, and intellectual abilities.

Yet this building almost destroyed me, and in doing so, 110 Tower altered my life's journey forever. I entered its doors, nearly holding my breath as I waited for my body to react to this familiar— and once nearly lethal—environment.

I inhaled cautiously in the lobby. Ironically, I knew instantly that whatever had been in this building and made me sick was now gone.

I felt nothing. The toxic building materials had finished outgassing and the ventilation system must have been redone.

I went everywhere in 110 Tower that day. I rode the elevators and visited the suite of offices where I'd experienced vertigo and blurred vision, aches, and fevers. I went to the fitness center and the shops, and hung out in the lobby. Still, no symptoms.

I wasn't surprised by this. As the new material odors—which we may perceive as pleasant dissipated over time, the building became safer.

Finally, almost a decade later, I had returned to 110 Tower, slayed the dragon, and walked out a free man. I had fought my way back. I was a survivor.

◆ ◆ ◆

As good as my life is now, I have not given up on my mission to alert mankind to the dangerous chemicals poisoning us all in our workplaces, homes, schools, and neighborhoods. I have lost track of the countless victims I've encountered whose lives have been permanently damaged or lost to this silent epidemic.

I've worked with residents in Naples, Florida, where a real estate developer was doing shoddy work; when it rained, all of his buildings leaked. Water intruded into their homes and the residents got sick from the mold. I've also counseled nurses made ill by mold in their hospitals and teachers made ill in their schools—along with their students. Through the years, I've helped factory workers who became sick while working on assembly lines. I've helped flight attendants poisoned by toxic air on planes, and people whose breathing has been forever compromised due to air pollution caused by oil refineries built near their homes. I've worked with 9/11 survivors and Gulf War vets.

In Long Beach, California, I consulted with workers who cleaned up an oil spill at a refinery without properly suiting up to protect themselves against the chemicals they were wading in—up to their chests. I've comforted women whose breast cancers were linked to their silicone implants, and victims of sick building syndrome.

The point is this: You can be an athletic guy like Dan Allen, coaching an elite college football team, or you can be a little girl whose family lives in Section 8 housing, like Neveah. You can be living in a neighborhood with a toxic site your city refuses to clean up, like the residents of Lincoln Park and Wingate Road in Fort Lauderdale; you can also be a postal worker doing her job in a rural area, like Judilyn Knight; or a guy like me, thinking he's on the fast track to success.

It doesn't matter who you are, where you work, or how you live. No one is immune. Wrongdoing is widespread, manifesting in people, governmental organizations, and corporations that are seemingly bland and harmless—just as Ted Bundy hid his evil beneath a thin veneer of "normal." Some corporate entities are truly evil, knowingly exposing victims for profit. Other companies choose to look the other way, rather than face the harmful consequences caused by their negligence. In either scenario, wrongdoers should be held accountable for their actions, because it's the only way to help protect victims and curtail this irresponsible behavior.

Our global pandemic is terrifying, yet many people choose to look the other way rather than face their own mortal vulnerability. Sadly, the human race is committing this ultimate crime against itself—and against future generations.

There are no geographic, economic, ethnic, political, or religious borders when it comes to environmental toxins. We are all at risk of being poisoned. However, everyone is not equally exposed to toxins. Those living in economically challenged circumstances are more likely to encounter toxins where they work and live. They are the least able to protect themselves legally and lack the necessary financial resources to flee from their proximity to environmental contamination.

As I learned during my years as a prosecutor and, later, as a toxic tort lawyer, those in power don't always do the right thing. It's up to us to fight for our own environmental health if we're going to save the humans and survive as a species.

♦ ♦ ♦

In a recent issue of *International Business Times,* one particular headline caught my attention: "Unhealthy Environment Was a Factor in Nearly a Quarter of Global Deaths in 2012."

As I read the article, my heart sank, even though I already knew all about the problem. According to the World Health Organization's latest report, environmental risk factors like climate change; the pollution of our air, soil, and water; and chemical exposures are responsible for nearly a quarter of all deaths worldwide—that's *12.6 million deaths* out of a total of 55.6 million.

There are plenty of other terrifying statistics out there. Worldwide, about 682 pounds of toxic chemicals are released into our air, land, and water every second by industrial facilities—that's approximately 10 million tons (over 21 billion pounds) of toxic chemicals released into our environment *each year.* Of these, over 2 million tons (over 4.5 billion pounds) per year are recognized carcinogens, according to the website *Worldometers,* which gathers statistics from the United Nations Environment Program and the EPA, among others.

Another recent study published in the journal *Environmental Health Perspectives* linked sixteen thousand premature births in the United States each year to air pollution. This is a costly health crisis: preterm births associated with particulate matter—a type of pollutant—led to more than $4 billion in economic costs in 2010 due to medical care and lost productivity resulting from disability. Not surprisingly, the affected populations tended to be concentrated in low-income communities composed of mostly minority residents.

Many governments around the world legislate to clean the air we breathe, but there is much more work to be done. *Voice of America* recently cited a new study by Massachusetts Institute of Technology reporting that nearly two hundred thousand deaths in the United States alone occur *each year* as a result of air pollution, with most related to emissions from road transportation and electrical power generation. "Wasteland," an article published in the December 2014 issue of *National Geographic* magazine, takes a good look at the hazardous waste sites in the United States. Although many have been cleaned up, many more remain. Nearly one in six Americans live near a toxic waste dump that is poisoning the ground beneath our schools, homes, and workplaces. Even where the waste has supposedly been cleaned up, as in the case of the Florida incinerator, it's often still there, just swept under the surface. Cancer is only one danger associated with these sites; birth defects is another.

Meanwhile, an article published in a March 2014 issue of the *Atlantic* magazine details the damage done to human brains—especially to the brains of developing infants and young children—by lead and other neurotoxins commonly found in our environment. The article cites my Environmental Health Foundation colleague, Dr. Landrigan, and a paper he co-authored spelling out the "silent pandemic" caused by twelve toxins found in everyday furniture and other common household products. These chemicals are linked to disorders like autism, attention deficit hyperactivity disorder (ADHD), and autism spectrum disorder.

The real issue here—as the writer points out in the *Atlantic* article—is not the twelve neurotoxins that Landrigan names as culprits (including lead, arsenic, DDT, and methylmercury, which are already regulated), but the many other chemicals pouring into our environment before they are proven to be 100 percent safe for human health.

Even if you don't live near a toxic waste dump and the air you're breathing seems clean, you and your family could be exposed to harmful chemical exposures through the water you drink. On March 27, 2016, a *New York Times* editorial by Mona Hanna-Attisha, a pediatrician at Hurley Children's Hospital and an assistant professor at Michigan State University's College of Human Medicine, reminded us that the Environmental Protection Agency's "action level" for lead contamination in drinking water is fifteen parts per billion. Recent tests of tap water in Flint, Michigan, reveal that 1,300 homes exceed that—with thirty-two of those families exposed to lead levels *above one thousand parts per billion.*

"For almost two years, Flint's children have been drinking water through lead-coated straws," wrote Hanna-Attisha.

People who believe they are immune to toxic dangers because they can afford homes in "nice" city neighborhoods or the suburbs are fooling themselves. Sure, your water and air might be free of harmful toxins, but what about your own backyard?

An article published in the March 28, 2016, issue of *Reader's Digest* titled "The Dark Side of the Perfectly Manicured American Lawn: Is It Giving You Cancer?" cites alarming facts about pesticide use. Despite the fact that Agent Orange was the notorious defoliant used in Vietnam—it was originally developed during World War II to destroy an enemy's rice crops—one of its key components, the pesticide 2,4-D, is still being widely used.

Today's worldwide annual sales of 2,4-D surpass $300 million. You probably have it in your own neighborhood, since it's commonly found in products used to keep our lawns green and weed free, despite the fact that several research studies link this toxin to reproductive health problems and genetic mutations, as well as to a variety of cancers.

Even far from crowded cities and suburban green lawns, rural residents are equally at risk of being poisoned. According to an article published in the June 13, 2011, issue of the *Atlantic* magazine, The Farmworkers Association of Florida conducted a survey in 2006 showing that 92 percent of the region's agricultural workers were exposed to pesticides through aerial spraying, as well as by touching poisoned plants and inhaling pesticides. Little wonder, then, that in a state where the rate of birth defects is 3 percent, a whopping *13 percent* of the farmworkers in the agricultural region of Florida near Apopka had children born with defects.

The bottom line? Whoever you are, wherever you live and work, you and your family are at risk of being poisoned without knowing it, unless you learn how to protect yourself.

♦ ♦ ♦

Our government is broken. As a former prosecutor, I believe every criminal is innocent until proven guilty. However, as a legal advocate for victims of environmental poisoning, and as a victim myself, I strongly believe that every chemical should be presumed guilty until proven innocent.

Many people mistakenly believe that if they buy a fertilizer for their lawn, a new carpet, or a gallon of paint, they are buying something that has been tested and deemed safe through various governmental regulations and channels, just like the drugs their doctors prescribe for them. I once believed this, too, but it couldn't be further from the truth.

When chemicals are developed for pharmaceutical purposes, they undergo rigorous safety testing using animal models and human exposure studies. These drugs aren't approved for market until after preclinical trials show they don't cause adverse health effects. When chemicals are developed for industry use, on the other hand, and they're not marketed for human consumption per se, these substances don't go through the same rigorous testing. They're only regulated *after the fact*, if data emerges showing that their use leads to toxic effects in people. This data emerges chronologically and cumulatively while the casualties continue. Many people are injured by chemical exposure before any regulation is put into place.

Several European countries have moved toward more rigorous testing of chemicals before they go on the market. The European Union has a chemical testing protocol called "REACH" (Registration, Evaluation, Authorization, and Restriction of Chemicals). This involves a multitiered approach to regulating chemicals, requiring in-depth testing only of chemicals produced in large amounts. In 2009, the European Parliament passed laws banning twenty-two pesticides linked to the disruption of human hormones or reproduction, or associated with cancer.

The United States lags behind in reforming chemical regulations because of our powerful chemical lobby. The only existing US law regulating chemicals is the Toxic Substances Control Act (TSCA); this law was passed in 1976 and requires testing only those chemicals that pose "an unreasonable risk." Even worse, at the time TSCA was passed, sixty-two thousand chemicals were grandfathered in because they were already on the market. Over twenty thousand new chemicals have been introduced since then.

This is wrong. The burden of proof should be placed upon industry to show that the chemicals they're manufacturing and using are safe for human use *before* being introduced into the marketplace. Instead, we wait until people become ill or die in large enough numbers to suspect a problem. Then we backtrack, trying to prove such chemicals are linked to illness.

Those who argue against chemical regulation claim such testing would be unduly expensive. They ask how companies could possibly make money with that financial burden. If manufacturers had to pass that burden on to consumers, it would be horrible for business!

There is persistent lobbying against any sort of chemical regulation, and safety laws don't get passed as a result. Meanwhile, humans around the world are paying the steepest price for this insanity.

Dr. Landrigan and his colleagues argue that our country needs stronger chemical safety legislation. Scientists realize it's not financially feasible to subject every chemical to long, randomized control studies prior to being brought to market. However, they point to the Tox21—the Toxicology in the Twenty-First Century program—as offering a potential solution, at least in the short term, because Tox21 is laying the groundwork for accelerated, large-scale testing. Some of this testing includes screening industrial chemicals through simple cell-based studies—in short, chemicals that cause cells in a petri dish to show a toxic reaction would be subjected to further testing.

As a collaborative effort between the National Institute of Environmental Health Sciences, the Environmental Protection Agency, and the Food and Drug Administration, the Tox21 project aims to develop better methods to quickly and efficiently test chemical compounds and determine whether they have the potential to cause biological disruption, human disease, or injury.

In the meantime, there has been an onslaught of class action lawsuits proving that specific chemicals *are* harmful. Many toxic tort lawsuits, like the ones I have described here, force companies to take responsibility for the harm they do through the poisons they manufacture and distribute. But that is too little, too late.

I see this issue from a number of perspectives. As a former victim of chemical poisoning and as a survivor, I understand both the personal and global issues at stake. I've prosecuted criminals and defended big business in the courtroom. As a legal avenger and an environmental health advocate, I'm hoping now to put a face on this issue—*my* face.

✦ ✦ ✦

My life span and quality of life have been severely compromised. That's what happens when your immune and nervous systems are injured by toxins. I'm resigned to that.

Yet, my life has meaning. My efforts have become a lightning rod for change because my personal story is not just another disease of the week.

Our species cannot adapt fast enough to survive the onslaught of chemicals pouring into our environment. Chemical poisoning is a risk we all face. This is why I wrote this book: to send up a flare, sound the alarm, and give a voice to this problem. We must face it now, before it's too late.

While I believe laws governing how and when companies bring chemicals to market should be changed, I'm not optimistic about that happening any time soon. We can't rely on our government to protect our health.

So what's the solution?

We must educate ourselves and each other. It's time to expose this ultimate crime—a crime so vicious that it leaves millions of victims in its wake; a crime so insidious that the villain is often invisible. We can no longer look away.

We must join together and become vigilant in protecting our own health and the lives of our family members because industry and government are obviously not doing it. We must be alert and knowledgeable about which chemicals are harmful. Then, we can modify our lifestyles to minimize our risk of toxic exposure.

I wish I had known, all those years ago, what I know now. I wish I'd identified my flu-like symptoms, runny eyes, blurred vision, fatigue, and many other symptoms as my body's reaction to a toxic workplace. What if I'd been smart enough to leave that 110 Tower? Who knows what my life would have been like, if I had trusted my instincts, instead of sweeping my symptoms under the rug?

But I believe everything happens for a reason. I heard that voice on the mountain summit with Ashlee, and I have embraced my wake-up call to help make a difference. I no longer care about keeping up with the Joneses. I treasure every moment I'm alive. Doctors told me I wouldn't survive beyond the age of forty, so I am grateful for every moment of life I am given.

One amazing day, my friends and family gathered to throw a surprise party for my fiftieth birthday in my brother's Miami Beach condo. My presence was perhaps as much of a surprise to many of the guests as it was to me, and I was overwhelmed by how much love was in that room.

It was wonderful that Ashlee had the opportunity to meet people from my past—my high school and college buddies, my law school colleagues, my family and friends—talk about me as a fierce fighter and a loyal friend. Hopefully, I can pass this hard-won wisdom on to my daughter. I owe her at least that much, and so much more. I wouldn't be here today if it weren't for Ashlee's support and her determination to find a cure for her dad.

My plight was preventable. You can prevent this from happening to you and your family. I urge you to take charge of your own health and destiny. Modify your lifestyle to minimize your risks. Start the process of protecting yourself against chemical exposures now, so that you and your loved ones can embrace every moment of a long and healthy life.

Appendix A: How to Modify Your Lifestyle to Minimize Chemical Injury

Multiple chemical sensitivity (MCS)—a diagnosis used to describe adverse symptoms caused by environmental exposures—remains a controversial diagnosis.

The concepts underlying MCS were developed by allergist Theron G. Randolph, MD (1906–1995), who believed his patients reacted and became ill when exposed to chemicals at doses far below levels normally considered safe. In the 1950s, he suggested that human failure in adapting to modern-day synthetic chemicals was causing widespread hypersensitivities to many environmental substances.

Other names for MCS that have emerged through the years include allergic toxemia, chemical sensitivity, ecologic illness, environmental illness, immune system dysregulation, total allergy syndrome, total immune disorder syndrome, and toxic response syndrome. Other related terms include sick building syndrome, Gulf War syndrome, and toxic carpet syndrome.

Whatever you choose to call it, people suffering from exposure to toxic chemicals experience symptoms that may include depression, irritability, an inability to concentrate, memory loss, digestive problems, fatigue, allergy symptoms, flu-like aches and pains, head-aches, and lack of coordination.

Mainstream medicine still doesn't understand a whole lot about the human body and how it reacts to chemicals in our environment. Many people—including physicians—remain in the dark about chemical sensitivity. It's difficult to put a descriptive term on symptoms that are difficult to pinpoint and often impossible to link to specific blood tests or diagnostic imaging.

Science has not yet caught up in diagnosing environmentally induced injury and illness. My test results showing brain lesions, strange blood counts, abnormal enzyme levels, and a suppressed immune system puzzled most physicians. They saw the smoke but couldn't find the gun that fired the bullet.

What should you do if you suspect you've been injured by toxins? Start with your personal physician and keep asking questions if you don't get answers. See specialists, too, and get the necessary tests to see if there are ways to treat your symptoms. Keep going until you find treatments that work for you.

Many doctors tell patients suffering from environmentally induced illnesses that it's all in their heads, because science is still in the Dark Ages. If you're sick, however, you owe it to yourself—and your family—to pay attention to your own body and do whatever it takes to find answers for yourself. You are your own best advocate.

Go to the best mainstream institutions, whether you're seeking legal or medical help. That's certainly what I did: from the Mayo Clinic to the Cleveland Clinic, I sought out experts who had earned recognition worldwide. Most universities and medical schools have environmental health departments. Check those out, too. Keep going until you find answers and relief for your symptoms.

If, over time, mainstream medicine fails you, and you believe you're suffering from an environmentally induced illness, I urge you to consider contacting the nearest physician affiliated with the American Academy of Environmental Medicine. (AAEM, originally founded by Dr. Randolph as the Society for Clinical Ecology, is made up of about five hundred osteopathic and medical physicians.) Through this network, you will at least find a physician who will listen to you with compassion, and who may have treatments your primary physician isn't aware of yet. Leave no stone unturned in your quest for treatment.

◆ ◆ ◆

It is my hope that you have found this book before becoming irreversibly injured by toxins in your environment. Whatever your situation, the fact that you're reading these pages means that you're looking for ways to protect your health—and your family's—from the poisons all around us.

The truth has been exposed in many, many research studies about how man-made poisons are harming us. I've built a powerful case in this book for the need to protect ourselves because our government has not done its job to keep us safe by regulating what's put into our environment.

Now it's your turn. By following the easy lifestyle modifications listed below, you can defend yourself and your family against environmental injury and death—before it's too late. If you'd like to download this list and other resources, visit my website (alanbell. me/resources).

TOP TWENTY-ONE LIFESTYLE TIPS

1. *Food.* Eat plants grown organically, with natural fertilizers, and make sure the meat you buy comes from animals not fed with chemicals, hormones, antibiotics, or pesticides. Avoid farm-raised fish. Eat wild-caught and smaller fish to minimize mercury exposure. Avoid tuna, sea bass, and swordfish. Cod, salmon, and pollack are better.

2. *Water.* Drink, bathe, and cook with filtered, chlorine-free water. Drink only water bottled in glass, not in plastic. Hundreds of contaminants have been found in tap water.

3. *Indoor air quality.* We spend 90 percent of our time indoors, where pollutants are up to five times higher than outdoors, so use ozone-free HEPA air purifiers. When vacuuming, use a HEPA-filtered unit. If you're building or renovating a home, consider installing a central vacuum cleaning system with a HEPA filter. Buy a test kit to determine if mold, radon, or asbestos are present in your home. Asbestos and radon are leading causes of lung cancer. Regularly open the windows in your house to let fresh air dilute any radon gas that has built up. Use tight sealing glass doors on your fireplace to minimize the fumes (carbon monoxide and nitrogen dioxide) that could seep into your home. Never use any type of scented air fresheners because they contain many synthetic toxic chemicals.

4. *Personal care products.* Most personal care products with synthetic fragrances contain toxic chemicals. Avoid perfume, cologne, and products with added fragrance. Use nontoxic sunscreen. Most sunscreens are chemical based and those should never be used. Buy sunscreens containing zinc oxide as their active ingredient. Read labels and avoid products that include the following:
    a. Words ending in "paraben"
    b. DMDM hydantoin
    c. Imidazolidinyl urea
    d. Methylchloroisothiazolinone
    e. Triclosan
    f. Triclocarban
    g. Triethanolamine (TEA)

5. *Children.* Don't buy disposable, plastic baby diapers. They contain toxic chemicals that infiltrate children's bodies. Use cloth diapers. When using personal care products for children:
    a. Use fewer products and use them less often.
    b. Don't trust claims. Read all labels and check ingredients.
    c. Buy fragrance-free products.
    d. Avoid the use of synthetic baby powder on newborns and infants. Use organic cornstarch instead.

6. *Cookware.* Don't cook with Teflon or nonstick pans. When cookware with nonstick coating is heated, the coating breaks down and leaches toxins into your food. Use cast-iron, stainless steel, or glass cookware.

7. *Plastics.* Avoid plastic baby bottles and food and drink containers made with bisphenol A (BPA). BPA is a common ingredient found in plastic and is associated with many health problems including birth defects and cancer. Use BPA-free plastic, glass, or metal containers. Only use plastic containers labeled one through five for food.

8. *Laundry products.* Buy fragrance-free detergent and fabric softeners. Read product labels. An increasing number of companies manufacture scent- and dye-free products. Use natural alternatives. For example, white vinegar is a natural fabric softener.

9. *Home cleaning products.* Although toxic cleaners kill germs, they pose health hazards. Use nontoxic home cleaning products. Many nontoxic cleaning products can now be found at most markets and stores. Read all labels and look for fragrance-free, chemical-free, and preservative-free items or use safe substitutes such as vinegar and baking soda.

10. *Clothing.* Buy clothing made with natural fibers such as cotton and wool. Avoid synthetic materials that don't breathe and are treated with flame retardants containing polybrominated diphenyl ethers (PBDEs). When you enter your home, leave your shoes outside to reduce the amount of dust-bound pollutants (including lead) you track in. Brush off the soles and tops of your shoes before you bring them inside.

11. *Dry cleaning.* Avoid dry cleaning your clothes. At a minimum, find a dry cleaner that uses less toxic materials or *wet* or *carbon dioxide* cleaning processes. Hang your clothes on a clothesline after they are cleaned to air out before wearing. The sun is a powerful detoxifier.

12. *Pesticides.* Don't use pesticides on your lawn or in your home. Use natural alternatives such as boric acid for ants and cockroaches and heat or microwaves to kill termites. Old-fashioned traps are great for eliminating mice and rats.

13. *Furniture.* Avoid glued particleboard furniture coated with toxic stain, flame retardants, and PDBEs. Use glass, metal, or solid wood furniture coated with nontoxic sealers and natural fabrics.

14. *Bedding.* Avoid materials treated with toxic flame retardants. Sleep on an organic cotton mattress and bedding instead of the standard toxic flame retardant–treated materials.

15. *Paints.* If you paint your home, use zero volatile organic compound (VOC) products.

16. *Electromagnetic frequencies.* Minimize exposure to electromagnetic frequencies (EMFs). Stay a safe distance from your television set and use low-EMF, flat-screen computer monitors instead

of cathode ray tube monitors. Don't hold your cell phone to your ears. Use a wired earpiece. Bluetooth earpieces emit radiation, and Wi-Fi areas create unhealthy EMF levels.

17. *Automobiles.* Buy a healthy automobile with low VOC materials. Leathers, fabrics, and plastics inside your vehicle emit toxic chemical vapors.

18. *Floor coverings.* Install ceramic tile, stone, or solid wood on your floors, with washable area rugs. Avoid synthetic wall-to-wall carpet containing petrochemical fibers coated with toxic stain resisters.

19. *Supplements.* Iodine supplements provide protection against exposure to petrochemical, thyroid-disrupting residues contained in water and substances found in your everyday environment. Pregnant women should use iodized salt to reduce thyroid disruption caused by environmental exposure. Large daily doses of vitamin D (4,000 IU) and buffered vitamin C (4,000 mg) are also powerful ways to boost your immune system and resist environmental toxins.

20. *Detoxify your body.* Cardiovascular exercise, sauna, or hot sea salt baths help you sweat and excrete toxins absorbed on a daily basis.

21. *Avoid scented products.* Products of all kinds with fragrances often contain chemicals. My mantra is "If it has a scent, don't spend a cent on it." Buy a scent-free alternative. At the very least, read the labels of all scented products, but understand that the listings are not a guarantee. The best policy is to play it safe and *avoid anything scented.* If you must have a scented product, go for those that have natural herbal scents, such as vanilla extract or flower-based products.

TOP TEN CHEMICALS TO AVOID

1. *Acrylamide.* Used in gel and binding agents and found in food packaging, cosmetics, and disposable diapers. You will also find it at the summer barbecue or fast-food restaurants because it is created by frying or baking starchy foods like potatoes and grains. Acrylamide can also be ingested from tobacco smoke or drinking water, and by touching products that contain the chemical. High doses of acrylamide exposure can lead to skin, eye, and upper respiratory infections.

2. *Atrazine.* More than 70 million pounds of this agricultural pesticide are sprayed on our croplands each year, most of it to protect corn. Agricultural workers inhale and absorb this pesticide, and it has also been found in ground and drinking water. High doses of atrazine found in animals have been linked to the delayed onset of puberty, impaired fertility, and reduced levels of the hormones prolactin and testosterone. The EPA is currently reviewing whether or not the chemical is carcinogenic in humans.

3. *Benzene.* This volatile chemical is a product of coal and petroleum production. It's also added to unleaded gasoline and industrial solvents, and it's a by-product of tobacco smoke. The compound offgasses from building materials and also occurs naturally. Humans typically inhale benzene in ambient air. The body absorbs it readily and sends particles to the brain, fatty tissue, and, in pregnant women, across the placenta. Exposure to high concentrations of benzene vapor can depress the central nervous system and lead to death.

4. *Bisphenol A.* Also known as BPA, this chemical is commonly used in plastics such as eyeglass lenses, auto parts, CDs, food

containers, plastic dinnerware, and toys. Exposure to BPA is thought primarily to happen when we eat foods that have come into contact with the chemical. It is highly toxic to some animals, interfering with brain and reproductive organ development. Studies in humans are murky, but have found a variety of possible health effects, including a possible association between BPA and heart disease.

5. *Long-chain perfluorinated chemicals (PFCs).* Fire-resistant PFCs are used in electronics, automotive parts, textiles, and in the construction and aerospace industries, not to mention nonstick cookware. It is unclear how the chemicals get into the human body, but one likely possibility is through diet. While scientists don't know with certainty if PFCs are harmful to human health, studies have found that high doses cause liver damage in rodents and monkeys.

6. *Methyl tert-butyl ether (MTBE).* MTBE was once commonly used as an additive in gas, but was eventually banned or limited in most states when it became clear that it could adversely affect water quality. MTBE is found in groundwater and in the air of cities where use is still permitted. Human exposure has been associated with headaches, nausea, dizziness, and respiratory tract infections.

7. *Percholate.* Primarily used in the defense and aerospace industries for rocket and missile production, it is also found in consumer items like fireworks and matches. Though it was once used to treat hyperthyroidism, it has since been deemed a contaminant. Water, milk, and high-water-content vegetables are thought to be the main exposure source for humans. Both animal and human studies have shown that percholate inhibits thyroid hormone production.

8. *Phthalates.* These industrial chemicals are used to make plastics flexible and resilient. They show up in many everyday products, including detergent, vinyl tiles, deodorant, garden hoses, plastic raincoats, and hair spray. They end up in the body when we swallow and inhale them and, less frequently, when our skin comes into contact with certain products. The health impacts of phthalates haven't yet been measured in humans, but they cause reproductive and liver disease in lab rats.

9. *Polybrominated diphenyl ethers (PBDEs).* Like PFCs, these chemicals are highly effective flame retardants and are used in plastics, wire insulation, and textiles. They're also frequently found in furniture and mattresses. People are exposed to them by consuming fish, fatty foods, and breast milk. Once in the body, they accumulate in fat tissue and little is known about how they are metabolized. In animals, PBDEs adversely affect thyroid function, brain development, and reproductive organs. Scientists don't yet know how PBDE exposure affects humans.

10. *Short-chain chlorinated paraffins (SCCPs).* After discovering that manufacturers had been using SCCPs without governmental approval, the EPA decided to investigate these chemicals. They are frequently used in plastics like PVC piping and as lubricants and coolants in metal manufacturing. SCCP levels have not been measured across the population, but according to the EPA, they have been detected in human breast milk and various Japanese and European food products. SCCPs have been shown to accumulate in animal tissue with a toxic effect.

Appendix B: Recommended Reading

Silent Spring by Rachel Carson (Houghton Mifflin, 1962, 2002). This groundbreaking bestseller alerted the world to the dangers of pesticides and their deadly, toxic effects. It is widely acknowledged as one of the most influential books of the twentieth century and for creating environmental awareness at a time when pesticides and other chemicals were hailed as major scientific advancements and thought to be harmless.

An Inconvenient Truth: The Planetary Emergency of Global Warming and What We Can Do About It by Al Gore (Rodale, 2006). This alarming book documents the effects of global warming on our planet and the consequences.

Slow Death by Rubber Duck: The Secret Danger of Everyday Things by Rick Smith and Bruce Laurie (Counterpoint, 2011). The authors use a variety of methods to test individual body burdens of toxic chemicals. They describe, for instance, how the innocuous rubber duck is infused with poisonous phthalates as well as common toxins in everything from Teflon to nonflammable pajamas. The book reminds us that what we do to our Earth, we do to ourselves.

Dodging the Toxic Bullet: How to Protect Yourself from Everyday Health Hazards by David R. Boyd (Greystone Books, 2010). This book identifies chemicals and toxins found in our air, food, water, and the products we use. It explains how we can limit our exposure and protect our health. The author also compares environmental safety protections in the United States, Canada, Australia, and Europe and identifies areas that need improvement.

Green Goes with Everything: Simple Steps to a Healthier Life and Cleaner Planet by Sloan Barnett (Atria, 2008). An informative book by a mother and television consumer advocate on how to avoid toxic substances we use on a regular basis in our homes. It focuses on items that are harmful to children and how to avoid or substitute them. The book examines a wide range of products and reviews each one of their pros and cons.

Toxic Free: How to Protect Your Health and Home from the Chemicals That Are Making You Sick by Debra Lynn Dadd (TarcherPerigee, 2011). An informative, easy-to-read book that covers toxic substances contained in our everyday products, what they do to our health, and how you can cut back or even eliminate your exposure to toxic substances in your own home. The author's website is also a great resource, listing manufacturers of toxin-free products of all kinds.

Raising Healthy Children in a Toxic World: 101 Smart Solutions for Every Family by Philip J. Landrigan, Herbert Needleman, and Mary Landrigan (Rodale, 2002). This book is filled with information and easy-to-follow checklists to help identify toxins in our homes, workplaces, and areas that children frequent. Each chapter includes questions that help readers zero in on the areas of importance to them. The book also gives practical recommendations on how readers can protect their families by reducing their exposure to toxins.

Our Stolen Future: Are We Threatening Our Fertility, Intelligence, and Survival? A Scientific Detective Story by Theo Colburn, Duanne Dumanoski, and John Peter Meyers (Plume, 1997). A scholarly and technical book that is also highly informative on how man-made contaminates have caused health problems such as infertility, immune-system breakdowns, autoimmune diseases, behavioral problems, and learning disabilities. It focuses on endocrine disruptors and identifies dangerous substances. This influential book is credited with encouraging the EPA to implement more stringent regulations.

How Everyday Products Make People Sick: Toxins at Home and in the Workplace by Paul Blane (University of California Press, 2007). The author's main thesis is that industry has produced toxins and factory processes that have poisoned large populations. He chastises governments and businesses for historically denying, ignoring, and weakening protections. To support his positions, he cites studies involving specific products, including glue, rubber cement, shoes, phosphorous matches, asbestos, and rayon.

Clean: The Revolutionary Program to Restore the Body's Natural Ability to Heal Itself by Alejandro Junger (Harper One, 2009, 2012). In this *New York Times* bestseller, Junger, a cardiologist, explains to readers how toxins accumulate in our bodies, disrupt our systems, and result in physical ailments. He believes that our world is filled with toxins, and every day we take in more of them. The book provides a one-month detoxification and nutrition program to clean up our bodies and restore our vitality and health.

A Civil Action by Jonathan Harr (Vintage, 1996). This bestseller tells the true story of the battle of a young lawyer, Jan Schlichtmann, to obtain legal damages for leukemia patients and their families from a company that dumped carcinogens polluting the local water supply.

This gripping book won the National Book Critics Circle Award, was made into a major motion picture, and created wide awareness about industrial pollution and its effects.

Tom's River: A Story of Science and Salvation by Dan Fagan (Island Press, 2013). This story of a cluster of childhood cancers in a New Jersey town can be considered a continuation of the issues first raised in *A Civil Action* and involving some of the same individuals, including attorney Jan Schlichtmann. *Publishers Weekly* hailed the book as "a crisp, hard-nosed probe into corporate arrogance and the power of public resistance." The story was a *New York Times* bestseller and won the 2014 Pulitzer Prize for general nonfiction.

The Edge and Beyond by Lance Morris, ND (Resonant Sound Therapy, 2014). Dr. Morris explains his approach to healing through understanding fascial membrane and his development of Resonant Sound Therapy and Resonant Movement Meditation. His book combines philosophy and science and offers practical advice we can use in our daily lives.

Appendix C: An Online Resource Guide for Nontoxic Living

How to Identify Foods without Pesticides and Poisons
www.foodnews.org/walletguide.php
www.greenamericatoday.org/PDF/TipSheetSafeSeafood.pdf
www.ewg.org/research/childrens-cereals

How to Make Sure Your Water Is Safe
www.ewg.org/tap-water/home

How to Check the Quality of the Air You Breathe
www.scorecard.org
www.epa.gov/airdata
www.epa.gov/myenvironment
www2.epa.gov/rmp/forms/vulnerable-zone-indicator-system
http://www.rtk.net/
www.toxictrends.org
www.toxmap.nlm.nih.gov/toxmap/

How to Buy Nontoxic Personal Care, Cleaning, and Children's Products
www.cosmeticsdatabase.com
www.cehn.org

www.ewg.org/2015sunscreen
www.ewg.org/guides/cleaners
www.healthy-legacy.squarespace.com/plastics-tips
www.npainfo.org

How to Test Your Home for Mold, Asbestos, Carbon Monoxide, Lead, and Other Toxins
www.prolabinc.com/products.asp

How to Select a Low-Radiation Cell Phone
www.s21.com/sar.htm

How to Avoid Harmful Chemicals
www.cdc.gov/exposurereport/index.html
www.atsdr.cdc.gov/toxprofiles/index.asp

To download a digital version of this list, visit alanbell.me/resources.

Appendix D: My Foundation's Founding Scientific Advisory Board

Iris Bell, MD, PhD, University of Arizona. Psychiatrist and university professor emeritus researching complementary and alternative medicine. She was chosen as one of the best doctors in the Pacific region of the United States. Dr. Bell has served on the faculties at Harvard Medical School; University of California, San Francisco; and the University of Arizona. She is a fellow of the American College of Nutrition and practices homeopathy and alternative medicine.

Eula Bingham, PhD, University of Cincinnati. Former scientific and policy advisor for the National Institute for Occupational Safety and Health, the Department of Labor, the National Academy of Sciences' Lead in Paint Commission, the Food and Drug Administration, and the Environmental Protection Agency. President Jimmy Carter appointed her director of the Occupational Safety and Health Administration, and she served through his administration. She later served as vice president and university dean for graduate studies and research at the University of Cincinnati and as a distinguished professor of environmental health.

David Christiani, MD, Harvard University. Professor of occupational medicine and epidemiology in the school's Departments of Environmental Health and Epidemiology whose research focuses on the interaction between human genes and our environment. He conducts studies worldwide on how genetic and acquired susceptibility to pulmonary and cardiovascular disease is linked to environmental exposures to toxins that include exposure to chemicals, indoor combustion products, the particles produced by coal-burning power plants, and bacteria in cotton.

Joan Cranmer, PhD, University of Arkansas. Neurotoxicologist and professor of pediatrics and pharmacology and toxicology at the University of Arkansas School of Medicine. Her research focuses on infant and child neurotoxicity, children's environmental health, and developmental neurotoxicology. Dr. Cranmer has more than seventy-four publications in peer-reviewed journals, proceedings, and edited books and has participated on many national and international advisory boards and expert committees, including a member of the National Institute of Environmental Health Advisory Council of the National Institutes of Health, and the Scientific Advisory Board of the National Egyptian Center for Toxicological Research.

Bernard Goldstein, MD, Rutgers University. Professor emeritus of environmental and occupational health and former dean of the University of Pittsburgh Graduate School of Public Health. He is a physician, board certified in internal medicine, hematology, and toxicology. Dr Goldstein is the author of over 150 publications in the peer-reviewed literature, as well as numerous reviews of environmental health studies. He is a member of the National Academies of Science Institute of Medicine and of the American Society for Clinical Investigation. His experience includes service as assistant administrator for Research and Development of the US Environmental Protection Agency and the founding director of the Environmental and Occupational Health

Sciences Institute, a joint program involving the University of Pittsburgh and Rutgers University Medical School.

John Groopman, PhD, Johns Hopkins University. Associate director of cancer prevention and control at the Johns Hopkins Cancer Center and professor and chair of the Department of Environmental Health Sciences at the Johns Hopkins School of Public Health. He is recognized for linking environmental exposure to liver cancer and conducted studies that demonstrated how mold-induced DNA damage can be reduced by antioxidant supplementation.

David Hoel, PhD, Medical University of South Carolina. Professor in the Department of Medicine and fellow of the American Academy of Arts and Sciences. He has served on numerous governmental and National Academy committees, including the Environmental Health Coalition, the US Environmental Protection Agency's Science Advisory Board and the National Academy of Sciences. His research has focused on linking low-dose radiation exposures to cancer.

Kaye Kilburn, MD, University of Southern California. Former director of Cardiopulmonary Research at Washington University School of Medicine, chief of Medical Services at a North Carolina Veterans Administration Hospital, and professor of Community Medicine in the Environmental Sciences Lab at Mount Sinai School of Medicine in New York. His studies have led to over 235 publications, of which 43 papers focused on neurobehavioral toxicology, and a book, *Chemical Brain Injury,* which explores the link between exposure to environmental toxins and brain injury.

Nancy Klimas, MD, Nova Southeastern University. Director, Institute for Neuro Immune Medicine; director, Clinical Immunology Research, Miami Veterans Administration; and professor emeritus, University of Miami, School of Medicine. Dr. Klimas conducts research on myalgic encephalomyelitis/chronic fatigue syndrome (ME/CFS), Gulf War illness (GWI), fibromyalgia, and other neuroimmune disorders. She is immediate past president of the International Association for Chronic Fatigue Syndrome and Myalgic Encephalopathy, and has advised three secretaries of Health and Human Services.

Hillel Koren, PhD. Dr. Koren's research focuses on the immunological mechanisms and environmental factors involved in asthma and other allergic diseases, and on the interconnection between human health and global climate change. He was the senior science advisor to the US Environmental Protection Agency's National Health and Environmental Effects Research Laboratory studying links between environmental exposure and asthma. He is chair of the Scientific Advisory Board of the Helmholtz Research Center for Environmental Health in Germany. With more than two hundred publications and contributions to four textbooks, Dr. Koren is a widely published author in the areas of immunology, environmental pulmonary cell biology, and molecular biology.

Philip Landrigan, MD, Mount Sinai Medical Center, New York. Dean for Global Health and chair of the Department of Preventive Medicine at the Mount Sinai School of Medicine. Dr. Landrigan is also the director of the Children's Environmental Health Center. A pediatrician, epidemiologist, and international leader in public health and preventive medicine, he is known for his many decades of work in protecting children against environmental threats to health, most notably lead and pesticides. His pioneering research on low-level lead toxicity helped to persuade the US government to mandate removal of lead from gasoline and paint, actions that have produced a 90 percent decline in incidence of childhood lead poisoning over the past twenty-five years, and he has been a leader in developing the National Children's Study, the largest study of children's health and the environment ever launched in the United States. The author of more than five hundred scientific papers and five books, he has also been centrally involved in the medical and epidemiologic victim studies from the World Trade Center attack on September 11, 2001.

John McLachlan, PhD, Tulane University. As scientific director of the National Institute of Environmental Health Sciences, he discovered how environmental chemicals alter fetal development. At Tulane, he established a program on the Environment and Women's Health and formed the nation's first Center in Environmental Astrobiology. His scientific findings have been published in over 150 journal articles, fifty book chapters, and five edited books. His work has focused on how exposure to environmental chemicals adversely affect affects human health including breast and endometrial cancers.

Herbert Needleman, MD, University of Pittsburgh. Pediatrician, child psychiatrist, researcher, and professor. Dr. Needleman studies neurodevelopmental damage caused by lead poisoning. He is a member of the Institute of Medicine and the founder of the Alliance to End Childhood Lead Poisoning. He has campaigned vigorously to educate parents and government panels about the dangers of lead poisoning, and played a key role in launching environmental safety measures that have reduced average blood lead levels by an estimated 78 percent between 1976 and 1991.

David Ozonoff, MD, Boston University. Chair of the Department of Environmental Health studying the health effects of toxic exposures. He is coeditor-in-chief of the online *Environmental Health Journal,* serves on several editorial journal boards, and is a fellow of the Johns Hopkins Society of Scholars.

John Peters, MD, University of Southern California. Dr. Peters focuses on the short- and long-term effects of air pollutants on children's health. Peters has published more than 150 research papers studying the health effects of air pollution, magnetic fields, asbestos, vinyl chloride, and other chemicals on human health.

J. Routt Reigart II, MD, Medical University of South Carolina. Professor emeritus and former director of the Division of General Pediatrics. His research interests include children's environmental health issues, general pediatrics, and toxicology (lead poisoning prevention and education). He was the chair of the Children's Health Protection Advisory Committee and a member of EPA and the US Department of Agriculture Tolerance Reassessment Advisory Committee. Dr. Reigart is an active participant in the Prioritization Committee for the Best Pharmaceuticals for Children program.

Glenn Sipes, PhD, University of Arizona. Head of the Department of Pharmacology in the University of Arizona College of Medicine and founding director of the Center for Toxicology and the Southwest Environmental Health Sciences Center. Dr. Sipes has also served as president of the Society of Toxicology, the International Union of Toxicology, and the Academy of Toxicological Sciences, has edited scientific journals, and was an advisor to the World Health Organization/Food and Agriculture.